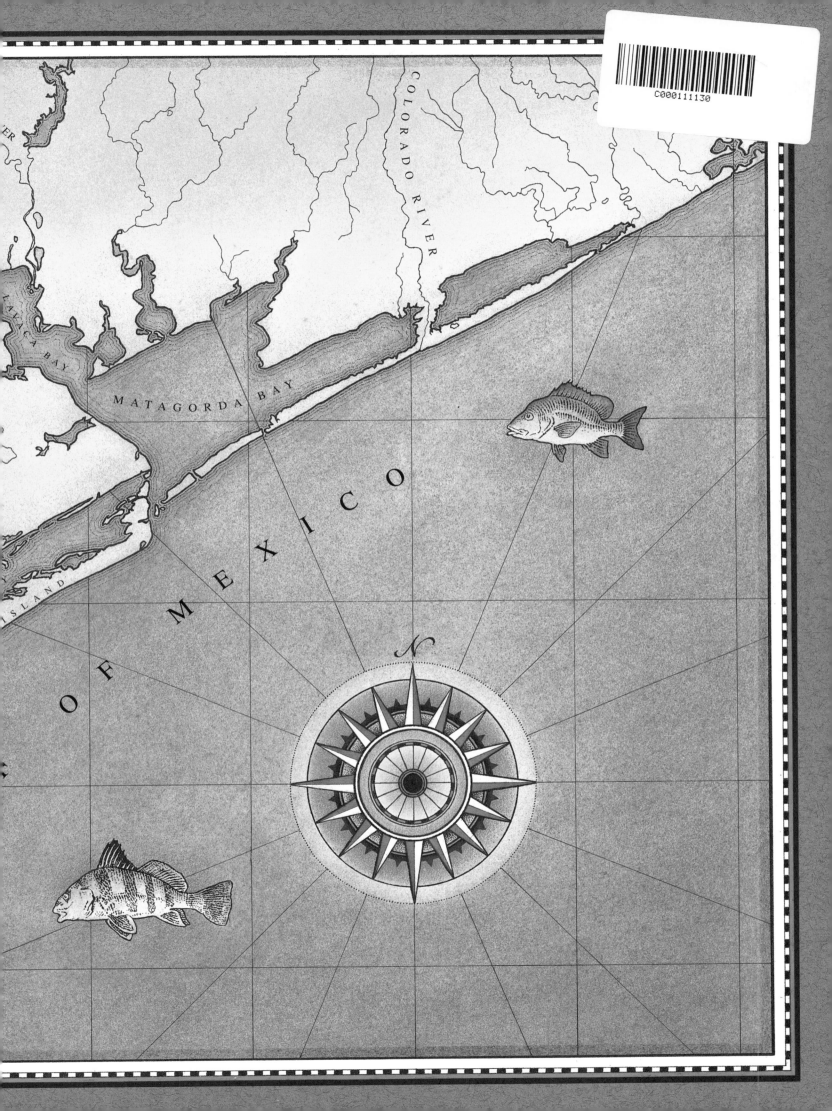

"If that San'tone River could talk, the tales it could tell."
Marye Murphy Greer

Marye Murphy Greer

Tom O'Connor Jr.

1915–1996

*Papa loved this land and these
people all his life. He taught me to
love them, too.*

Mary O'Connor Braman

1910–1992

*My adored "Auntie Mame," who
was my mother, my friend, my
teacher, and my hero.*

Dennis O'Connor (III)

1961–1996

*My beloved second son, my
"Shooting Star."*

Tales from the SANTONE River Bottom

To Graham —
Colleague, Friend & Mentor

James J. Connor
1998 —

Wexford Publishing

The San'tone River bottom.

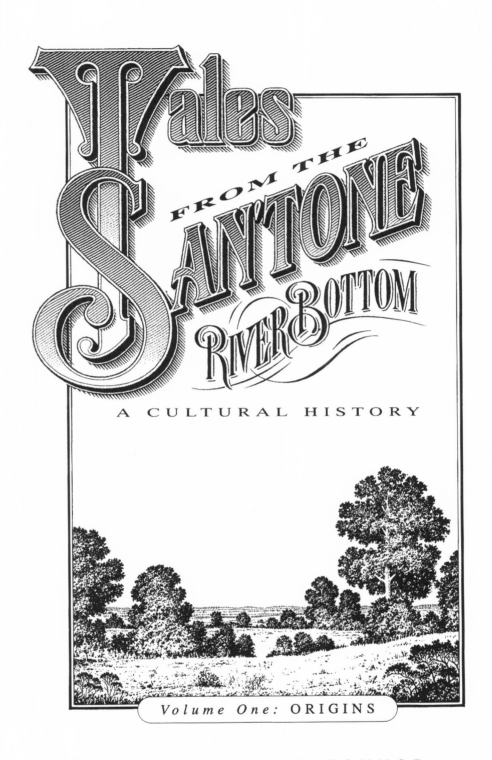

Tales FROM THE Santone RiverBottom

A CULTURAL HISTORY

Volume One: ORIGINS

By LOUISE S. O'CONNOR

TALES FROM THE SAN'TONE RIVER BOTTOM
A CULTURAL HISTORY

Volume One: ORIGINS
First Edition, 1998

By Louise S. O'Connor

First Printing

Wexford Publishing
106 W. Juan Linn
Victoria, Texas 77901-8022
512-576-4000
www.wexfordpublishing.com

Illustrations by John Wilson

ISBN: 0-9624821-1-0
Library of Congress Catalog Card Number: 98-88499

Texas Coastal Bend Series, No. 2

Also in this series:
CRYIN' FOR DAYLIGHT: *A Ranching Culture in the Texas Coastal Bend*

CONTENTS

TALES FROM THE SAN'TONE RIVER BOTTOM

Foreword

Louise Stoner O'Connor has asked me and my wife, Margaret Stoner McLean, to write a foreword for this latest volume of hers, entitled *Tales from the San'tone River Bottom*. We are glad to do so, but I can foresee that it will have to be done in two parts for the simple reason that we approach this study from two entirely different points of view. Margaret was born in the area; her ancestors have lived there for more than a century and a half; she has heard about it all of her life. Therefore, when she hears the "tales" in this volume, it is like a homecoming and family reunion for her.

I, on the other hand, did not know a thing about this area until I married Margaret and began to hear about it. Therefore, I come to the subject as an outsider and am forced to pass judgment on Louise's work strictly from what is contained in the book. I am happy to report, however, that I find its contents completely self-explanatory.

A word of caution: this work is in a class by itself—a reporting and analysis of the beginnings of civilization in a region. Therefore, it should not be judged by the same narrow criteria that critics usually employ: "Does it have unity, coherence, and emphasis?" It does. The unity is the geographic area of the San Antonio River region, the coherence is the organization which Louise has given to her material, and the emphasis has been given by the speakers whose interviews were tape-recorded.

There are a very large number of these contributors and every one of them is carefully listed and identified in the book. Their voices and their "tales" rise from these pages as though the speakers are sitting right with you. So the reader is getting the story first-hand. Louise reports it exactly as it was recorded. There is no question about its authenticity.

Louise spent fifteen years going to see these people, gaining their trust, and getting them to talk freely, a project which was greatly facilitated by the fact that she had been born there, and the people whom she was interviewing had known her, and her family, for generations. It is amazing to see the freedom with which they frankly told her everything, both good and bad, even down to what some might consider embarrassing, personal family details. From it all we get a very definite feeling for the region, beginning with the Indian tribes who were already there, and then following the successive waves of immigration: the Spanish, the French, the Mexicans, the Irish, some Germans, Anglo-Americans, and possibly the most influential of all, a very large contribution from Africa.

In fact, you might say that Louise has taken a "vacuum cleaner" (her tape recorder and her camera) and retrieved these gems before they have fallen through the cracks of history—and has brought them to light where we can all see, "hear," and enjoy them.

I am very grateful to her for having allowed me the privilege of contributing my part to this foreword. I have never read a more moving description of how people actually lived in Texas.

Malcolm D. McLean, Ph.D.

Malcolm McLean is former Associate Dean of Arts and Sciences, Texas Christian University, and Professor of Spanish and History, The University of Texas at Arlington. He is the compiler and editor of PAPERS CONCERNING ROBERTSON'S COLONY IN TEXAS *(19 vols., Arlington: The UTA Press, 1974–1993) as well as a Fellow and Life Member of the Texas State Historical Association and Fellow of the Texas Institute of Letters.*

In 1989, when Louise Stoner O'Connor published her volume entitled *Cryin' for Daylight*, I just loved it! It told the story of people, places, and happenings that I have known all my life. It left me wanting and needing more. Louise has done it again with *Tales from the San'tone River Bottom*!

Historians generally tell only about history. Louise O'Connor has chosen to use a new approach, letting the people themselves tell their own story, in their own words through the new approach of oral history. Using transcriptions of those interviewed, she lets them tell their own tales. In using such an approach, she is giving the world a fifty-yard-line seat to the real drama which cannot be duplicated anywhere else.

These tales show the beginning of a beautiful, colorful, and unique presentation of the manner in which the people who lived along the San Antonio River from 1834 to the present time have left us a heritage not found elsewhere. This is one example of why Texans are so unique that no one definition fits everyone. The story is of the Texans who have roots in the San Antonio River bottom, but because of the changes in the family lifestyles and economic needs over the years, some have had to move to other areas. The Wellington family, part of the Stoner family, and even the O'Connors themselves are examples.

The reader must realize that the main objective of both books is the preservation of more than the bare facts. As a historian, Louise O'Connor not only brings out the visual images of the land, the animals, the people, but also blends the sensual feelings of the earth, trees, contours of the river, and all manner of natural elements it contains. No one has ever gotten as close to the people of any area as she did to the people who have lived here for several generations.

It is written with much more insight than is frequently found in many of the books of historical significance.

The San'tone River must have taken an especially strong magnetic hold on the teenager Tom O'Connor when he arrived in Texas in 1834 with the Power-Hewetson Colony. In Ireland, the place of his birth, people of the Catholic faith were not allowed to own property, hold office, or practice their faith. If he left a written record of his thoughts concerning what he saw when he first visited the San Antonio River, which is flowing through what is now the O'Connor Ranches, I do not know about it. He was wise enough to leave it to his great-great-granddaughter, Louise Stoner O'Connor, to tell the story of the land, the people, the animals and other creatures living there, and to give the historical importance of it all.

Through her insight, love of the land and people, and with the aid of all technological advances, including the computer, she is now approaching the year 2000. I have no doubt that the material she has preserved by all methods will make it safely into the new century. I look forward to more volumes in this series of tales.

Margaret Stoner McLean, B.S.E.E.

Margaret McLean spent ten years as Microfilm Newspaper Archivist at the Amon Carter Museum, Fort Worth, and was the Texas Researcher for Thomas W. Streeter's 5-volume BIBLIOGRAPHY OF TEXAS, 1795–1845 (Cambridge: Harvard University Press, 1955–1960). She also worked as Microfilm Research Specialist, Texas Microfilm Center, Presidio La Bahía, Goliad.

Preface

When I began this oral history project more than fifteen years ago, I thought *Cryin' for Daylight,* my first book, would be my contribution to historical preservation and I could return to retirement. This was not to be. Once again, I find myself producing another book about the Texas Coastal Bend culture.

Cryin' for Daylight recorded the working lives of the people in the ranching culture that is the foundation of three counties of the Texas Coastal Bend: Refugio, Victoria, and Goliad. Its primary focus was on the men and women who worked the cattle and engaged in those aspects of ranching that made it a famous, if not legendary, occupation. It examined the daily activities of these cowhands and ranchers and only occasionally hinted at their rich personal lives apart from their work.

While collecting this material, I realized that the interviews were not just about ranch life. They revealed a wealth of background information about the different cultures of the Coastal Bend—Hispanic, European, African-American, and Celtic. Here was a wealth of stories, all with fascinating glimpses of Coastal Bend history, folklore, social customs, and other details of a way of life that is fast disappearing. This material provides valuable documentation in itself, as important and compelling as the ranch life that was the subject of *Cryin' for Daylight.* By the end of the second year of interviewing, I realized that I would not get off the hook with only one book. *Tales from the San'tone River Bottom* began to take shape, and I started asking culture-related questions in each interview.

As I delved deeper, I began to realize, yet again, that a single volume would not be enough to contain all the information I had amassed on the cultures of the San Antonio River. *Tales from the San'tone River Bottom* would have to consist of two volumes, maybe three. About the same time, a book on the Irish settlers of the Coastal Bend began to rear its head. And other themes in the extensive material suggested additional volumes. Thus was born the Texas Coastal Bend Series.

Tales from the San'tone River Bottom is the story of the convergence of the American Indian, African, Mexican, and Celtic cultures in the vicinity of the lower San Antonio River. It is an area of the Coastal Bend that is distinctive for its cultural mix. These groups settled along the river bottom where a source of water was guaranteed. Thus, the river bottom became the center of this culture, surrounded by ranches and farms of all sizes. The oral narratives in this book show us the enormously complex support system that grew up around the ranches. It was a network of people and communities that created a body of folklore, universal in many respects, that ultimately defines this area of the Coastal Bend.

In each culture, and in the combining of these cultures, the people were comfortable with themselves, each other, and their role in the community. That sense of comfort produced a high degree of satisfaction in their lives regardless of the hardships that would invade their world on a regular basis. The concept of hard work as something "bad" does not exist among the people I interviewed. It was part of life. It was how everyone lived each day. It was what one did.

They knew how to cope with life as it was, and they took great pride in knowing nothing was too tough for them to handle. To this day, they still express satisfaction in the fact that they provided for their families even in the toughest times. This made for a deeply satisfying life, for each person clearly recognized his own worth to himself and to the community.

From their lifestyle, the people of the river bottom learned sharing, reasoned obedience, nurturing values, trust, an understanding of nature and the natural order of the universe. Out of this evolved strict moral and behavioral codes by which they lived. It was a belief system based on a common understanding that one's honor was one's prized possession, and that it superseded racial, cultural, and age differences.

Most of the narratives describe life as it was in the first half of this century. In this environment, people lived in intimate contact with nature and one another. Nature and a strong sense of community shaped their lives and their attitudes about almost everything. Even the people who moved into town or out of this culture are still, in one way or another, strongly affected by their early lives. They retain their strong connection to the earth, the animals, and the traditions of their forebears.

Many of these aspects of a traditional, rural lifestyle are unknown to urbanites of today. Therefore, the preservation of information about the primary culture and its support

Kathryn Stoner O'Connor in the La Bahía office, ca. 1960.

system is of critical importance. This is a culture rich in its connection to nature, God, and to each individual.

The element that unites these diverse people into a cohesive cultural unit is the land. Coexisting with the land is what this book is about. Those whose experience is restricted to urban life will, I hope, find much to think about and much to enrich their lives in these stories from the San Antonio River bottom.

Oral history preserves how history "got lived." For this reason, I have worked hard to avoid presentism, which is the inappropriate application of today's attitudes, morals, and social mores to the past. I must ask my readers to avoid it as well. To do otherwise would be to falsify history. It was the way it was, and "political correctness" has no place here. Anyone who is offended by the way things were should read no further.

> *As a ship leaves its wake on the ocean*
> *And a jet leaves its wake in the sky*
> *So may my journey on life's broad pathway*
> *Leave the message that I've been by.*

Kathryn Stoner O'Connor, Diaries, 1963

As you read this book, you will soon become aware of the footprints of my beloved grandmother, Kathryn Stoner O'Connor (1883–1979). Throughout her long and productive life, she researched the history of the Coastal Bend of Texas and left a large and interesting body of work. I have used it liberally in researching the historical background for this volume. Her influence is everywhere in this book and in my consciousness.

Granny grew up in a nineteenth-century Texas ranching family, married into one, and continued to live on a ranch until her death. She was a very strong influence in and on my life from my earliest recollection. She helped my father raise my sister, Kathryn, and me after our mother passed away in 1955. She was there when needed, often on a daily basis. We spent summer vacations with her at the Melon Creek Ranch and continued to do so long after we were both married and had children of our own.

I would spend countless hours with her in her library at the ranch during the heat of the afternoon, listening to her stories of early Texas, our family history, and her counsel on what needed to be done to preserve the history of our state. Many are the times I have ended an eighteen-hour day by shaking my fist at the heavens, and at her in particular, for having, unbeknownst to me, programmed me to feel compelled to do this historical work.

Granny came from a family of writers, the most notable of whom was Victor Marion Rose, an early Texas historian and journalist. Not many women lived her lifestyle of ranching combined with Southern gentility, and few of those who did wrote well. She added greatly to the store of knowledge we now have about many aspects of the history of our state. Her literary ability, her understanding of historical preservation, and the time frame in which she lived have preserved for all of us a unique insight into our past.

Her mentors in Texas history were Carlos E. Castañeda, Eugene C. Barker, and Herbert Bolton. Many of her handwritten notes and margin notations were taken from their work and, therefore, can be considered as source materials for much of this book. Granny was profoundly deaf from the age of thirty-five, and this no doubt contributed greatly to her passion for reading any and everything she could get her hands on. Any book, manuscript, paper, or letter pertaining to history that fell into her hands bore her copious margin notes. Some of my favorite commentary from Granny's pencil is to be found in margin notes of her copies of the works of J. Frank Dobie. Each volume contained lengthy personal inscriptions to her. They were great friends, yet adversaries at the same time. They frequently saw history and the future quite differently, and this difference produced some very humorous and historically valuable exchanges between them, either in letters or Granny's commentary in the margins.

I would often be allowed to have tea with Granny and her lady friends who came to visit. Two who remain vivid in my memory are Miss Madie Mitchell (Simmons) and Eulalia Marmion Coward. When Granny was feeling particularly racy, we would be offered a little daiquiri.

These spry octogenarians would often sit around and ponder the sad state of their friends, commenting that they all were dead, in wheelchairs, or *non compus mentis* at best. Granny and her friends were still active and healthy and could not understand the deterioration in their peers. Physical and mental deterioration was quite beyond their comprehension. Granny wrote her first book at eighty-three and Eulalia was riding camels in Egypt and mining for diamonds in Arkansas at the age of ninety-one. Miss Madie led a somewhat more sedate life, but continued to be mentally alert and active around her home and suffered no loss of strong opinions.

Eulalia Marmion Coward.

These spirited women taught me about daily life in earlier times and about the changes they had seen. They were especially informative about life in the Old South, the social conventions of which were still present in daily life even into their middle years. Some of their attitudes and beliefs were peculiar to their rather unique and unusual station in life. Born and reared in one century, they came to maturity in another. As young married women in the early twentieth century, they saw the world around them changing as automobiles, telephones, and airplanes altered forever the way they lived. They accepted the fact that change is part of the human condition and viewed it with equanimity.

From their conversations, I unwittingly absorbed much to prepare for my current work. They taught me the value of preserving knowledge from a bygone era and gave me an interest in other times and approaches to living. They began to introduce me to the concept that certain traditional ways had remained the same, or should remain the same, regardless of changes in the world. In a subtle manner, they instilled an understanding that some approaches to life are universally proper and should be preserved.

The stories these women told trained me to listen to aspects of history and daily life quite different from the history of ranching taught to me by my father, Tom O'Connor Jr. Papa taught me in a different setting. His classroom was the outdoor world of cowpens, the prairies, and the river bottoms. In that setting, we children gained insight into the people who lived and worked close to nature. There, he taught me, by example and by his stories, to listen attentively when people talk and tell tales. Granny taught me to listen to the rest of the story, and that is what is contained in this book.

Thank you, Granny, for your contributions to my life and to historical preservation in Texas.

At her death, my grandmother bequeathed to me the O'Connor family papers. With the realization that my project was expanding, I began working with my cousins Margaret

Madie Mitchell Simmons.

Stoner McLean and Malcolm McLean. I had been around both of these Texas historians as a child, for Margaret was my grandmother's niece. They, too, were interested in preserving their family papers. After several visits, we realized that we had the basis of a valuable archive that needed a home.

This collaboration led to the birth of the Texas Coastal Bend Collection, which will be housed at the Center for American History at the University of Texas at Austin. It will consist of the O'Connor Collection and other important family collections, supplemented with additional archival material from the Coastal Bend. Any other papers of value that need a home will be welcome in this collection.

The Coastal Bend of Texas is relatively untouched as far as historical preservation is concerned. It has been closed to research since the first settlers arrived. Few have been allowed to study this culture, and fewer have written about it from the inside. It is my dream and my life's work to make this unique society come alive for the rest of the world.

Marye Murphy Greer: Well, you promised Miss Kate that you would write this history, didn't you?

Louise O'Connor: No, ma'am, I just promised Miss Kate that I wouldn't be a drunk old rich lady, that's all I promised her! She said, "You just simply cannot drink yourself to death and sit around and be rich!" I said, "Yes, ma'am, how do I not do that?" She said, "Listen to what I'm saying to you!" I said, "Yes, ma'am!"

This book would not have been possible without the help of many people: Tommy Tijerina, project manager and enthusiastic supporter of my work; Norma Simmons, general life source for the whole group and expert transcriber of great quantities of material; Leah Bianchi, a complete life-support machine; Terry Wayland, superb photographic archivist; Margaret Eakin, research associate and friend; Alison Tartt, consulting editor; Dick Reeves, award-winning book designer, opinion-giver, and blame-taker; and Townes Van Zandt and Guy Clark, who taught me how to write.

I am also deeply grateful to my household staff, who keep the whole ship afloat; my masseuses and my acupuncturist, bodyworkers, and chiropractor, who have kept me alive for two decades; and my children, grandchildren, family, and friends for enduring me during this process. Special thanks go to Dr. Johnnie Fisher, coping coach; Robert Murdock, my great supporter; Tim Wilson; Virginia Drake Lebermann, my daughter, friend, inspiration, and strength; Margaret and Malcolm McLean, for their friendship, their support of the project, and their willingness to share their knowledge of Texas history; my sister Kathryn O'Connor Counts and my cousin D. H. Braman Jr., for their support, love, and permission to do this work; and my cousin Nancy O'Connor, for her invaluable contribution to this entire project.

Most of all, I thank all those who allowed me to interview them and without whom none of this would be possible. The oral interviews are the heart and soul of this book, as they were in *Cryin' for Daylight*. Each voice is unique; each story is different. There is, however, a recurring thread that binds them together—their connection with the earth and with their neighbors.

I still remember the very first person I interviewed—an old cowhand named L. V. Terrell who had been given the task of being "compadre" to my sister and me as children. This job consisted of teaching us to ride a horse, going with us on horseback picnics, and being general nanny, protector, and teacher when we were engaged in ranching activities and play. After the first day of interviewing, L. V. suggested we call in Abel Pérez, another tophand he had worked with all his life. Then Nancy O'Connor suggested that we call in Milam Thompson. From that day on, we added to the list of interviewees by threes and fours until the final count is now close to five hundred contributors.

The people interviewed for this oral history project are remarkable in their ability to impart information and express feelings. I am constantly amazed by their powerful insights and the beautiful verbal pictures and colorful scenes they draw. Their talents strongly disprove the modern notion that one can accomplish little without literacy and formal education. Their observations about their lives are the stuff of history.

My collaborators have changed my life permanently. Just knowing them is precious to me. They are a unique and endangered species who deserve the recognition they are now getting.

I wish every day that I had started this project many years earlier, but I am grateful to have reached those who are left. The end of that era and this kind of people has come, and the world will not be the better for it.

I give it to you as they gave it to me.

Louise S. O'Connor

The author annoying Dennis Williams and Tom O'Connor Jr., O'Connor River Ranch, 1980s.

TALES FROM THE SAN'TONE RIVER BOTTOM

CHAPTER ONE

The San Antonio River

"Small, meandering, unassuming, the San Antonio River is a sparkling river of life."

V. G. Vickers

From my earliest recollection, there has been a river in my life called the San'tone. It has always been a reminder to me that no matter where I was, I had a home and a place where I belonged.

I grew up being told stories of how the river and the vast plains of the Coastal Bend of Texas had cast their spell on my great-great-grandfather, Thomas O'Connor (I). He immigrated to this area from Ireland in 1834 with the Power-Hewetson Colony. At this time, the English Penal Codes, a set of punitive decrees against the Irish, were in effect. Life was hard for Irish Catholics in their homeland in the nine-

The San Antonio River at the Fagan Bridge, 1940.

teenth-century. Catholics were not allowed to own property, hold office, or practice the Catholic faith. The hardship and oppression in his native land gave Thomas O'Connor, only a teenager, an even greater appreciation of the opportunity presented by the government of Mexico in offering colonists like himself a seemingly endless supply of water and land in Texas.

My ancestor lived on the banks of the San Antonio River and was buried there in accordance with his wishes. As a local historian has commented, "One who has once known the San Antonio River intimately seems never to overcome the longing to return to it."[1]

The Spell of the River

Just about everyone in the Texas Coastal Bend calls it "the San'tone." People who have spent any time on or around the river also acknowledge that there is something unique about it. It is unique among Texas rivers, especially its neighbor to the east, the Guadalupe. As rivers go, the San Antonio is small, shallow, and slow-moving. People who know both rivers say the San'tone is a benevolent friend and benefactor, while they fear the size and power of the Guadalupe. Other rivers simply do not have the same strong emotional hold on people as the San'tone.

Bella French came under its spell in the 1800s. She published a magazine called *The Sketch Book*, which contains articles on Texas history. In 1877 she moved to Austin and, while there, married John M. Swisher in 1878. A poem she wrote about the San Antonio River leads one to wonder if peyote also grew along the banks of this river, but it is a delightful concept either way. For the sake of brevity, I have used here only the essential parts of the poem.

The sweet San Antonio River.

The San Antonio River

A most very thing winding in, winding out
Overshadowed by leaflets that quiver in the breezes
Which toss the clear wavelets
Flows the sweet San Antonio River.

Under bridges, by churches, near ruins most grand
With its numerous gladsome surprises
In its grandeur of landscape on every hand
From the beautiful spring where it rises.

I sat down near the source on one glorious day
When the sweet mockingbirds, a great number
Were each piping forth its melodious lay
And I think that I dropped into slumber.

For up from the foxgloves of every hue
From all points of those emerald bowers
Groups of fairies come forth to my wondering view
Quite as numberless as those sweet flowers.

One ran down to the spring with a wee larkspur cup
Oh, has nature a tinier daughter?
And the pure little goblet she brimful filled up
With the beautiful shimmering water.

Then I said, "Fairy Queen, can you tell me, I pray,
From whence came this glorious river?"
In a silvery voice, replied the fair fay,
"Yes, a woman's bright tear was the giver."

I awoke, out of sight went the strange little fay,
But to where it was not for my knowing.
Yet, as then, on its way, winding in, winding out,
Flows the sweet San Antonio River.[2]

The Gentle Friend

"When you get in that bottom, everything is strange. Man, it was rough! We didn't get lost, we just couldn't find our way, all the trees and stuff. When I first went to goin' down there, there was moss hangin' all in those trees and everything else. You couldn't find your way in that."

Ralph Bego

The Guadalupe River and the San'tone River are very different from each other. The Guadalupe is full of sand bars and has sand sides. The San'tone River is sand bottom and mud sides. You can't get out of the San'tone River without getting your feet muddy.

They're both water, trees, and wildlife; but the Guadalupe was by far the bigger river until around 1967 when Hurricane Beulah reamed out the San'tone River and made it much bigger. It changed lots of sand bars.

The San'tone River used to be like a little bitty stream. Children played up and down it just like they do in small streams. The Guadalupe is a big river, and it always was. Even the buckeyes are different on each river. Buckeyes are poisonous to cattle unless they are raised on it, then they can eat all they want. It's the leaves on the plant that can kill cattle. The buckeyes on the Guadalupe have longer flowers than the San'tone. The two varieties never mix.

Eunice Huber, Emily Smolik Buckert, Martin Huber, David Huber

I spent a lot of time in the Guadalupe River bottom before I went to work for the O'Connor ranches. Then I spent a lot of time in the San'tone River bottom. It has always been the best catfish river around. The Guadalupe was thick, brushy, wild, and uninhabited.

Darden Jacob

Jim Whitney and "Black Moccasin" at the old Stoner Crossing of the Guadalupe River.

You know, life centered around the San Antonio River. To me, the unique thing about it is that you don't hear the Guadalupe River mentioned in the same context at all.

P. K. Stubblefield

Coming down to the bottom was a special treat because we were not allowed to go down there unless we had somebody with us. We always wanted to go there because it was forbidden territory. They were afraid we would fall in the river and

Scene on the Guadalupe River at Tivoli, 1911.

drown. I guess it was just the idea of exploring. We wanted to explore and see if we could find buried treasure. We'd hunt eggs and look for deer.

Things we take for granted, nobody had back then. The isolation down here was just incredible. They brought stuff from Goliad down the river. Like my father used to say, the best land in the world is the forks of the San Antonio River and the Guadalupe.

Marye Murphy Greer

Everyone looked up to the San Antonio River. It's special to people, even more special than the Guadalupe. I have no idea why, I just don't know. People from the Guadalupe would come here to fish. I really think the size had something to do with it. The Guadalupe is big enough to be scary.

John Freeman Lott

The Guadalupe River had whirlpools and sinkholes. A lot of people drowned in that river. It looked smooth on top, but sinkholes would pull you down. The San'tone River had better banks than the Guadalupe. The Guadalupe would cave in. When it floods, the San'tone River will clear up much faster than the Guadalupe. The San'tone River was like a gentle friend. These two rivers come together near Tivoli. We didn't mess with the Guadalupe. It was dangerous and crooked as a dog's hind leg. The Guadalupe fed lots of people during the Depression with hunting and fishing. It was close to town where people felt the Depression more. Everybody knew each other on the San'tone River and the Guadalupe, but the two groups didn't mix much. They were too far apart. There were some communities along the Guadalupe, but none like Lewis's Bend.

K. J. Oliver, Jesse Jones, Johnny Robinson, Pete Brown, Reverend Mack Williams

When you see either river, you know it. There is a different feeling to each. The San'tone is more remote and we have a distinct river bottom. The Guadalupe doesn't have that distinctive second dropoff, and it is more public. It is nearer large towns. There is no public access to the San'tone River. It is private property on both sides. The Guadalupe has public access along both sides.

There is a lot of magic and history along the San'tone River. It has a little different history, too. The people and the country are different.

David Huber

Some people were born in the woods and some were born on the prairies. They were very different experiences. It was like two different worlds, that bottom and the prairies. I was a prairie man. We lived out there on the bald prairie at Butler's Mott. Food supplies were scarce out there, not like the bottom. Trees always fascinated me when I went down to the bottom. I didn't see many of them. They were unusual to me. There was a lot of animal noise in those river bottoms.

Reverend Mack Williams

Yeah, there was lots of difference in being by the river than up on the prairie.

Henry Sievers Jr.

River with a Past

Many important events have unfolded along the banks of the San Antonio River. It is considered the most historic in Texas. In its journey to the coast, it passes great landmarks of Texas history and cuts through the rich grasslands on which the Spanish and later immigrants established the cattle and cotton industries. The river nurtured and sustained the people and their work as they shaped the cultural mix that is now the Texas Coastal Bend.

The river's primary source is not within the city of San Antonio, as many believe, but from subterranean streams in neighboring Bandera County. They also form the Medina River to the west. This groundwater, part of the Edwards Aquifer system, rises to the surface in San Antonio as a complex of springs that in the past numbered as many as one hundred.

From its headwaters on the grounds of Incarnate Word College, the river heads south, bisecting the city and inviting visitors to the 2.5-mile downtown stretch known as Paseo del Río. Below the city of San Antonio, the river joins the Medina and flows southeast across the coastal plain, cutting through Wilson, Karnes, and Goliad counties. It then forms the boundary between Refugio and Victoria counties. After its 180-mile journey, the San Antonio converges with the Guadalupe above San Antonio Bay. Until recent times, the river's spring-fed tributaries ensured a relatively constant flow of water along its entire course.

The Spanish named the river in honor of St. Anthony of Padua when a 1691 expedition camped on its banks on June 13, the saint's feast day. Led by the provincial

Front gate to La Bahía, Katherine Brownson and Fleming Smith, February 17, 1924.

governor of Texas, Domingo Terán de los Ríos, the party was seeking a route for the Camino Real. With the establishment of the presidio San Antonio de Béxar and its mission San Antonio de Valero, in 1718, the San Antonio River acquired its first permanent settlement. By the early 1730s, a string of four additional missions occupied the banks of the San Antonio River to the south: Mission Nuestra Señora de la Purísma Concepción, Mission San José y San Miguel de Aguayo, Mission San Juan Capistrano, and Mission San Francisco de la Espada. All except San José had been relocated from their original locations in East Texas.

COASTAL BEND RIVERS AND MISSIONS

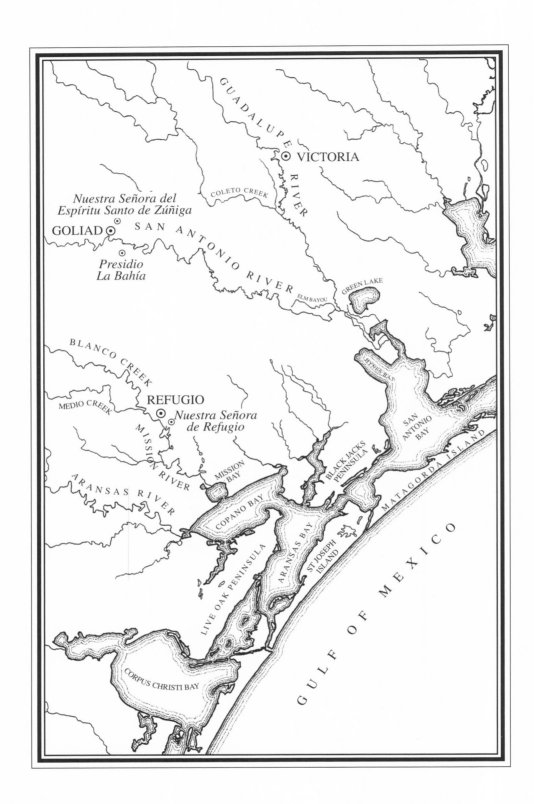

The arrival of colonists from Spain's Canary Islands gave the river—and what was to become Texas—its first organized civil settlement and the first official municipality in Texas. It was known as Villa de San Fernando. By 1775, the area was the center of Spanish colonial rule.

About fourteen miles downstream, where the San Antonio joins the Medina, is the site of an early-day settlement that goes back to perhaps the seventeenth century. Known as Las Islitas, it was inhabited by small-scale farmers and ranchers of Spanish and Indian descent. The settlement marked an important river crossing, El Paso de Borrega, or Sheep Crossing.

Farther downstream, on the river's west bank in the vicinity of present-day Floresville, is the site of Rancho de las Cabras, an outpost of Mission San Francisco de la Espada. Ruins from its stone chapel and ranch house, which served as quarters for cowboys and shepherds, still remain. The property has been designated a historic site and is now owned by the National Park Service.

The next stretch of the river is marked by steep earthen banks and a series of characteristic twists and turns. The spring-fed Cibolo Creek enters from the east, but the water continues to move slowly. The gently rolling to hilly terrain, with its sandy loams, begins to give way to the grasslands and post oak savannahs of the coastal prairie.

On the banks of the river at Goliad we find the mid-eighteenth-century mission

Gus Schulze and Fritz Neumann on Forest Fisher's boat at Mosqueet Landing, San Antonio River, just east of the Hwy. 35 bridge, 1910.

complex consisting of Mission Nuestra Señora del Espíritu Santo de Zúñiga and Presidio La Bahía—what my grandmother called "sites [where] many of the most stirring episodes in Texas history took place."[3] A Spanish emissary sent by the crown in 1767 to inspect the mission complex wrote that the San Antonio de Béjar, as he called it, was "a large river, whose shady and pleasant banks are covered with sabines, willows, walnuts, oaks and many other trees." He went on to describe the waterway as plentiful with "a great many eels, bagres, piltones, pullones, mojarras and other kinds of fish."[4]

This section of the river is part of the San Antonio River Valley Rural Historic District and is listed on the National Register of Historic Places.[5] The forty-three-square-mile area encompasses the river and river banks, densely wooded areas, floodplains, and rolling hills. The district also includes a portion of the old La Bahía–Béxar Road. Lying near the confluence of Cabeza Creek and the San Antonio River, it connected Goliad and San Antonio. The little cotton-processing town of Riverdale once flourished on the south bank.

Goliad is the last town on the river these days, and as it flows south, it becomes more isolated and meandering. A few miles below Goliad, it becomes the boundary between Refugio and Victoria counties. The tiny settlements that once dotted the river banks—Hall's Point, Carlos Ranch, Lewis's Bend, and Anaqua—are long since abandoned.

However, the rich black alluvial soil still remains and the river's banks are still lined with elm, willow, sycamore, and pecan trees of monumental stature. Other vegetation from the era of exploration remains, but it has been greatly altered by the occupation of domestic animals. The increase in wildlife, which also affects the flora of the area, is due, in large part, to the successful screwworm eradication program of recent years.

As the San Antonio nears the Gulf, it converges with the Guadalupe at the site of old Mesquite Landing, or Paraje de los Mosquitos. This swampy area was a rendezvous point of the Karankawas. As settlement occurred, it became a landing point for seagoing vessels carrying supplies for the inland missions. During this era, it was known as El Muelle Viejo (Old Wharf). A short-lived Spanish mission was located in the vicinity before its eventual relocation to Refugio. Spaniards, Mexicans, and Texians built fortifications here at various times. Mesquite Landing was also on an early-day trail that ran between Indianola and Chihuahua.[6]

After the San Antonio empties into the Guadalupe, these waters flow slowly onward to form lagoons and marshes along the coast. The river bank is now only inches above the slow waters. Herons, glossy ibis, cranes, gulls, ducks, geese, and pink roseate spoonbills fill the landscape. Dunes built by the prevailing winds give some variety to the otherwise flat horizon. At the end, these waters leave the land to become part of the Gulf of Mexico.

The Spirit of the River Bottom

River bottoms are very special places that encompass the low-lying grasslands along a watercourse. The river is full of life, and its banks are lush with trees, shrubs, vines, and other plants. Here nature is a powerful force, for a river bottom has always been, and to great extent still is, wild country. In today's world, a river bottom is one of the few places left to get away from the stress of the modern world. There is something primordial there. It can heal the soul.

In interviewing people who had lived in the San Antonio River bottom, I soon realized that they possessed a special knowledge, a sensitivity and spirituality that came from their constant daily contact with the natural world. Their reminiscences give us the opportunity to examine the possibility that the human race has lost much to urbanization and formal education.

The Music of the River Bottom

"You could scowl down in that river bottom and you could hear your voice two miles."

Milam Thompson

When I would walk down there, I would hear the trees singing, the wind blowing, and the limbs rubbing together. I would walk through the bottom on a windy day and the trees sang to me. There are leaves crunching and blowing together. Owls are making noises.

There is a difference in river bottoms and other areas. The shade, the smell, does something to me. In the spring when certain trees is blooming, it does me good to ride through and smell. Plum trees have a good smell. The vines would make me a seat. Being around nature will eventually affect you.

Sounds are another thing that entertained me as a child. There is a many a sound in this world. Every bird is different. I was never lonesome, there were too many sounds.

A child turns to whatever environment he is in. Birds sing, frogs holler, and crickets make that special sound. Each one is different and you get to know them. It depends on how you were brought up whether these sounds affect you.

All this comes from a river bottom and woods. I ain't no money-makin' man, but there ain't no way you can starve me. I'll survive in anybody's country as long as I am out of town.

Milam Thompson

There is all kind of music down in that bottom. Bugs, frogs, and birds makin' a concert early in the mornin' and in the evenin'. Mournin' doves are a lonesome sound, but it gives us inspiration. It's nature talkin'. Some people live a lifetime and never hear these things. This river was our way of life. It was all we knew.

Nathaniel Youngblood

The main thing I love about going down in the river bottom is to listen to a thunderstorm. God, it sounds so fine rolling down that river.

Kai Buckert

Heavenly Garden

When I was young, I would take my gun and my fishing pole down with those colored people on the San'tone River. It was beautiful down there in Lewis's Bend. They were wonderful people.

That bottom was all trimmed up and they had farms up and down that river. As far as you could see, there would be pretty grass and squirrels everywhere.

They had grafted pecan trees down there, and there was an old bridge across the San'tone River. These people lived up and down that river and farmed.

I would shoot squirrels and catch fish walking in a line from one house to the other. I enjoyed the company of those old people. I'm not sure I remember their names.

Back then, the handshake was real important. They knew how your heart was. You didn't have to explain it to them. That is the difference between then and now.

It was like being in a garden. As far as you could see down under those oak trees and pecan trees was perfectly clean. It was like being in heaven.

Copano camphouse, Tom O'Connor's (II) ranch, Charlie Williams, cook.

Time didn't mean anything and those people enjoyed life. They had a little church they went to.

The houses down there were little old shacks, but they were neat and clean. They would cook for me as I moved up and down the river.

It was like I belonged to them.

E. "Spec" Phillips, D.V.M.

Lee McConnell, his wife Fannie, their daughter, and her children.

This River Is My Home: John Freeman Lott Remembers

I know pretty much every inch of this San'tone River. I have been on this river a many a year. Down through history, people have tried to tame the earth. If you go against nature, you are seldom successful. When people come down here and use this river, I am resentful. It's not mine, but I can't help resenting their intrusion. There was a time when it seemed like I was the only one on it. The river wasn't polluted then. It was alive.

This river has meant a lot to me. I particularly love the cypress, sycamore, and cottonwood trees, and a many hot day after cow work, we would head for the river to cool off.

Many animals live in this bottom. Wild turkeys, fish, coons, all kinds of things make this place their home. When I was a child, there were ducks everywhere down here. I'm glad I grew up before we got game wardens. It is impossible to feel free and wild since they came along. Most of the land up and down this river was O'Connor land.

They never minded anyone going in their bottom to hunt or fish. Nobody used to try to stop people going down to the river until people turned mean and careless and quit respecting other people's property.

She is a good-sized river. I once knew an old Negro man named Bingo. Everyone else took off their guns and leggin's and boots to swim the river. He couldn't swim, so he left his gear on so he could sink and walk across the river underwater to the other side.

There was lots of treasure-hunting in those days. People would come from all over to dig. They even had divining rods, some of them. They would dig holes you could put a Model-T Ford in.

There are some big old catfish down here. The yellow cat is not a scavenger. You could use live bait on him. The blue cat scavenges. He will take dead bait. Used to be white-winged dove around here, but you don't see them much anymore.

There are panthers around here, too, or at least there used to be. Back in 1915, some children didn't know what one was, so they shot him with a .12 gauge shotgun, then beat him to death. When they found out what it was, they almost died. Panthers are beautiful animals.

My grandfather had given me a "white powder wonder" when

"There was lots of varmints in that bottom—possums, coons, wildcats. Everything was fatter in the bottom. It was life."

Richard Harris

"Who would have thought all this good stuff would happen to us when we were roaming around this river bottom barefooted with pasteboard in our shoes? We were mostly freed slaves from Lewis Plantation after the Civil War and became squatters in the Bend. We even poured wiggletails out of the water and drank it."

S. W. "Toney" Lott

I was around eight years old, a single-barreled shotgun. I was proud of that gun. I'd go down to the old lake here after school and kill me a dove or two for my lunch. Mama would fry it and I would take the dove in my lunch. I liked to eat 'em. Every weekend I walked to the place out here. I'd do it pretty quick. I wasn't going to stay in town. Thought nothin' of it. I'd do ten or twelve miles in an hour and a half.

This river was enjoyed around here in Riverdale. We had a regular swimming hole. There was a big old cypress tree with a rope over the swimming hole. We'd drop twenty feet off the bluff into the river. I'd rather go to Riverdale as a boy than New York City.

All this talk makes me long for my childhood. I never get tired of looking at those old trees. They're beautiful. Everything about them is beautiful. You couldn't take the country out of me if you tried.

The river has cut down quite a bit since my childhood. One of the prettiest sights I ever saw was a bunch of wild turkeys drinking water on a clay bank in the middle of the river.

Down our way on the river, there used to be a lot of "river rats" who fished for a living. This was during the Depression when everyone was starving to death. They would sell live fish in town on Thursday. People used to eat fish on Fridays in this area.

The river has improved over the past few years, but it was a lot better when I was young. Now, I'm eighty-five years old, you know, but when I was a boy that river was clear, not polluted like now. All these tenant farmers drank water out of the river.

It was more like a spring-fed stream, clear. I remember one time with Dad right up here not too far up the river. Threw out a long line with perch on it—four, five hooks, you know, stations on a throwline, with perch on it. It barely hit the water and we grabbed it and pulled it in and it had a bass on it. To catch a bass out of the river, it's got to be clear.

Victor Weber (left) with friends on the San Antonio River.

At one time when I was young, you could go down there to the river and play outta bait and find a mussel. There was a big bank of them and you could dig them out big as your hand. Take a knife and split 'em open like an oyster and use that mussel for bait.

I saved some shells from the old days and now they're coming back. I know where a bag full of mussels is right down in that river now. They're there, they're coming back. Some young boys found a bunch last summer.

When I was a teenager, we used to go the Armour Fagan ranch and fish. In

*"I used to go to the river bot-
tom in a wagon with my mother
and father. There was burr oak,
wild plum, redhaw and black-
haw. There's an oak tree over
there that had a limb pointing
down and Richard [Harris] and
all of them used to dig, my
Lord, they have dug looking for
that treasure that's supposed to
be buried there!"*

Zilpah Daniel Edwards

those days people didn't have radios, television, nothin' like that. We would go
down in their bottom and pitch two or three tents and stay a month. It would be
Hattie and Hatch, Cousin Henry and Cousin Ella, and their child Virginia May. It
would be me, Uncle Happy and Aunt Helen, and their kid Butch. We had a spring-
board and a swing, and we'd drop down in that river. I didn't want to live anywhere
but on that river. You could always get in the shade of a tree. In those days, there
was no restrictions.

The first deer I ever killed, I was fifteen or sixteen and I killed it over here in
the Martínez Thicket. Mr. Jim [O'Connor] and I were real good buddies. I had some
land leased next to him at Clip. There weren't many deer back in those days
because the screwworms ate up the young. Mr. Jim sent me to a mesquite flat and I
shot my first deer on the O'Connor ranch. Everyone who had river frontage was
happy to let people use it.

This river is my home.

John Freeman Lott

*The river bottom when the trees
were heavy with moss.*

CHAPTER TWO

They Met Us at the Boat

"I used to tell my husband, 'My family came over on the Mayflower.' And he said, 'Hell, woman, mine met the Mayflower.'"

Jeanette Johnstone Perkins

The banks of the San Antonio River, as it traverses the Coastal Bend, once harbored many ethnic communities. Although small, they were the centers of rural life in the late nineteenth century and early twentieth century.

These communities were the heart of a unique culture. They were populated by Hispanics, Mexicans, blacks, and whites. The Hispanics and Mexicans carved out farms and ranches from the old Spanish and Mexican land grants. Blacks, who can trace their origins to slaves brought to Texas in the pre–Civil War era, and whites of

Old boat on Copano Bay.

European and Celtic extraction all lived in harmony. The binding force was the land and the ranching culture that grew from it.

To fully appreciate this culture, it helps to understand how the different groups came to possess, utilize, and share the land. Although this same land was a major source of early-day conflicts, it also became the unifying force that fused the black, white, Hispanic, and Mexican cultures that are the foundation of the Coastal Bend ranching industry.

We All Got Along

"When the water gets high down here, you wish the Indians still had it."

Thomas P. Traylor

Everyone worked together and all adopted the same community friendship. There was no racial problem in this area. Even Santa Anna's soldiers lived here after the Revolution. People had to get along to survive. Even though the cultures were very different, they got along. It was German, Irish, black, Mexican—and nobody else was welcome.

Earl Albrecht

No matter what color you were, you did the same things. We had the same experiences. We all still talk about the same things today.

Black, white, and Spanish all lived down here together. Everyone got along, mostly. Down here we all shared, whites and black alike. We often used the word "podnah" and we meant it. The Spanish and the blacks were friends, too.

Here, if you were a civilized person, you were treated like a civilized person. Sure, there was segregation, but it was not quite the same thing as in other places. I never felt threatened by the white man.

The only way I can see it is like this. We just all got along. We shared and took care of each other. Several whites have said to me that without some of the black women, they wouldn't have survived. They cared for them along with their own children, whether they were paid to do it or not. It may not have been that way up the country, but it sure was here.

Reverend Mack Williams

This had to be the last of the Karankawas. The photo was taken at present-day Aransas National Wildlife Refuge.

The Karankawas

Those of us who are members of early pioneering families in this region of Texas should remember that when our ancestors arrived on the Texas coast, they were greeted as they got off the boat by the native Indian tribes.

The juxtaposition of cultures in this region goes back to 1528, more than four centuries ago, when Alvar Núñez Cabeza de Vaca, two other Spaniards, and a black Moor from North Africa named Estevan found themselves in the land of the Karankawas. This was the first meeting in Texas of the three cultures—Native American, European, and African. These cultures were to meld, after a struggle, to become the unique mix of the Texas Coastal Bend region. The explorers, the remnants of an expedition for the Spanish government, had washed ashore along the coast and had been rescued by the Indians. The group was attempting to make their way on foot to Mexico, which was the only civilization in North America. In Cabeza de Vaca's *Narratives,* the first book published about the Coastal Bend, we have an account of this eight-year odyssey. It is remarkable for its detailed descriptions of Indian life and the land he and his party crossed.[1]

Equally remarkable is the relationship that evolved from this encounter between the different cultures. Cabeza de Vaca lost his conqueror's arrogance and began to view Estevan as his partner and the natives as fellow human beings deserving empathy.[2] In the course of his wanderings, Cabeza de Vaca had the opportunity to

"Reverend Weathers told me one time that an Indian would put on a hog hide and crawl right up to you. He said that one time, three of them were crawlin' up on him and he thought they were hogs and shot one. He didn't know they were Indians."

Milam Thompson

apply simple healing remedies that were well known to European society. Using this knowledge with some of the natives he encountered, he became an esteemed medicine man in their eyes. He also attained a position as a respected intermediary between the Karankawas and unfriendly tribes. This mutual respect among diverse cultures prevails today in the San Antonio River bottom.

The term Karankawa, meaning "dog-lover," was originally applied only to the boating people of the coast. Some say they occupied an area no farther north and east than Galveston Island, while the sandbars and lagoons were occupied by the Attacapas, another seafaring people. In time, the term was extended to several small subgroups or bands of coastal people who shared a common language and culture. The Karankawas went as far north as Goliad looking for food or trading for corn at the mission there. Farther inland, between the San Antonio and Guadalupe rivers, lived the Coahuilteco-speaking

Mrs. Strauch (left) was captured by Indians, then returned later near Copano Bay.

Aranama and Tamique.[3]

Using the accumulated knowledge of generation upon generation, the Karankawas and other tribes of the region lived the nomadic existence of hunters and gatherers. They were intimately familiar with the resources of the land and its waters. Their lifestyle was based on

"As a race they have withered from the land. Their arrows are broken and their springs are dried up. Their cabins are in dust. Their Council fires have long since gone out on the shores and their war cry is fast dying away to the untrodden West.

Slowly and sadly they climb the mountains and read their doom in the setting Sun. They are shrinking before the mighty tide which is pressing them away. They must soon hear the roar of the last wave that will settle over them forever.

Ages hence, the inquisitive white man, as he stands by some growing city, will ponder on the structure of their disturbed remains and wonder to what manner of person they belonged. They will live only in the songs and chronicles of their exterminators. Let these be faithful to their rude virtues as men, and pay tribute to their unhappy fate as a people!"

**Sam Houston,
address to U.S. Senate**

Karankawa Indian, Coastal Bend.

the seasons and was highly adapted to the area they occupied. They sustained themselves on what was available in that place at that time. Their diet consisted of decayed fish, alligator, carrion, snails, worms, crab, conch, water birds, snakes, the prickly pear tuna, and the roots of marsh plants, which were pounded to powder for a tortilla-like bread. Chile was their preferred seasoning instead of salt. Archaeological remains indicate that they also ate deer, javelinas, an occasional buffalo, bears, and other smaller mammals, such as rabbits. Mussels and oysters, turtles, porpoises, various species of fish and birds, and other wild foods were no doubt part of their diet.[4]

The Karankawas were people of large stature, tall and muscular. Cabeza de Vaca's journal and the accounts of later visitors to the region describe the men as being over eight feet tall and the women in the seven-foot range. John J. Linn, an Irish immigrant to Victoria County in 1829, described Antonio, a Karankawa chief, as the most beautiful specimen of physical manhood he had ever seen. The Karankawas carried huge bows and arrows, along with shields made of animal hides. They dressed scantily in buffalo skins and smeared their faces with alligator grease and dirt to protect against mosquitoes. Their housing was carried on sleds that they dragged along with them, and half-wild wolf-dogs often accompanied them.[5]

The fate of the Karankawas is, of course, well known. Among the first of the Texas Indians to meet Europeans, they were also the first Coastal Bend culture to lose out in the evolutionary process of history. The Karankawas were never broken to the yoke, despite the paternalistic approach of the Spanish missionaries in trying to get them to convert to Christianity and a sedentary, agricultural way of life. During the early years of Spanish rule, they appeared to adjust somewhat to colonial culture. At least, they included the missions among their ecological resources by visiting the missions as part of their seasonal rounds in search of meat and grain. March and April was the time when they would normally leave their coastal fishing camps and go inland to the river bottoms and prairies. The Spanish were upset with this roving lifestyle of the Indians. They wanted them to live at the mission settlements on a permanent basis. Although the missions failed in that regard, they did succeed in creating a bridge between the two cultures.

It was not until Anglo-American settlement of Texas began that the Karankawas became hostile. This hostility arose when they were forced to abandon their homelands. They also began refusing contact with the new settlers. Finally, defrauded of their land and deprived of their only friends, the missionaries, the Indians sank into abject poverty. In most cases, the remaining vestiges of these tribes of giants wandered off to mingle with the last free tribes in northern Mexico.

According to an article in the December 14, 1934, issue of *The Refugio Timely Remarks*, "The tribe continued to exist in Refugio until the year 1843, when about forty or fifty men, women, and children, the sole remnant of a once powerful tribe, secured permission from the Mexican government to migrate to that country, and left our country, never to return. This remnant settled in the Mexican state of Tamaulipas and were never heard of again."

My grandmother's papers contain several notes about the Karankawas. Commenting on a story about a fierce storm in 1818 or 1819 that purportedly swept away and drowned the last band of Karankawas off a point of timber in the Brazos River, she wrote that this was "very wrong" and that they were known to be in the San Antonio River area as late as 1930.[6] Some of the older people in the town of

Tivoli remember the last known Karankawa Indian in the area as a huge man of great height who was the local mail carrier until 1930.

The Descendants of Goliath

There were lots of Indian mounds around. They were crescent-shaped and fifty to one hundred feet wide and three hundred feet long. They were made by the Karankawas. The old forts [missions] were trying to civilize the Indians. They were part of the cannibal tribes around here. They didn't like to stay in the bottoms, and they didn't want to be around the other Indians. They ruled over the small Indians.

I once saw an old circle of live oaks over one thousand years old. Under them was a bunch of eight-foot-tall Indian skeletons. They were lying on their sides, frozen to death. Alfonso Pérez was an old Portuguese man. He called the Karankawas "the descendants of Goliath." The tallest one we dug up was eight feet, nine and a quarter inches tall. The women were over seven feet. The last known Karankawa Indian was a mail carrier in Tivoli around 1930. He carried the mail afoot all the way to Copano and back. I know that for a fact.

Earl Albrecht

As Tall as a Tank

I knew José Figueroa. He was full Indian blood. All his life, he work cattle. He was born around 1836, when Texas was independent, and he spent all his life on the O'Connor ranch. He was almost one hundred years old when he died.

Also, there was Jesús Mascoro. He was an Indian about as high as that tank over yonder. His hands were about that long. I think he was a Karankawa, and long legs, too.

One time when we was at the O'Connor River Ranch, Mr. Sitterle sent for him to break some horses. When he got there, Mr. Sitterle asked him how many people he needed to help him break the horses. Mascoro looked at Sitterle and said, "You see that rope, that whip, that quirt over there on my horse? That's all I need." He broke ninety horses for the O'Connor in one year. Nobody ever did do a thing like that around here before.

Víctor Rodríguez

The Legend of Indian Point

There's an old road down on the river. Lewis [or Louis] Terrell told me that there's an old cottonwood tree there. The reason they called it Indian Point was because an Indian would get up in that tree and he'd whistle like a bird. People would come by and stop in their buggy and he'd shoot them with an arrow. That's the story. It's when you go into the ranch from Fannin, the first pasture. At one time there was a ferry on that river.

James K. "Spec" New

Karankawa Indian maiden, Coastal Bend.

The Spaniards

The first permanent settlers along the San Antonio River were the Franciscan missionaries. They were accompanied by Spanish soldiers stationed at each mission's presidio to protect it from the French and hostile Indians. These priests and soldiers from the northern provinces of New Spain were sent to Texas with supplies and livestock to create a self-sustaining agrarian system.

The typical colonial mission was a compound with a chapel, offices, kitchen, granary and mill, carpentry and blacksmith shops, and facilities for weaving their own textiles. The mission's pastures and cultivated fields produced food for man and animals alike.

Civilian settlements, or pueblos, grew up around the presidios. Retired soldiers and their relatives and families, Christianized Indians, and a growing number of merchants made up these surrounding communities. The merchants were important additions to the population because the missions were not allowed to engage in trade.

To provide an early warning system in case of attack by hostile Indians, the presidio soldiers were encouraged to establish small ranches on mission pasturelands at some distance from the mission-presidio complex. These outposts were capable of quick and forceful response to outside aggression. This system was to prove very problematic later on.

With the arrival of a dozen or so families from the Canary Islands in 1731, Texas received its first European colonists. They were sent by Spain to establish Villa de San Fernando on the banks of the San Antonio River. They were the only

Mission Nuestra Señora de Refugio.

such group to arrive during Spanish rule.[7] By the middle of the eighteenth century, there was a cultural blend of Spanish peninsulares, creoles, mestizos, and mixed-race offspring of various Spanish-Indian unions.

When it became obvious that the missions were failing to achieve their objective, the Spanish government began to view them as a financial liability. In 1793, at present-day Refugio, Spain built its last mission, Nuestra Señora del Refugio. Its purpose was to protect the port of Copano from pirates and smugglers while making one last-ditch attempt to convert the Karankawas to Christianity.

At the time the Spanish missions were established, large tracts of land had been awarded by the king to support them. Now there was growing pressure from the area's civilians to obtain title to the lands. There was increasing conflict between the secular ranches and the missions. The ranchers claimed that the missions controlled the best pastureland, while the missionaries accused the ranchers of rustling unbranded stock.

When the missions were finally secularized in the 1790s, mission lands, stock, and other property were turned over to the civil authorities to be distributed to settlers who applied for them. Although the Indians were eligible to apply for land grants, they had no concept of private ownership of land. Their only interest in cattle was to hunt them for food.[8] As a consequence, they did not acquire any of the mission lands available to them and continued to live a subsistence lifestyle in the river bottoms and on the prairies of the Coastal Bend.

The method of surveying the land for private ownership was done in a very rudimentary and haphazard way. This worked well as long as the country was sparsely settled and the neighbors were friendly. Then things began to change.

From the Time of Columbus

You know, there was a fella I met once who ran away from Santa Anna. Joe García lived to be 129 years old. He was servin' with Santa Anna. He did not want to fight Texas, and he didn't want to go back to Mexico. He was very young. He was

Presidio La Bahía, Goliad. It was established in 1721 and is the oldest fort west of the Mississippi.

originally from San Luis Potosí. He went to El Paso and helped build the railroad to New Orleans. He used to work for Mr. Welder and he lived to be 129 years old. He worked cattle the rest of his life after he left Santa Anna.

When he died, we were all goin' to collect for his funeral, but John Welder did the whole funeral because he worked for him. He died without no folks. Who could have folks left at 129?

The world belongs to the good Lord. He gives people as long as He wants. Some people don't believe it.

Jesús Ybarbo, Gaffney Ranch, 1950.

You know, the roots of the Spanish tradition, they been workin' cattle longer than anybody else. The Mexican peoples was one of the first workin' cattle around this country.

They even learned to make their own ropes and saddles from the Spanish. Even the colored peoples learned to work cattle from the Mexicans and the Spanish. It wasn't in their roots like it was the others.

The De La Garzas got here many years before the DeLeóns. Carlos was the commander and chief for the whole area between the Guadalupe and San Antonio rivers. The DeLeóns got to Victoria in 1824. When they all got here, they brought hogs, sheep, chickens, horses, cows, oxen, and seed. They brought whatever they needed, those peoples did. They came from Columbus, you know. When the revolution in Texas started, they went back to Mexico and then came back many years later after things calmed down. My family came back because they were afraid their son would be put in the Mexican army.

There used to not be any border patrol on the river [Rio Grande]. My great-grandfather used to bring people over in a boat for ten cents. Some of the people didn't have the money to pay that, so they would give him hogs, chickens, eggs, or something else.

They tell me through the history, I hear, that they had a hard time at La Bahía when they came over, but they all wanted to stay together and live together. Anaqua

Pete De La Garza and Julián Tijerina Sr., old Williams ranch, ca. 1930.

was where the Mexicans gathered, just like the colored peoples gathered at Lewis's Bend. Ojo de Agua was another place they gathered.

The De La Garza cemetery got started when the O'Connors and the Fagans gave land for us Mexican peoples to bury. When my great-grandfather come here, someone died and there was no place to bury them. He was a very religious man and he walked over to Mr. Dennis O'Connor's [I] and asked him, and Mr. Dennis talked to Mr. Pete Fagan. They gave them a place inside the Fagan cemetery and all my peoples are buried there and we have the right to go in there always.

I can even remember seein' the cows with the four-foot-long horns. Rafael [De La Garza] used to tell me about them. He said they came from the Spanish. He said they were even bigger when he was a young man. He said some of them you couldn't even get into a railroad car, and if you could, it was one horn at a time.

Víctor Rodríguez

Janie O'Riley and Rafael De La Garza, 1920s.

The Mexicans

When the Mexican Revolution erupted in 1810, it eventually brought an end to Spanish rule in Texas. The missions were practically abandoned and settlers had moved onto the land in increasing numbers. The newcomers joined the established Tejano families along the San Antonio River. The earliest ranchers in the area carried names such as Arocha, Becerra, Flores, De La Garza, Guerra, Peña, Pérez, Rodríguez, Tijerina, and Ybarbo.

The most notable ranching dynasty was that of Don Carlos De La Garza, the son of a Mexican soldier who was garrisoned at Goliad. Don Carlos had started a subsistence ranching operation along the north side of the San Antonio River. In 1834 he received a land grant encompassing the ranch as well as the village known as Carlos Ranch, which had grown up around the river crossing. A member of a pioneer family in the area described Carlos Ranch as a Mexican village composed of "highly educated and wealthy people" who were "just as intellectual and cultured in those days as the country can now boast of."[9]

In my interviews I have discovered a great dichotomy among the descendants of the pioneer Spanish and Mexican families as to where their cultural loyalties lie. Many still feel strongly that they are Spanish, while others regard themselves as Mexicans. Occasionally, I find a person who believes himself to be almost pure Indian and identifies more with the Indian traditions than either the Spanish or Mexican cultures.

The Indian Tradition in the Mexican

In my family, we are more Indian. Mexicans have fifty-two Indian tribes and each one of these is different, so sometime they don't know or understand each other even as Mexican-Americans.

There are so many different ideas and ways, it is difficult to understand each other in our own culture.

There are still so many tribal influences on those of us with Indian blood in us. We cannot even understand each other's feelings at times. Those of us with more Indian in us are much more superstitious than the Spanish who brought in the Christian religion.

Carlos De La Garza came in here long before even Martín DeLeón, and they were both Spanish. Each got a Spanish land grant. José [de] Escandón was a Spanish count who sent the first Spanish over here. The Portillas and the Benavides

"The De La Garza ranch was a big ranch at one time. I was told a steamboat used to come up the river to the ranch."

Johnny De La Garza

were some early people who came in with the Spanish also. These people raised cattle and horses when they got here.

Even though these people lost their lands in a series of revolutions, they still work on this land for the new owners. Because we once owned this land is one reason we are so attached to it and work it like it is still ours. We feel like we still own it.

Spain gave up the land in the Mexican Revolution and Mexico gave up the land in the Texas Revolution. Everything was fair. Ultimately, God chooses what will happen. It was in the Víctoria treaty after the Texas Revolution that the De La Garzas could keep their land because they helped many Texans during the war. Any Mexican that was here was allowed to keep their land and their citizenship. Many lost land because they did not file their claims right. There was a lot of monkey business, too, after the revolution. The big fish ate the little fish and the big fish changed the laws.

So be it, God's will.

Víctor Rodríguez

Our Heritage

Actually, we were raised with a mixture of the Anglo and the Mexican culture. We are half Irish also. Our mother was an O'Riley. They were Irish and came over here when the O'Connors did from Ireland. We don't really think about what we are. Our life wasn't much like Mexican. We did speak Spanish in the home, but it was mostly our father that spoke Spanish. Our mother, Janie O'Riley [De La Garza], spoke mostly English.

Louise De La Garza Mace, Johnny De La Garza, Julia O'Riley Rodríguez, Mary Lucy De La Garza Adams, Beatrice De La Garza Nava

My ancestors were from Spain. Don Carlos De La Garza was born at La Bahía in 1801. His father was a military man. Around 1829, Don Carlos married Tomasita in the La Bahía chapel. That same year, they moved to the Carlos Ranch on the San Antonio River. I identify more with the Spanish influence. We were allowed to keep our land after the Revolution.

Alejandro De La Garza

Our family was from Spain. There were a few of our ancestors who had red hair and blue eyes. When the Spaniards came to Mexico, my family began to move to this country.

Julián Tijerina

My ancestors were both Indian and Spanish, but the Spanish traits are stronger. My family was from Goliad at La Bahía. This is where they had some land. Through the generations, the land was divided, so there was no loss of land except by division. I

Ynocente De La Garza Amador.

do not have any resentment that there is none left for me. I do know that there is history in that land, a history of my family and their contributions to society.

Margaret Pérez-Salazar Rubio

I was born on the De La Garza ranch in 1902. My father's name was Jesús De La Garza, and my mother was Julia Ybarbo. When I was eight, my father died. He had lots of horses, cows, and mules. I am kind of an aunt to everyone. Víctor's dad [Juan Menchaca Rodríguez] was my godfather. My mother and Jesús Ybarbo's father were from Nacogdoches. Julián's [Tijerina] grandmother, Jesús' father, and my mother were brother and sisters. My mother was very pretty. She had red hair and blue eyes and was very fair-skinned. She looked like an American.

People in those days were very poor, but my mother had plenty to eat. After my daddy died, my mother was the boss of the family. When my mother died, we inherited the land and split it among us. There was a restriction on the land when she inherited it that she could not sell it. She had to pass it on to her family. Her life was about staying home and taking care of the family. She made all the decisions at the ranch. She was well respected by all the people, who called her "Mama Julia." She let other families camp out by the river and get water. After the Revolution, the De La Garzas were the only ones to have maintained their lands.

Ynocente "Tía Minnie" De La Garza Amador

The Pérez family: Arnulfo, Pancho Sr., Pancho Jr., and Linda Pérez.

My family was from the province of Andalucía in southern Spain. They, together with other immigrants to the New World, came through the Canary Islands to New Orleans. From there, they went up the Mississippi River and Red River to Nacogdoches. Our family was driven from the area in the 1770s and began traveling towards San Antonio. Several dropped out of the procession between Goliad and San Antonio. Our family came to his area of Texas from that journey.

Jesús Ybarbo

We Are Friends

"You all keep digging in history, we're all gonna come from Spain with Columbus."

Julián Tijerina

I was born on the O'Connor ranch called El Oso in 1931. My great-grandparent was Antonio De La Garza, the last of the big rancheros. His wife was Ponposa Bontan, the daughter of Manuel Becerra. I am from the Carlos De La Garza family. He remained loyal to Mexico in the Texas Revolution, but helped his Texan friends. The rest of the family fought for Texas independence. They were all Spanish land grant holders.

Both José María and Paulino were spies for Colonel Fannin. Carlos was alone in his family as a Mexican loyal. Aunt Salomé said Carlos was on the land in 1824, but he never got title. He was applying to Power and Vidaurri to perfect his title. He was born at La Bahía in 1801. His father was born there also in 1778. He was Antonio De La Garza.

Manuel Becerra was also born at La Bahía in 1765. He was an *alcalde* of Goliad in 1834. He granted over sixty thousand acres for the settlers. He was the last explorer in Texas for the Spanish regime. He signed the peace treaty with the Karankawas and the Cocos for the town of Goliad on May 27, 1827. He was a *procurador* or councilman and law officer at the time.

These men were the early frontiersmen, and they came to La Bahía. It was like a beacon shining in the north for people to come to. The Carlos Ranch was like this

Last survivors of the Texas Revolution, 1906.

also. Everyone in Mexico knew of these places and would come to them. Many of these came as soldiers to protect the area from the Indians. Everyone was very fearful of the Indians.

Just knowing that my family did some honorable things for the Irish makes me happy. The relationship between our families has been long and friendly. My research shows that in spite of their different loyalties, the De La Garzas and the Irish in the area remained close friends. They fought on different sides, but they have always been friends.

The Europeans learned ranching from the Spanish and Mexicans. They learned

Earliest Ranches in the San Antonio River Valley

La Mora
Laguna de las Ánimas
Las Cabras
Los Chayopínes
Los Corralitos de Reyes
Rancho Amoladeras
Rancho de Capitán Piscina
Rancho Guerra
San Antonio del Cíbolo
San Bartolo
San Rafael
Señor San José

from the days of the missions and that knowledge was brought from Spain. They also brought the Catholic religion with them.

Our family stayed with Mexico because of patriotism. They did not approve of having Protestant Americans here. They did not mind the Irish, but the North Americans were not friendly to the Spanish and Mexicans. Their views were very different. Even Austin's colony was mostly Protestant and the De La Garzas didn't go for that. It was probably religious problems. They objected strongly to the Protestants and would never bow to anything American.

The Tijerinas were living on the Carlos Ranch and were related to the De La Garzas. That is all I know about them. They were either related through the mother's or the father's families. I do not think we are related to the Rodríguez family.

The Carlos Ranch was in operation before 1824. It was a settlement for the family and a stronghold for the area. Many people were running from the political problems in Mexico. The ranch was 5,535 acres. He lost that to the Texans after the Revolution and the governor or someone told him to get out.

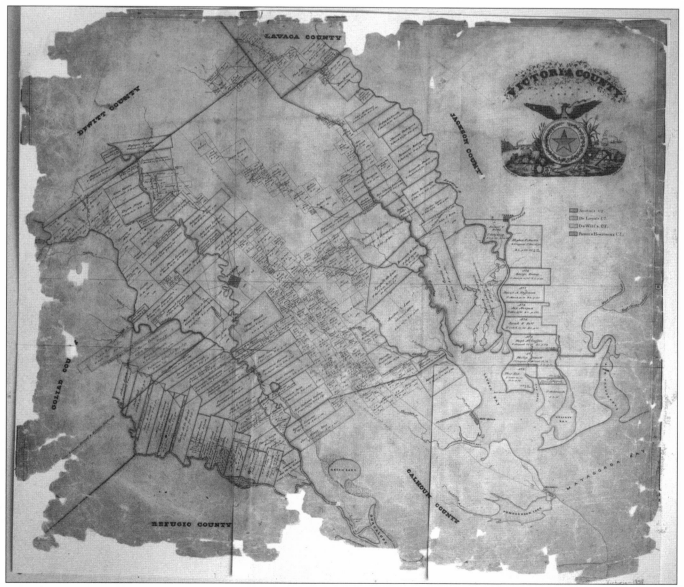

Map of Victoria County, 1858. Courtesy of Texas General Land Office, Austin.

Manuel Becerra had 8,856 acres granted to him by Francisco Vidaurri in 1834 in the Copano area somewhere. When Carlos lost his ranch in 1836, he wound up on a portion of 2,214 acres of the Becerra grant. His wife bought this land from the Becerras probably because Texas was still after him when the Revolution was over. Probably, they would let her buy land—so what? She was Antonia Cruz, Carlos' second wife. Antonia bought this land from María Josepha Becerra, old Manuel's eldest daughter. They were married in Refugio County in September 1840. Francisco De La Garza, Carlos' younger brother, got the 2,214 acres.

Carlos De La Garza was an honorable person, well thought of, and in spite of the troubles with Texas, they would not hurt him because he was brave and honorable. He did a lot for the settlers here.

The attitude of the Irish toward the family was friendly. Carlos was born here, and if the Irish had wanted to kill him after the Revolution, they would have. All of this area was Irish after the Revolution and I guess they would not allow anyone to harm their friends, the De La Garzas. In those days a friend was a real friend. They would die for you.

The women of that time all owned their own land and had their own brands. Many even ran the land themselves. I have a letter from Ponposa Bontan saying that the Americans were killing the Mexicans in 1870. I have no proof of any of this except this letter. It seems that the ones who fought on the Texas side got land for fighting for Texas, and Carlos and the ones who remained on the Mexican side got theirs confiscated.

Abel Rubio

"The Reading of the Texas Declaration of Independence," painting by Charles and Fanny Normann. James Power (in dark clothes) is seated beside Sam Houston who is in left front chair. Collection of the Joe Fultz Estate, Navasota. Courtesy of the Star of the Republic Museum.

The Rancheros

Carlos De La Garza came here way before Martín DeLeón. Most of these came here so early they came from Spain. De La Garza was a leader over here. The De La Garzas, Tijerinas, Benavides, Portillas, and Placedos were all here long before the Texas Revolution. Maybe they were here for over one hundred years. They were here along the San Antonio River. They never built towns or cities, just ranches. They were rancheros. Francisco Tijerina was here long before the Revolution.

We all lost our lands in the revolutions here in Texas. No, we really didn't lose it, it just passed from one brother to another. We accept that things get divided in time, but at the same time, the memory is there and the history is there and we identify with the fact that our families were part of the creation of this state.

We contributed then and we still contribute to our society. In 1821, Spain just gave it up and then it belonged to Mexico. Any Mexican that was here was allowed to keep his land, but many of them didn't go and register so they could keep their land. Then, when Texas won the next revolution, the old Spanish claims were not registered, and even though they had lived there all their lives, they did not have legal claim to the land. The new laws changed all that ownership.

The people just didn't understand what they had to do. Still, some of them had land along the river that they were allowed to keep. Carlos De La Garza kept his because he helped Texans in the Revolution. His ranch was a horse ranch and they either had work raising horses or cutting wood for the corrals and for the fences. They also grew vegetables, corn, and potatoes on the ranch and during the winter they picked pecans. That is how they kept themselves going from the land that they had owned since the Spanish were here.

Alejandro De La Garza, Elías De La Garza, Víctor Rodríguez, Margaret Pérez-Salazar Rubio, Mary Luz Pérez De La Garza, Teresa Escalona Tijerina, San Juana De Los Santos Martínez, Anita Martínez, Julián Tijerina

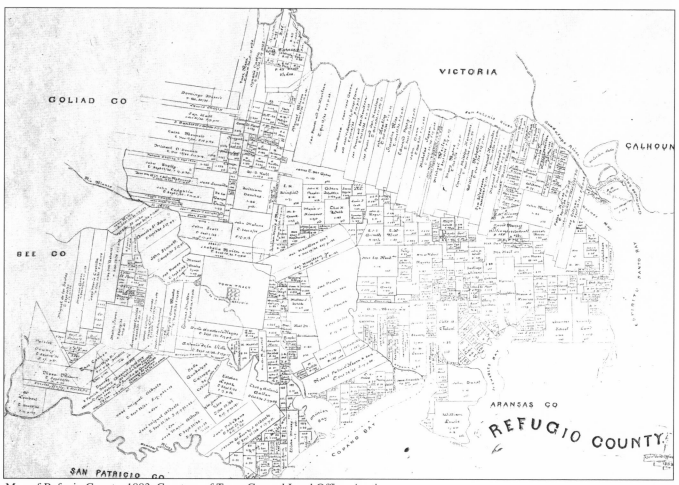

Map of Refugio County, 1883. Courtesy of Texas General Land Office, Austin.

The Irish

As Mexico struggled to form a national government, there was much confusion and chaos in the land. Needless to say, it was magnified on Mexico's northern frontier. There, the instability facilitated the Anglo-American and European colonization of Texas.

Desperately in need of a population of loyal citizens to deter encroachment from the United States, Mexico launched a program of colonizing its northern frontier. In other areas of the state, many of the colonists were of European and European-American descent. Here in the Coastal Bend, the majority of the colonists came from Ireland.

By 1830, conditions between the Mexican government and the colonists had deteriorated to the point that revolution against Mexico was inevitable. Open warfare began in 1835 and Texas won its independence in 1836.

Under this colonization system, the government of the state of Coahuila and Texas contracted with immigration agents called empresarios. These agents received large grants of land and agreed to import colonists of the Catholic faith. The empresarios were to be responsible for the colonists' welfare and settlement in their new home and were to keep the colony progressing and safe from danger. Each settler, for a nominal fee, could receive up to a league (4,428 acres) of pastureland and a *labor* (177 acres) of land for cultivation. In return, the settlers were expected to adhere to Mexican law, uphold the Catholic faith, and abide by the traditions of their new country.

Inspired by the success of Stephen F. Austin and his colonists, James Hewetson interested a fellow Irishman, James Power, in forming a joint venture to establish a colony of Irish Catholic and Mexican families in the Coastal Bend. Hewetson had immigrated to Mexico in the 1820s and was living in Saltillo, where he carried on a successful mercantile and manufacturing business. James Power came to Mexico about the same time and married the daughter of an army officer. Like Hewetson, Power became a Mexican citizen.

Power and Hewetson applied for a contract in 1826 but did not receive their grant until 1828. The grant finally included the littoral leagues between the Guadalupe and Lavaca rivers and between the

John J. O'Brien, Refugio, early 1900s.

John J. Power, son of Phillip and Mary Louisa Luque Power and brother of Mary Agnes Power Shay.

Terms from the Old Land Grants

arpent—an old French unit of land equivalent to about 0.85 acre
caballería—a parcel of about 105 acres; originally, the amount of land considered necessary to keep one horse in fit condition to serve the king
fanega—the amount of land required for sowing one and a half bushels of grain
hacienda—an estate of 5 or more square leagues
huebra—the amount of land plowed by a yoke of oxen in one day
labor—one million square varas, or 177.1 acres
legua—a league, or 4,428.4 acres
sitio—a league
vara—the standard linear unit for measuring land; officially defined as the equivalent of about 32.9 inches but highly variable in practice; by the empresario period, the more convenient 33^1/3-inch vara had been silently adopted by most surveyors in Texas

James Hewetson.

Guadalupe and Nueces rivers. By 1831, they had also acquired the lands of the Refugio mission.

A conflict arose between Martín DeLeón, another empresario, and Power and Hewetson because they had been given overlapping grants. The dispute was settled by granting the lands from Coleto Creek to the mouth of the Nueces as the northern border of the Power-Hewetson grant. Around this time, James Hewetson obviously tired of the struggle to establish the colony in Texas. Being a successful businessman in Mexico and having married a wealthy and well-connected widow, he turned his part of the colonial grant over to James Power. He never again had anything to do with the huge grant of land to the north, nor did he concern himself with its colonists.

Power, a native of County Wexford, Ireland, returned there in 1833 in the hope of enticing his friends and relatives to join his Texas enterprise. Included in the group were a number of his relatives named O'Brien and O'Connor. His young nephew, Thomas O'Connor, may have become Power's "honcho" for the new colony even before they left Ireland. Family records indicate that O'Connor arrived before the rest of the group and, soon after, began managing land, cattle, and business transactions for his uncle.

From left: Martin O'Connor and Tom O'Connor (II), L. A. Fritz, Charlie Webb, Dan Mitchell, and friends.

Approximately 350 Irish immigrants embarked on the voyage, but roughly half died from an outbreak of cholera, which had first arrived in the United States in 1832 from India. The survivors came ashore at Copano in 1834 and were joined by a group of Mexican colonists from Coahuila. Many settled in present-day Refugio and San Patricio counties.

Most of the settlers, having been tenant farmers in their native Ireland, were astonished by the vast coastal plains and lush river bottoms of Texas. By 1836, the O'Connor, Fagan, McDonough, Teal, Fox, O'Brien, Bower, Perry, and Davis families

"Half of Goliad County at one time belonged to the Ybarbos. His name was Marie Jesús Ybarbo. All of our property is Ybarbo grant land."

June Pettus

from the Power-Hewetson Colony were firmly entrenched on the south side of the river. The Teals, Sidicks, and O'Rileys lived on the north bank at Carlos Ranch with the early Mexican settlers.

The Power-Hewetson Colony, the neighboring McGloin-McMullen Irish Colony at San Patricio, and the De León Colony at Victoria settled down and prospered in spite of revolution, primitive frontier conditions, and frequent Indian raids. In accordance with the requirements of the colonial grants, they also started schools and churches.

When Our Ancestors Arrived

Judge George Amery.

Delores Power.

John Batiste Sidick.

Janie O'Riley.

James Joseph Murphy.

This area down here was perfect for survival living. Everything that was needed was here. The Spanish mission system didn't work because they couldn't settle the Indians. The United States and the French were pressing the Spanish and then the Mexican government, so they needed to bring in immigrants to fill the empty space.

The Irish were brought over here because they were Catholic and were eager to escape the problems in their own country. They were looking for cheap land and they didn't worry about what they were going to do with it.

Agnes Murphy.

The major interest here was in the land. Later, the land began to pay off. When the markets were developed, the wealth began to build.

This country is livestock country and water has helped it become valuable, productive, and profitable. Good water is the most important commodity for any settled region, and has been the key to success for the Coastal Bend.

A ranch cannot survive without good water. Every major area of this country was developed on water. Our excellent water sources here enabled us to develop very early on. The original Tom O'Connor [I] was instrumental in promoting water systems in Texas. Port O'Connor was named for him. He was even trying to get an intercoastal canal built.

Most settlers came in here by water, not overland. Everything had to come in by water and out by water. There was very little trade overland, even into Mexico.

This area developed because of its proximity to good water, both fresh and salt. That is why our ranching business developed so early. The water enabled them to raise cattle and to carry on trade with the outside world.

The merchant class in the early days lived on the coast. There were factories and all kinds of trade. Everything was freighted inland by ox cart before the railroads and roadways came in.

Dennis O'Connor (I) with sons (from left) Tom, Martin, and Joe, 1885.

The seaports were very important in the early days. There was a lot of trade between the Coastal Bend and New Orleans. They even tried to send cattle to New Orleans by boat but that was not successful. There were no roads or railroads, so water transportation was essential to settlement and progress. The rivers and the bays and Gulf were all very important. Populations flock around water and we were no exception here in the Coastal Bend.

Thomas M. O'Connor (II)

The African-Americans

"We were oxened off."

Zearlee Robinson Wesley

People of African descent have lived in Texas, although not continuously, for four centuries. Like Estevan, the Moor who accompanied Cabeza de Vaca to the Coastal Bend in 1528, African slaves and servants arrived with other Spaniards who came to the region as explorers, missionaries, and government officials. By 1792, almost 15 percent of the population, around 3,100 persons, were of African descent.

During Spanish and Mexican rule, the free blacks had all the same rights as other citizens and could own land and hold office. In the era of the empresarios, Mexican policy regarding slavery was vague and often contradictory. While slavery was not expressly prohibited in the new colonies, the slave trade was illegal and all slaves born within the empire were to be freed at the age of fourteen. In 1829, Mexico freed all slaves and banned further slave importation. By 1832, "peonage" was accommodated, but with a ten-year limit. However, there were always exemptions, and Mexico was never committed to the full abolition of slavery. This was mainly because of the threat of protest from the Anglo-American settlers.

After the Texas Revolution, slavery became an institution and was tied to the production of cotton in the eastern and coastal regions. Even the free African-Americans could no longer hold office, own property, or marry outside their race. A few were allowed to retain their land through petitions.

The Coastal Bend was mostly cattle country, but the Lewis plantation and several others around the San Antonio River were notable exceptions. The Hispanics, who

Churning on the Kyle ranch. (This woman may have been a Kyle slave.)

had been working cattle for centuries in the area, remained the cowhands. The blacks were mostly engaged in agriculture and domestic work until later in the century. After Emancipation, the freed slaves had several options. They could remain with their former owners as hired hands, tenant farmers, and domestics, or they could move on and establish emancipation communities on unclaimed or purchased land. Often, along the San Antonio River, they did both. They would reside in their small settlements and communities and farm at a subsistence level and also go out to the large ranches to work for cash.

In 1889 a landowner near Berclair, a relative newcomer to the area from England, made the following entries in his journal:

9th Sunday. Harold brought over two Hutt Boys & another Boy call'd Kemp was already here, so sisc of us sat down to dinner. Best the nigger brought his mother & two children to look at the land for sale. His older brother failed to come from Beeville so nothing settled.

10th Monday. Went down to see Mrs. Wilson to ask her opinion about selling land to niggers. She say[s] they are no inconvenience as neighbours if not too near our homestead but an advantage as regards getting cheap labour at any time required. They are taking them all round. Better than low down white people. This corroborates my own opinion.[10]

Many blacks became expert cowboys and legendary cooks on the Coastal Bend ranches, participating in the great trail drives. The coming of the railroads ended this era in the history of the ranching industry.

Mildred Koontz with Aunt Hattie Green Allen at St. Joseph Catholic Church in Inez. Hattie's parents were sold into slavery separately.

Aunt Belle Roy

Assisting Grandma Wood in the running of her large household was a remarkable black woman known as Aunt Belle Roy. She was highly regarded, said Grandmother, and you minded her promptly. "I'd have just as soon thought of disobeying God as disobeying Aunt Belle," recalled Grandmother.

She, Aunt Belle, had been a slave, brought to St. Mary's from New Orleans. This is the tale Grandmother told (which she got from Aunt Belle) of the end of the Civil War and the freeing of Aunt Belle and her family. St. Mary's had heard

Barbara Novella Lott, Nathaniel Youngblood's mother.

rumors that the war was coming to an end, but they were only rumors 'til a schooner came into port from New York, carrying newspapers about the surrender at Appomattox. Grandpa Wood read the papers and came into the kitchen.

"You are free now, Aunt Belle," said he, "the war is over," and he read her the newspaper account. "Since you are free now, Aunt Belle, I would like to know what you want to do." "I've been well-treated here," said Aunt Belle, "and I do not wish to leave, but I would like to be paid for what I do." "That is right and fair," said Grandpa Wood. "How much would you like to be paid?" She named a sum and they shook hands on it.

Grandmother once asked her grandfather why he, a northerner, had had slaves. "I didn't believe in slavery at all, but I had to have some help for your Grandmother Nancy. I would get an Irish girl to help her and one of my cowboys would set eyes on her and she would be married and gone before a year was up."

Besides being a wonderful housekeeper, said Grandmother, Aunt Belle was equally gifted as a midwife. So good was she at midwifing that Grandpa Wood freed her from her housekeeping post in the later years to be a traveling "nurse aide" whenever someone was having a baby in the large Wood family. Aunt Belle would come a month before the baby was expected and stay until the baby was a month old. She came for the birth of my mother and her brothers and sisters. "I cannot tell you how good it was to see Aunt Belle's face at the door," said Grandmother. "When I saw her, I knew that I would live and my baby would live

Charlie Lewis Sr., Lottie Lewis Mumphord, Kim Lewis, Elie Lewis Smith, Lenora Lewis Johnson, Elmer Lewis, and "Wild Man" Hand Shaw.

and everything would be alright. I really had more faith in her than I did in the doctor." Mother has, to this day, a small worn baby quilt made for her by Aunt Belle while waiting for her arrival.

Grandmother once queried Aunt Belle on her days in slavery. "I was always very well treated," said Aunt Belle. "I don't have anything at all to complain of, but now I can go where I want to go."

Mary Elizabeth Welder Knight

How We Got Our Land

St. Paul Community was about nine miles northwest of Goliad. It was settled by ex-slaves. Stories have it that some of the people bought their land with gamblin' money and some with treasure money. A lot of the men would go out coon huntin' and sell the hides.

We were country folk. There were some hard times and some good times. God came first in our community.

Della May McDow Bennett, Allie Fay Moore Robinson, Ruby Lee Youngblood Edwards, Vernell Gray Shelton

I've heard my grandmother say she worked a whole year after she was freed to buy a horse. A lot of the women took in laundry and ironing. My daddy used to drive cattle up the Chisholm Trail for the Pettus family.

Della May McDow Bennett

Henry Williams, uncle of Reverend Mack Williams.

Grannie Andrews, mother of Minnie Spriggs, with her granddaughter, Entora Spriggs.

Jodie Shaw, midwife in Refugio and daughter-in-law of "Wild Man" Hand Shaw.

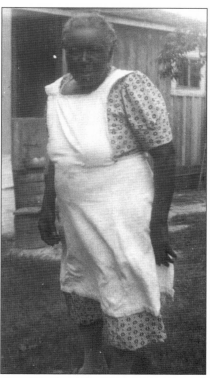

Aunt Hattie at the Koontz home, Inez.

The Black Jacks was an old community after slavery times. They turned them loose down there. My grandfather was one of them, and they fished. They fenced up some two hundred odd acres. That was all they could afford. They said it cost two bits an acre. They farmed and had a little garden. That's the way they made their livin'.

Royal McKinley Williams

"I can remember no fences around here. The big ranches were put together early. Old Man Tom O'Connor worked for wages like anyone, and when he got a little money he'd buy some land. When he bought it, the others had to go."

Herbert "Buster" Bickford

Buster Bickford.

Grandpa raised horses here when it was still open prairie. He was on the Santa Fe Expedition and wound up in jail in Mexico. Sam Houston told them not to go.

There were lots of people in this area went on that expedition. They were goin' to take New Mexico and make it a state. They had a guide and he took them into a range of mountains somewhere above El Paso or thereabouts.

He sold them out and marched them into Mexico and there were the Mexican troops waitin' for them. They were in jail there for over a year and had to walk back to Texas with cowhide and sacks on their feet.

When he got back, he married a girl from Lewis Plantation, Sarah Lewis. Everyone was ranchers around here and so was my family. It was 1854 when he settled here and had one girl. There was good relations until she married Ed Phelps. That was Mary Bickford. Now, here come Mary and Ed and wanted half of his land. They went to court and she got a child's share out of half. That caused hard feelin's and some feudin' started. Later, Ed Phelps rounded up all the horses and left outta here and was never heard from again.

Around 1914 or 1915, an article came out in the *Houston Chronicle* about an explosion in a San Antonio lawyer's office and the lawyer was killed. I looked at it and saw Ed Phelps Jr. was the guy. My old aunt looked into it and found out it was Phelps's son. She wanted to just let it go, so we did. No more feudin'.

It had been constant fightin' and it cost us lots of land. The Bickfords were losers and alcoholics. They were constantly in trouble. The stigma stuck with my family. If one person did something wrong, the whole family was guilty back in them days.

My grandfather lost land because he was a Confederate and because of some trouble back in those times. There was a lot of buyin' out of trouble with land. I never held any grudges about any of it. I think Dennis O'Connor [I] got some of that Lewis land through marriage, but I don't know what happened to it. I don't really know how Lewis got this land. Probably bought it for nothin' like everyone else did.

The De La Garzas and Tijerinas owned all the land around here once and they lost it in the revolutions. My grandfather sold 'em slaves. They were loyal to Mexico and they got burned out by the Texans. That's the way it is in war. Land changed hands after all the wars.

Well, after the Civil War, Tijerina didn't have no money, couldn't pay the taxes. The Terrells come in and paid the damn taxes and took it. I've known a hundred Tijerinas and everyone one of them come from right up here. I think they got a Spanish land grant. They've all been good people and right to the top. They just lost everything in the wars.

There was a lot of those people were disloyal to Texas and when the Texans sent out fourteen or fifteen men with Winchesters, those Mexicans didn't come back. Hell, everybody was on the side of the Texans. The Mexicans were disloyal to the cause and they wanted to take Texas back for Mexico and they weren't about to get by with that. At least, that's the way my daddy looked at it. Leave it with them what's got it.

You take the De Leóns—why, hell, they owned half of Victoria County and tried to claim half of Refugio County. They finally sold it to somebody else for about fifteen cents an acre. All these wars took a lot of people out.

Now a bunch of 'em are tryin' to jump all these people done found oil on their land. Back when those people got it, it wasn't worth nothin'. Then they struck oil and here they come. That's happened a lot around here over the years.

I think it belongs to the people live on it now. Those old families went back to Mexico and tried to stir up another revolution against Texas. I'd rather live with people I can get along with.

Herbert "Buster" Bickford

Imaginin'

They call me "Jim," but I was born Santiago DeLeón on the Lower Mission Valley Road in 1913. I was born on the last tract of land belongin' to the DeLeóns. My father was Octavio DeLeón and his father was Patricio DeLeón. Patricio was a grandson of Don Martín De León, the founder of Victoria.

I am the fifth generation from Martín De León. At one time my family owned much land in this area. He was given a land grant by the Spanish government to bring people to this area of Texas to settle. The grant was finally given by Guadalupe Hidalgo, the president of Mexico, and Martín was to make a settled place out of the wilderness. Mexico had become independent from Spain. The Spaniards had ruled here for three hundred years. There was a lot of buffalo in Don Martín's time.

My imagination tells me a lot of things about the past. Some of it I get from readin' and some of it I just imagine. Then I put it all together. All of this area around here I call my past. They tell me that Don Martín had around a million acres of land around here. You can imagine how big that was.

I often tell the schoolchildren about how Don Martín got along in the wilderness. At the time of Don Martín it was wilderness. Now it is not.

Don Martín had a lot of land and he could dispose of it any way he wanted to. He was authorized by the president of Mexico, Guadalupe Hidalgo. Don Martín got lonely in this wilderness and wanted to have a party. Now, that's imagination. I imagine a friend of his came over and told him he had a lot of tomato plants at his house, in fact, he was pretty well blessed with a good crop of tomatoes, pumpkins, maybe watermelons, or whatever they planted in gardens in those days.

The friend brought Don Martín some fruits he had from his garden as a little gift. Don Martín knew the guy was plantin' on his land, but he ignored it. He was so glad to get the gifts from the man and he asked him how long he had been plantin' there. The man answered Don Martín that he had been there awhile. De León told the man how nice he thought the gift was and wanted the man to feel good when he gave him the forty acres of land he was plantin' on. He also offered the forty acres of land for the man's boots.

Don Martín said he could use a good pair of boots because there were so many rattlesnakes around and since they seemed to have the same size feet, he would trade him for the land. The man agreed to it. What De León wanted most was the company of the guy around him. He wanted him to stick to the place and it would only cost him a pair of boots to stay until the last day of his life.

"We were Watusis, so they say."

Althia Lewis Burns Franklin

Another story I imagine is one where Don Martín De León had a little go-in with the Cibola Indians in the area. They would always come and ask De León for cattle because he had so many. His cattle would go out there and eat all that grass that was in abundance. The Indians called my ancestor "Vacamucha." It means lots of cows. He was their protector. The chief would tell Martín that he needed some cattle for his people. Don Martín gave them gladly. They had a pretty good size tribe and three or four cattle would be eaten up in one meal.

These things I imagine, that another tribe of Indians would come and try to beat the Indians protected by Don Martín. There was jealousy goin' on from the other tribe. They would come and fight De León's Indians. I guess it was only a natural thing to happen.

Don Martín had been goin' out to Monterrey and one time he came back with a jackass and a gun and he mounted the gun on the jackass's back and shot at the enemy Indians. Pow! Wom! and it probably killed four or five of those enemy Indians. Killed the jackasses, too.

There is another story about some acreage on the Calle De Los Diez Amigos. When Martín came to Victoria to make plans for the beginnin' of the town of Victoria, he was ridin' alone, like a lone wolf. He throwed his saddle right on the De León Plaza, which was full of huisache. He picked up his prayer book that had the Twelve Truths of the World in it. He was lyin' on his saddle, readin' the book

Víctor Rodríguez.

The prayer pamphlets "Las Doce Verdades del Mundo" and "La Mano Poderosa."

and readin' the Twelve Truths when he heard a horse comin' up. He pulled out his gun and the horse moved away. This happened several times and the next mornin' when he had scratched up a little fire to make his coffee, he heard the horse's hooves again. Don Martín was waitin' for the closer steppin' of the horse when he saw a gun barrel stickin' out of the fog and a man said, "No que nada usted. I want nothing with you."

De León challenged him and said he must have wanted somethin' to have come so many times, and the man admitted he had been sent to kill him and asked where all the twelve people were that were protecting him. Don Martín said there was no one protecting him or watching over him. The man said he had seen many people around Don Martín.

He got down off his horse and sat by the fire having coffee with De León. After talkin' with him for a while, he realized there was no one with him the night before and tears began runnin' down his face. This story was brought down in the family maybe through Aunt Susie. It has much to do with the Twelve Truths of the World, Las Doce Verdades del Mundo. It is about the Twelve Apostles that accompanied Jesús on His journey through life.

All the names of De La Garza, Tijerina, Ybarbos, I have heard many times. They came here with each other, they were good friends and neighbors. They were a different group than the De Leóns. I think Don Martín did marry a De La Garza by the name of Patricia. I do not know if she was kin to the De La Garzas of the San Antonio River.

All these things were passed down in my family as true. I imagine them. I am happy with what I have.

Santiago "Jim" DeLeón

CHAPTER THREE

River Bottom Communities: Centers of the World

"Back then, if you ran out of somethin', there was no goin' to town to get it right fast. All the families out here supplied each other. You see somebody comin' to the house in a high lope, and they generally got what they needed. That's the way we grew up out here."

Herbert "Buster" Bickford

Maps of the lower San Antonio River basin are dotted with place-names that mark the region's development over four centuries. Communities were formed as settlers banded together for safety and company. Often these settlements grew up around a commercial operation such as a mill, ferry, or trading post. With the growth of commerce, small towns developed to support cotton-processing, shipping, and other activities. Other communities got their start as freedmen's colonies. Many settlements were formed on private ranchland to accommodate ranch hands and their families. Some of the old river communities are still viable. Others are proverbial wide places in the road, with no indication of what thriving little towns they used to be. Many are gone entirely, and not even the old landmarks remain.

During the Spanish-Mexican era, Refugio, Goliad, Victoria, and the coastal settlement of Copano were the most important towns in the region. Refugio and

Hotel Leah at Austwell, ca. 1912.

Goliad had grown up as civilian settlements around the missions, and Victoria had grown steadily over time from De León's colony on the Guadalupe River. Copano, south of Refugio on Copano Bay, was the deepest port in Texas. Almost all imported

RIVER BOTTOM COMMUNITIES

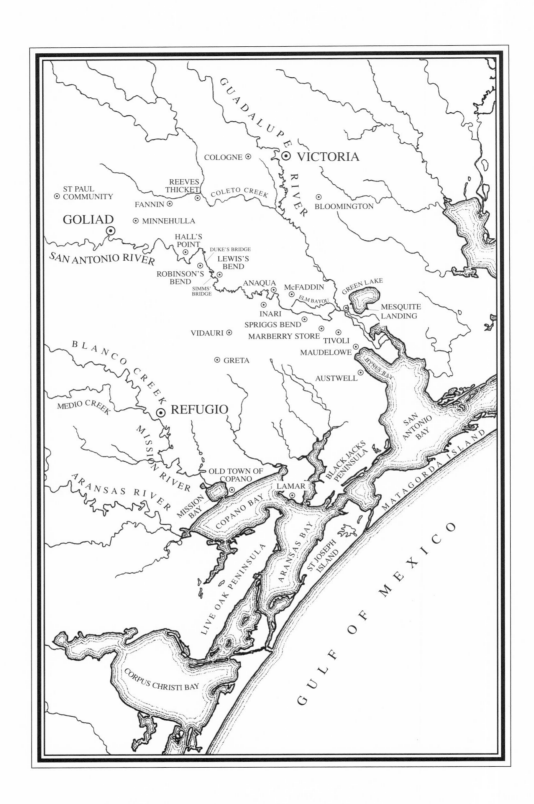

GUADALUPE RIVER

COLOGNE ⊙   ⊙ VICTORIA

ST PAUL
⊙ COMMUNITY

REEVES
THICKET
⊙

COLETO CREEK

⊙ BLOOMINGTON

FANNIN ⊙

GOLIAD
⊙   ⊙ MINNEHULLA

HALL'S
POINT
⊙

DUKE'S BRIDGE

SAN ANTONIO RIVER

LEWIS'S
BEND
⊙

ROBINSON'S
BEND
⊙

SIMMS'
BRIDGE

ANAQUA
⊙   McFADDIN
⊙

GREEN LAKE

ELM BAYOU

MESQUITE
LANDING

INARI
⊙

SPRIGGS BEND
⊙

VIDAURI ⊙   MARBERRY STORE

TIVOLI
⊙

MAUDELOWE
⊙

⊙ GRETA

HYNES BAY

BLANCO CREEK

AUSTWELL ⊙

SAN
ANTONIO
BAY

MEDIO CREEK

⊙ REFUGIO

MISSION RIVER

ARANSAS RIVER

OLD TOWN OF
COPANO

BLACK JACKS
PENINSULA

MISSION
BAY

LAMAR
⊙

COPANO BAY

ARANSAS BAY

ST JOSEPH
ISLAND

MATAGORDA ISLAND

LIVE OAK PENINSULA

GULF OF MEXICO

CORPUS CHRISTI BAY

supplies passed through its customhouse, and numerous groups of Spanish and Mexican soldiers and settlers, including Irish immigrants, entered Texas here. Copano, like port cities today, was also a center of smuggling activities.

The coastal towns of Lamar (1839) and Indianola (1844) both came into being as a result of the influx of German settlers headed for the Hill Country. Other than these few places, there was little development in the Coastal Bend during the years of the Republic.

It was not until Texas joined the Union that the area economy fully recovered from the devastation caused by the Revolution. With the rise of mercantilism and renewed immigration in the late 1840s and 1850s, communities grew up between the San Antonio and Guadalupe rivers and along Coleto Creek. These settlements —Charco, Perdido (now Fannin), Coletoville, Steiner, Meyersville, Raisin— developed as agricultural hubs serving the surrounding farms and were generally marked by a church, a school, and a locally owned store that handled general merchandise of all sorts.

In 1857 the coastal townsite of St. Mary's was platted on Copano Bay near present Bayside. The port town became an import center for longleaf pine and other building materials, and by the time of the Civil War there was regular freight and passenger service into St. Mary's. From here goods were shipped to Refugio, Goliad, San Antonio, and other points. For a time, St. Mary's served as the seat of Refugio County.

County road crew building the low-water bridge at Raisin.

The Civil War brought another episode of economic setback to the Coastal Bend. The coastal communities were ravaged by the Union blockade and shelling, and the interior was stripped of crops and livestock to support the Confederate army. During the prolonged Reconstruction era, there was a consolidation of land holdings as high taxes forced people to leave the land or go bankrupt. Their property was bought by those who were smart enough not to buy into the Confederacy and had kept their money in gold or currency other than the worthless Confederate paper money. This created vast tracts of land that would later provide lucrative opportunities for subdivision. Black families, now freed, formed their own communities. This gave rise to Manahuilla, Cologne, the Black Jacks, and Lewis's Bend.

As the railroads came through the Coastal Bend in the 1880s and the cotton economy boomed, little towns sprang up all along the railroad line, spelling the doom of others that were not so fortunate as to be near the tracks. With the advent of the railroads, everything changed. Fences began to go up, and land speculators seized land as fast as they could. Folks who had managed to hold on to their land during the hard times, when it wouldn't bring six dollars an acre, now had the opportunity to sell off town lots at two or three hundred dollars each if the railroad came through their property. Communities established to support the railroad crews became important trade centers for shipping cattle and cotton. The little towns of Austwell, Maudelowe, Inari, Vidauri, and Greta all got their start when the St. Louis, Brownsville and Mexico Railway pushed through the area in the early 1900s. McFaddin and Tivoli, which centered around the ranch commissary, also got a boost from their proximity to the railroad. Wherever the railroad placed a station, there was a need for cattle pens, warehouses, a cotton gin, hardware stores, blacksmiths, and a host of other services required by the surrounding farms and ranches.

With improved transportation and a booming economy, a few communities were established as "company towns." In the Coastal Bend these were towns bankrolled by real estate promoters or investment groups, usually local, to support

Main Street in Tivoli, 1913.

the surrounding cotton farms and cattle ranches.

Riverdale was a typical company town. Situated about ten miles above Goliad where the Berclair-Charco road crossed the San Antonio River, Riverdale was formed in 1913 by the Riverdale Gin and Milling Company and the Riverdale Mercantile Company, which also established nearby Angel City. In towns of this kind, the gin company would set up the cotton gin, weigh station, and other structures needed to process the crop. The mercantile company built the stores and rented them to private operators of barber shops, drugstores, saloons, general stores,

Church at Lamar, 1917. Photo by J. D. Mitchell.

blacksmith shops, and livery stables. The investors might also fund houses, a school, and other buildings to create a viable community. Like nearby Angel City, Riverdale suffered the fate of many river bottom communities that broke up after World War II.

These tiny places often consisted of only a few houses. At best, there may have been a small store that contained a post office. If there was a church that was also used as the school, it was considered very "uptown."

Although tiny and insignificant even by the standards of the day, every one of these communities was important to the people who lived there. These places were their homes, their base of operation, and a communal gathering place for those who lived too far away from a large village.

Travel was hard in the Coastal Bend until the middle of this century. The earth here is either sandy or black alluvial soil that becomes impassable with any amount of rainfall at all, and it often rains here. The average yearly rainfall is thirty-seven inches and can double that amount in a wet year.

Until after World War II, when paved roads and four-wheel-drive vehicles became prevalent, much of this country could be impassable

Austwell in 1913.

for months at a time. It was necessary for people to be able to get to supplies, to church, to medical care, and to visit one another from time to time.

Places such as Lewis's Bend, Hall's Point, and the Black Jacks kept people in the area from being hopelessly isolated for long periods of time. They were of great importance for a number of other reasons also. Even if people did not live in one of these wide places in the road, they would often stop off at several as they traveled.

The trip from Goliad to Lamar could take several days in all kinds of weather.

Shepley Avenue, Bloomington.

Original mill at Depot and Goodwin, several blocks off Main Street in Victoria.

Texas weather is unpredictable at best and the Coastal Bend is no exception. Dangerous weather could appear unexpectedly and quickly in a time before weather information and reports were part of daily life.

Many a person has sought refuge from inclement weather conditions in these settlements. People in those days would take in travelers and give them a bed and food in the hope that someone would do the same for them when they were in need.

These places existed in a time when people were more trustworthy, and this enabled the human race to be kinder to one another. It was still frontier down here and people needed one another for survival. It was not only safe to take people in, except in the rarest of situations, but it was expected of all who lived along the trails and roads of the region. It was a serious social *faux pas* not to be a Good Samaritan in those days.

As you read the narratives about these tiny places, you will find they were spiritual as well as physical homes for the people who inhabited them. They are still fondly remembered by the occupants as well as by those who only visited occasionally. Some are still in existence, but very few. Most were abandoned or moved long ago, and yet they remain in the hearts and minds of those who knew them.

Some are of more historical significance than others, but all were, at one time, important to the residents of the Texas Coastal Bend. Their histories give voice to one more aspect of life along the San Antonio River and its environs.

Early Crossings: Carlos Ranch and Anaqua

Ferries were an important mode of travel before bridges were constructed in the late nineteenth century. They were natural places for settlements to develop.

El Oso, or Terrell Crossing, was about nine or ten miles below Goliad. A ferry operated here, owned by Thomas Marshall Duke. An iron bridge was built here in

San Antonio River ferry crossing at the end of Commercial Street, Goliad, ca. 1884. The ferry was owned and operated by George L. Turner. Photo courtesy of Goliad County Historical Commission.

1900 after the ferry was swept away by heavy spring rains. This point on the river later became known as Duke's Bridge. Farther downstream on the south bank, Thomas O'Connor (I) operated a ferry and built the first O'Connor ranch home. It was here that he made saddletrees from mesquite wood and traded them for cattle.

The most important of the early crossings on this stretch of the river were Carlos Ranch and Anaqua, for both were situated where the two main roads between Refugio and Victoria crossed the San Antonio River. Settlements had developed at these points by the start of the Mexican era.

The Mexican village known various-ly as Carlos Ranch, Carlos Rancho, and Carlos Crossing was located on the north bank of the river about twelve miles below Goliad. Carlos De La Garza ran a commissary and operated a ferry here, assisted by John Bower, who lived on the opposite bank and was a signer of the Texas Declaration of Independence.

Bower and George B. Amery also ran a store here. In addition, Carlos Ranch had a smithy, a Catholic church, and a boys' school.[1] The village began to fade when Don Carlos died in 1882 and his widow sold off most of the land to area ranchers. The post office was discontinued in 1886.

About five miles downstream from Carlos Ranch was the site of Anaqua,

San Antonio Ferry Rates

1847

Animals, per head	5¢
Single man	5¢
Man and horse	10¢
Two-wheeled vehicles	25¢
Wagon or carriage	50¢

1870

Each head of sheep, hogs, or goats	2¢
Each head of horses or cattle	5¢
Man on foot	5¢
Man and horse	10¢
Carriage with one or more horses	50¢
Wagon with one or two horses or one yoke of oxen	50¢
Wagon with two yoke of oxen or two span of horses	75¢
Wagon with more than two yoke of oxen or two span of horses	$1

Bob Garnett with his gramophone and dog in Anaqua.

another early-day ferry crossing. Located on the north bank below where the Missouri-Pacific bridge and present-day U.S. 77 cross the river, Anaqua was a trad-ing post established by Irish colonists who arrived in the 1820s. Previously, Cabeza de Vaca had visited the site when it was a camp used by the Anaqua tribe, which he referred to in his *Narratives* as "Iguaces." So my grandmother claimed that Anaqua was "possibly the first site in Texas to receive a name."[2] A post office—at first con-sisting of nothing more than a box nailed to an anaqua tree—was established in 1852, serving a wide area.

An 1855 visitor to Anaqua described the river here as follows:

"My daddy used to carry mail from Anaqua to Tivoli. He made fifteen dollars a month for once-a-week delivery. The mailbox was on an anaqua tree. That's how it got its name. There used to be good dances there."

Herbert "Buster" Bickford

. . . turbid, winding, with a current of above five miles an hour. Its channel is about fifty feet below the level of the prairie, and the banks, often precipitous, where the water has undermined them, show sand, with a deep, blank [black] alluvium overlying it, and containing shells of Anodonta, Bulime and Helices of species now living. . . . the pecan tree, I saw here for the first time. . . .

I spent most of the forenoon on the banks of the river, shadowed by the moss-draped trees, and lulled by the murmur of the water among the fallen trunks. The cardinal grosbeak showed its scarlet plumage in the light green of the willow that dabbled its leaves in the river just where it took a short turn under a high, thicket-crowned, caving bank.[3]

Anaqua had a chapel, built by Carlos De La Garza about 1820, as well as a school. In the early 1900s, a telephone line was installed from Victoria to Anaqua. F. P. Marberry then established a store and gin on the river bank across from Anaqua. Upstream from Anaqua was the settlement of Warbonnett, where James A. Warburton had established a general store in the 1890s. Anaqua was eventually eclipsed by nearby McFaddin, and the post office was closed by 1919.[4]

Pupils of the Anaqua school.

The Anaqua School

Anaqua was settled by the French in the late 1700s. It was solid anaqua trees in that area years ago. The soil around there was reddish sand and a road went by there on the way to the river bottom. The school was right there on the San Antonio River road. It was a one-teacher school in one room. We had no water and the school had bad floors. We stuck paper in the floor to keep the cold and animals out. The desks were long benches. Our teachers were Mattie Crawford and Eulalia Marmion

Anaqua school picnic.

Coward. They taught us the three R's. We didn't get much of the sophisticated stuff until we went into town. We had a blackboard to write on and we had to go to the Amerys to get water.

Volney Warburton

I went to school in Anaqua with Miss Kate Stoner [O'Connor]. I stepped in a bucket one day and Miss Kate reminded me of it *mucho* years later. We went to school with all the Amerys, Miss Blanche [Stoner Warburton], and Cornelius Simms and his sisters.

Judge George B. Amery had court at Anaqua in his home. He was a judge of the law. He wasn't tough, he was just an ordinary white man. He was big friends of the Murphys. There was John Amery there, too. He was a little older than me. He died of a heart attack in 1946 or '47. There weren't no big trials there, just little ones.

Judge Amery told me when they first come here they lived on the O'Connor ranch just below the railroad. He said he was born in Refugio County. He said his daddy used to run the ferry boat.

Anaqua was a Mexican gatherin' place, kind of like Lewis's Bend was for blacks.

Rafael De La Garza

The Marberry home.

Most of the kids in this area didn't get much schoolin' because of cotton-pickin' time. The Mexican children went to Anaqua, and the black children went to Lewis's Bend.

This was the world down here. In those days you only heard the news once in a while. There was no communications with the outside world, not even newspapers. We never knew about the weather until it got here. Everybody went by the signs.

Jesús Ybarbo

The Legend of Gregorio Cortez

Butler Williams, father of Reverend Mack Williams.

He was an outlaw from Mexico. His brother was in jail in Goliad. He came by Anaqua when my father was there.

A horse was always kept at Anaqua so if someone's horse got tired they could take the rested horse and return for theirs later. Gregorio borrowed the horse and went to Goliad. There was a big gunfight and his brother was killed.

He came back to Anaqua and told my father the story. He said the posse was after him and wanted to know which way Papa would tell the posse he had gone.

Papa said he would tell the truth. Cortez drew down on him. Papa came out with a skinning knife and Cortez gave him his knife. I still have that knife. He took his horse and went on.

They caught him in Karnes City. He killed Brack Morris, the sheriff, and a fella named Grover shot Gregorio.

Andrew Scott, a horse trader, bought the horse.

Reverend Mack Williams

Anaqua Snapshot

We would come home over the Old Road, and everybody had to stop at the Adlers and have coffee. It was expected. There were Fagans and Sidicks, and Grandma Murphy had a ferry boat down here. She also had a store at Carlos Lake. That's where you cross the San Antonio River bottom.

When we came out of town, we would have to stop at Amery's and see Birdie. It was expected. Anaqua was the town out here then. Lillian was Birdie's sister. Their brother John never did marry. He ran the post office and was a rancher.

Zilpah Daniel Edwards

Nothin' Here But Friends

Butler Williams, my father, was the first colored school trustee at Anaqua. This was 1896. He was also the constable and peace officer. He was given a pistol to control the peace. Aus Avery said to him, "You don't need no pistol, Butler. There ain't nothin' here but old friends."

Sure enough, two years later, they came down and took his gun away because he didn't use it. He never arrested anybody, he just fussed at 'em.

Reverend Mack Williams

Rememberin' Anaqua

Anaqua is right on the road where it turns off from the Warburton. The Amerys were there. He was a judge, George Amery. He married people.

I can remember when Mr. Tom O'Connor [II] would ride from the Buck Ranch to see Miss Kate Stoner. I remember when they were married. He had a little horse named Tommy Hunt. He bought it from Tommy Hunt.

The Buck Ranch is right on Highway 77. Roger Williams has it now. Old Man Dennis built the house there for Dr. Buck so he would be nearby. He was from Oklahoma, red-headed, and they named the ranch after him.

They had to haul the lumber for the house from Goliad. I remember the old log cabins. They had to be sealed up with clay and moss. They was good, too. No wind got in 'em.

Rafael De La Garza

The Amerys: Anaqua "Aristocracy"

George Bramled Amery was born in Cincinnati in 1847. His wife's name was Alice Grey. Her father died of yellow fever in Indianola. George H. Amery was the son of Alice and George.

The Amerys were English, and Grandad was a member of the Shaker sect. We have some articles he wrote for the *Cincinnati Enquirer* back in those days. They

Mary G. "Birdie" Amery (center) and Lillian Amery (upper right) at Amery home in Anaqua.

were rather communistic, but then the Shakers were communal in those times. They went back to the old Christian way of handling things.

The farm where I grew up was founded by Judge Phelps, a rancher and lawyer, in 1856. Grandad came to Texas and bought the farm in 1880. They started out somewhere around the Stubbs house and then moved to Anaqua. It's called the old Amery Place at Anaqua.

I am curious about his education, because he was a German teacher and justice of the peace. We always thought he was a county judge, but according to all we can find, he was a J.P. He was also a county commissioner.

Aunt Mary, Miss Birdie, was the oldest of the children, then John, George Henry, and Lillian. Miss Birdie, that's how everyone knew her down there. Uncle John was the quintessential cowboy. He was foreman for the Sam Williams ranch. His wife's name was May Williams. They had a radio and we would visit up there all the time.

Anaqua had a general store and a post office as well as a cotton gin. When I was a child, I found chunks of equipment and Dad said it was from the old cotton gin.

Two old spinsters from the Shaker colony lived with Grandmother and Grandaddy. Their names were Lucy Woodward and Nancy Hughes. I have no idea what the story was. Maybe they were friends of the family back in Cincinnati.

When we went to live at Anaqua, the old school was still there. It originally belonged to Rob Williams. That whole place was my security as a child. The thirties and forties were ups and downs for my father, and so when he was down, we would come to the old home place. That's why it was security to me.

When I was in school at Anaqua, there were two rooms. The young ones were in one room, and the older ones in the second room. There was no division between the two areas. The teacher was Miss Wright. During World War II, she joined the FBI.

Mary G. "Birdie" Amery, George B. Amery's daughter.

The Williamses were the closest neighbors. We would visit back and forth with them, the Gaffneys, and occasionally the Stoners. Anything past the Gaffneys was way gone. There weren't many people down here in that time. Our friends the Pickerings would come down and stay with us also.

We had no car in those days. We only had horses, and my father hated them and thought they were only for work. Uncle John was very different. He was on one all day. I grew up with two versions of horses in my family.

There were very few people we were allowed to associate with. It really was

George B. and Alice Grey Amery.

snobbish. I think it came over with the English. There was a caste system. The Irish came over here dirt poor, but when they built up what they had, they assumed the caste system also. We were very gracious to those that were supposed to be inferior to us. It makes me cringe to think of it. We were always very gracious to those down the next step.

It was always a very strange and rigid thing, and it wasn't just about black or white or Mexican. This went on among the white community very strongly. There were whites that weren't acceptable in the white community. I was allowed to have Mexican friends, but they were not allowed in my home.

The Amerys had position, but they never had money. My grandfather was an intellectual, and he liked to teach and be the justice of the peace. My family was rather liberal for the times. The happenings down in Duval County really upset them. That sort of behavior truly outraged them. They must have kept a lot of their attitudes to themselves because I was never aware of any ostracism. We were accorded a sort of prestige in the river bottom. It never occurred to me that we were poor, because we had social status in the San Antonio River bottom.

Jean Amery Wieser

Marberry Store, ca. 1915. It was established by F. P. Marberry on the San Antonio River across from Anaqua.

The Marberry Store

In the early 1890s, Francis Peter Marberry, my uncle, moved to Archer City, Texas, near Wichita Falls. In 1898 the family moved to Anaqua, Texas, one of the earliest named towns in Texas. In 1890 it boasted a population of twenty-five. Anaqua was a thriving little community on the west bank of the San Antonio River about twenty miles southwest of Victoria.

Immediately on arrival, Pete built a store and a little distance away a cotton

Pete Marberry.

gin, which shortly was completely destroyed by fire. Actually, the store was on Martin O'Connor land on the east side of the river and about three miles downstream from the village and the ferry crossing of the river.

In 1900 my father, E. P. [Page] Stubblefield, Mavis Marberry's younger brother, came from New Concord, Kentucky, to work in the store. In late 1904 Page returned to Kentucky and took a sales position with the O. E. Harvick jewelry company of Vienna, Illinois, a manufacturer and dealer. He traveled mostly in those states adjacent to Kentucky.

In 1906, Pete [Marberry] bought a small ranch adjacent to the Peter Fagan ranch eight miles west of Tivoli. It was a narrow piece of land extending across what is now Highway 239 and then across the San Antonio River, with a small acreage extending into Victoria County. Pete's son, Roy, operated the ranch for his lifetime. By 1988, Roy's sister, Mary Lucy, was the only surviving family member and she, along with Roy's widow, Anna Kate Sessions, sold the ranch to Roger Williams.

Also in 1906 the St. Louis, Brownsville and Mexico Railway was completed and traversed from Houston to Brownsville. The railroad tracks came between the store and the San Antonio River. Before the railroad, most merchandise was shipped by wagon from Victoria. The store stock embraced clothing, dry goods, groceries, ranch necessities, and personal needs from Grover's Chill Tonic to caskets for the deceased.

The Holeman house.

With the coming of the railroad, both Vidauri and Inari came into being. Inari was nearest the store, and the *Victoria Advocate* reports visitors from and to Inari. In fact, it reported the arrival of Mavis Marberry's parents at Inari from New Concord, Kentucky, in 1907.

The railroad changed the total market scene. Page Stubblefield returned to Inari in 1907, and he and Pete Marberry formed a partnership and arranged with the J. A. McFaddin family for a store location at Marianna (now McFaddin). It served the McFaddin ranch as its commissary, as well as the other ranching establishments in

"I can remember when McFaddin was Marianna. Two brothers lived there named Dave and Jim McFaddin. They were big men— over three hundred pounds. They smoked pipes."

Rafael De La Garza

the area. This seemed to be a good arrangement for all. By 1910 the McFaddin ranch determined to construct its own commissary, and the McFaddin Mercantile Company came into being.

Later, in 1910, Pete Marberry sold his interest in the Marianna store stock to Page Stubblefield and his brother, Kelly; they moved the stock to a store location at Bloomington. Meanwhile, in 1913, Pete Marberry entered into a partnership with Martin O'Connor establishing the Maudelowe Mercantile Company at Maudelowe, Texas, a little settlement between Tivoli and Austwell in Refugio County. This store continued until Pete Marberry's health failed in 1926. Martin O'Connor then purchased the store and hired Pete's son, R. K. Marberry, to manage it.

P. K. Stubblefield

Ranch Communities: Hall's Point, Morrowville, and McFaddin

On the large ranches in the Coastal Bend, settlements often grew up from the clusters of houses that were provided to the ranch hands and their families. The ranch commissary served as a general store, and there was usually a church or chapel that could also be used as a school.

Hall's Point was located on the Terrell ranch on a bend in the river just before it leaves Goliad County and marks the dividing line between Victoria and Refugio

A busy day at Marianna, December 1910.

counties. It was sometimes called Pajarito de Sangre (Bloody Little Bird). According to local legend, an Indian chief named Little Bird was shot here in 1812 by a party of Americans from the Gutiérrez-Magee expedition, which occupied the presidio at Goliad. Several other murders have been associated with Hall's Point. In 1842, seven Mexican traders were ambushed and shot here by a band of outlaws, reputedly the Mustang Gray [Mabry B. Gray] gang. Perhaps the most famous incident at Hall's Point was the 1911 murder of a levee builder, Charles Gosnell, whose wife arranged his death with the help of her lover. As my grandmother wrote, "The numerous murders reported to have been committed here are sufficient to explain why this point of timber won the name of Pajarite [Pajarito] de Sangre . . . and how a superstitious person passing through it at night could see ghosts and apparitions, as well as hear all kinds of weird sounds and doleful songs."[5]

McFaddin began as a settlement on the ranch established by James A. McFaddin in the 1870s at Kemper's Bluff, south of the Guadalupe River. Constructing a levee along the river, he drained thousands of acres of swampland and began raising cotton. His son, Allen "Al" Minor McFaddin, joined his father in the ranching business and became an expert in breeding Brahman cattle. By the turn of the century, the McFaddin ranches were engaged in numerous businesses, such as meat-packing plants, cotton gins, and grain elevators. Originally the ranch community was known as McFaddin Ranch. When the railroad came through in 1906, the station on the ranch was named Marianna, after Marianna Sewell, the wife of a former mayor of Houston.

In the 1920s, the town took back the name McFaddin. In addition to a post office, McFaddin had a school, Catholic church, general mercantile, cotton gin, and machine shop. The development of the oil industry around McFaddin in the 1930s ensured the town's future. Today McFaddin's estimated population is about 55.

Blood Run All Around

There was houses and a schoolhouse, and the church was in the schoolhouse. There wasn't no store, though. That is the way I remember it. The real Hall's Point was where Uncle Steve Holliman lived in that hollow.

Uncle Steve used to say that in the time of Sam Houston, when they was fightin' that war, he seen blood run all around dead men's bodies. I heard him say that a many a time.

I don't know what battle they fought along there, but there was one. Uncle Steve would always talk about the blood runnin' and Sam Houston. You can still go through Hall's Point today. Every time I go over there, I always think about all that.

There was fightin' in this area during the Civil War, too. Uncle Steve talked about that and the Revolution and how he was down at Hall's Point. Uncle Steve knew Sam Houston personally. They know Uncle lived to be 116 years old, but he nor anyone else knew how old he really was. They just knew he could account for 116 years.

Hall's Point has seen a lot of history in its day. It must miss havin' people around.

In school, we studied readin', writin', arithmetic, history, geography, and memory work. We had to memorize "The Midnight Ride of Paul Revere," the Constitution, Preamble, the Bill of Rights, and the Amendments.

> Our Alma Mater was:
>
> *I love the name of Hall's Point,*
> *Hall's Point, my home sweet home,*
> *I love the sunshine,*
> *I love the flowers,*
> *That's where I spend most of my happy, happy hours.*

Althia Lewis Burns Franklin

"Hall's Point, that's where I was born. Once upon a time, there was a community out there. It was a pretty big community, in fact."

Zearlee Robinson Wesley

"I went to school in Hall's Point—out from Fannin. It used to be a community, but now this place is out in a pasture, I would say Miss Terrell's. It's a private road, not a public road. You can reach it goin' like you go out to the Fleming Prairie and you see this road that says Fannin Road. You take that Fannin Road and you go right over that Hall Point, and then you go into Fannin."

Laura Virginia Lewis Evans

Morrowville

My family came in here when the O'Connors came. My grandfather sold off the land. He was highly educated, but didn't have any horse sense. He was a tobacco farmer in North Carolina, and he thought a cowboy was a disgrace to humanity. My daddy was a cowboy.

The O'Connors bought the land. Old Man O'Connor believed in that land, and it looks like he was right. When a man gets too much education, he doesn't have enough horse sense.

A cattle buyer bought from all the little ranchers. They all sold to itinerant cattle buyers. That was the only way the little fella had. The big ranches shipped on the railroads. Those big old wild steers were trapped when they came in to water. Some of them were nine or ten years old. They were so wild, they would sometimes kill themselves.

I was born here on the river in 1905 right over there in the second house on the hill. My Grandfather Perry owned slaves around here. I don't know where he came from, but the Morrows came from North Carolina.

Perry built a house here out of shells he carried from the bay in oxcarts. It had

The Edward Perry home constructed with shells from the bay.

Henry Morrow on Charlie, early 1950s, on the Roger Williams ranch.

thick walls and sally ports for the guns in the walls to shoot Indians. One day my grandfather had to shoot an Indian. There were a bunch of Karankawas ran all over this country.

I went to the Morrowville school. It was right there where Leo Scott's house is. It was eventually moved to the O'Connor ranch, then to Fagan's, and then to Tivoli. There were sharecroppers all up and down that river.

Henry Morrow

"Earl Albrecht was from the McFaddin ranch, born and raised over there. There were several brothers. They had a little meat market right next to the McFaddin store. He was a tall boy, quiet, never did say much. There was Earl, Lyle, and 'Sweetie.' They always called him 'Sweetie.' He was the little one."

Jesús Ybarbo

There were *thousands* of people living in McFaddin. There was a depot, a gin, and a store. Everybody did their trading there. Nobody much lives there now, but I remember when they built the McFaddin store. The Stubblefields had a store there before.

The De La Garza cemetery was down here and lots of others, too. The Sample cemetery was on the river road, and there is a cemetery at the back of the Buck Ranch. Simms are buried around here, too. Sully Simms lived on the Murphy near Miss Aggie's.

Richard Harris

Emancipation Communities: Cologne, Manahuilla, Lewis's Bend, and the Black Jacks

Emancipation was announced in 1863, but the news did not arrive in Texas until June 19, 1865. This monumental event gave rise to numerous black colonies throughout the Coastal Bend.

Cologne, for example, was founded in 1870 by two former slaves who operated a freight line from Indianola to Victoria and Beeville. The partners purchased five hundred acres of land on Perdido Creek in Goliad County and encouraged friends

Cowboys on the McFaddin ranch.

to join in the enterprise. First called the Colony, then Perdido Community, it acquired the name Centerville because of its location midway between Goliad and Victoria. When the railroad arrived in 1886, it was renamed Ira, and a decade later, Cologne—because the rendering plants here made it "such a sweet-smelling place."[6] The 1990 population of Cologne was estimated at 85.

The black settlement of Manahuilla was located west of Fannin on Manahuilla Creek. St. Paul and several other black settlements were in this vicinity. A church and a few families are still at Manahuilla today.

In the San Antonio River bottom, several black communities grew up after the Civil War. Lewis's Bend, the largest, developed at the Seabourne (also Seabron, Seabourn) Lewis plantation when the war ended and the slaves were freed. Spriggs Bend and Robinson's Bend were other black settlements along the river.

The Black Jacks was located on the Blackjack Peninsula, which was named for the black jack tree. The settlement was widely scattered in this area of heavy brush country, starting north of the Aransas County line. All that was here was scrub oak, red bay, and, farther in, mesquite, mosquitoes, and alligators.

Early land grants belonged to the Brundrett, Dietrich, Hynes, Dubois, and Kuykendall families. It then belonged to Horace McDowell and subsequently became Aransas National Wildlife Refuge. It has always been an area with lots of wildlife. The only way to get out of this area in the early days was by boat to Seadrift and a train from Bloomington to Victoria. A number of the cowboys came from this area of the Texas Coast.

Although these communities are long gone, they live on in the hearts and minds of those who knew them.

Manahuilla = Freedom

Manahuilla was started in about 1886. The church started then. There was no church at the beginning. The community started before that. The first church was

John Brundrett Jr. at gable house on Blackjack Peninsula, 1916.

started in a brush arbor. We all descended from slaves. We were owned by families all over the area.

Manahuilla is an Indian name. It is called Minnewee and we call it Minnehulla. It has even been called Minneway. What the real meaning of the word is, we don't really know, but in older times, the people said this community was "any way" of making a living.

Most of this area was owned by blacks. The Millers were the only white family out here. This community was formed after Emancipation. The land was cheap and

Horace Hammon McDowell.

they could afford it. Finally, the whites got it because they beat our people out of it. The blacks would get in economic trouble, and the whites would take it. A lot of this land was not registered, and business was done with a handshake and word of mouth.

Everybody here had their occupations. Some were farmers, some were ranchers. Some people were living on other people's places. There was a lot of tenant farming. Most people made their living dirt-farming and making syrup to sell. Peanuts and potatoes were another crop we all lived on. We mainly lived off the land. We had sweet potatoes and milk and butter.

As kids we would play church. We built our little churches on the side of the road in the wind by the woods.

This is the best life out in the country—freedom. It was a lot of hard work, but there was neighborliness and closeness. If you were in need, it was amazing how people would help you. That's why our community was so close. We knew each other and knew when anyone was suffering, when anyone was in trouble.

The people around this community were doing alright. Even though they weren't with the big ranches, they had everything they needed.

Vernell Gray Shelton, Ruby Lee Youngblood Edwards, Allie Fay Moore Robinson

St. Paul

I was born in the St. Paul community in 1917. This twenty acres was bought for one hundred dollars. They mostly farmed. The men in my family was mostly cowhands. They worked for the O'Connors and the Pettuses. My daddy was paid a dollar a day or about twenty dollars a month.

Most of the houses around here were clapboard, plain wooden shingles and wood floors. You see through the slits and see chickens under the house. The fireplaces were made of mud and that was where the food was cooked. The food was plain—cowboy stew, chili, biscuits and molasses, and sweet potatoes and roastin' ears.

When I was born, the church was already there. It was just an old sittin' room with a blackboard, plain windows, and a big bell in the back. That was the church house. Well, they had a wood heater in there, too, when it got cold. That was the church house and the schoolhouse, too.

Whenever somebody died, my daddy would ring the bell. They'd be sick for a good long while, then they would just pass away. He'd go and get this old bell and bang, bang, bang. Boy, that bell, I'm tellin' you. I don't know what happened to that old bell. I've seen bells here in San Antonio that weren't that big. It was real wide, the bell part was real wide. It stood up like this and was set out on a pallet. He had a platform built for it.

Uncle John Ray's Cemetery was right down the road. They gave him this little property for buryin' and they called it Uncle John Ray's Cemetery. My grandfather is buried out there. He died one day at St. Paul and they buried him there the next day. There wasn't no undertakers comin' out to embalm. They went to town and got the casket and laid him on a coolin' board. They carried him to the graveyard in a wagon, and people that had cars that knew Uncle Frank followed. Some of them walked, some with wagons, some with buggies, and some of them with what kind of car they had. That's the way they traveled in those days.

Miss Ada was my first schoolteacher. Miss Earline Cunningham was our second schoolteacher. When I went to school, they learned us the ABC's first. You would learn the ABC's and then learn how to put it together and spell. You know, learn how to spell "boy" and "girl" and like that. That was our lesson, like that, alright. We learned a little rhyme. It went like this:

Oh, had a little dog
The little dog liked me.
I loved the little dog.

Little Boy Blue, come blow your horn
Sheep's in the meadow
The cow's in the corn.

That was all in riddle books.

We lived in San Antonio durin' the school year and then we would come back out to St. Paul in the summer. We all worked in the fields in the summer, even the women. Grandpa would be openin' a furrow, and Grandmother would be followin' him with Old Nellie and a walkin' planter. She be walkin' behind, plantin' corn. They would be keepin' the weeds out also. She would pick the cotton, too, to have a little money to go to town with.

Daddy would work on places along the river and go fishin'. He would catch lots of yellow catfish. They wasn't nothin' but stomach and big mouths. We used to catch fish in the Manahuilla, Dry Creek, and Cabeza. We would make a pole out of long willow runners, a bobber out of wine barrel corks, and use a hook on the bottom with worms. We dug our own worms in the woodpile.

That Manahuilla comes right out in St. Paul and goes right through it. We also had a well there.

We had big hog killin's in St. Paul when the weather got cold and put all the meat in a smokehouse. Another big deal there was havin' dances and gamblin'. There were certain places where these gatherin's were held. We also did a lot of hound huntin' in the early days.

I lived there until 1934, then I moved to San Antonio. We didn't sell our land until around '81.

Joe Duncan, collected by Patsy Light, January 6, 1995

Spriggs Bend

I was born on our family ranch near where Tivoli was founded. That was in 1902. It was real near the San'tone River. My father, Charles Ross Bickford, was born on this same ranch where I live now.

It is on Spriggs Bend on the river, but it used to be called Bickford Bend on the old maps. Some colored people by the name of Spriggs used to live there. They had around one hundred head of horses. The woman was an old midwife. Old Mary Dean brought me in and all the older Fagans and Duboises.

There was a swimmin' hole in the river. Everybody in Tivoli learned to swim in that hole.

I was schooled at Marberry's, Tivoli, and in Beeville. There was a black, a

Mexican, and a white school. Then the KKK came in and started their own school.

There weren't any doctors for miles around. The nearest one was in Victoria. My grandmother's favorite doctor was old Dr. Braman. He'd come stay until she got well. She paid him off one time with five horses.

There's nothing there now but some chiny trees. It went on the map in 1850.

Herbert "Buster" Bickford

Spriggs Bend was by the San Antonio River. It was special. It was home. It was where all the activities were.

Ruby Lee Youngblood Edwards, Della May McDow Bennett

Hog-killing time on the Melon Creek Ranch, January 1947.

Robinson's Bend

The first I ever knowed of Louis Power was livin' up on Robinson's Bend with Uncle Charlie. Even after he moved away, it was called Robinson's Bend. I was a boy. I believe I went to Uncle Charlie's when I was about six or seven years old. Mr. Louis and Uncle Charlie was big friends. They had hogs over there at the Duke Ranch together. That was when I first met Mr. Louis. We would go over there and pen hogs, build fence, first one thing and then another like that.

Milam Thompson

Life in the Black Jacks

"The people that lived in the Black Jacks used to baptize in the bay."

Reverend Mack Williams

Almost the entire Blackjack Peninsula was owned at one time by Cyrus Lucas. When the crash came in 1929, he lost it. It was then sold to the U.S. government. Mr. Lucas had purchased everything in that area starting as early as the 1870s. If anyone lost their land for taxes, Mr. Lucas would buy it up.

Apparently, Mr. Lucas was the first one there. His brand **L** was established in 1872. He started out with a small ranch, and then Papa went to work for him in 1899 and remained down there through 1907. Grandfather became his foreman and lived down there long enough for he and Mr. Lucas to become good friends.

He sold some of it to the St. Charles Ranch and then bought some land from the Faulkners. This is where my grandfather lived, at the old Faulkner. There was a post office, a postmistress, a school and such.

Mr. Lucas did not live on the ranch itself. He came from around Berclair and would come down and visit every once in a while and stay with Grandfather. Grandfather could tell some tales about how isolated they were down there. It was such a lonely and desolate place. When they moved out there, you were talking about some real isolation.

Grandfather was hired in 1899, but he didn't go down there until 1900. My grandmother had an uncle in Rockport. When they went to the ranch, like all old houses, it

Camping in the Black Jacks.

wasn't the best—no screens, just a typical old ranch house. At first, they lived in the area of the Cow Camp, then they moved to Faulkner, where the post office was and the place they voted. Some of the children went to the school there also.

You had the McDowells, three families of Brundretts, the Dietrichs, the Duboises. There was a Mr. Roddy who lived on an island and ran a ranch. They all had three-story houses. The McDowells had a gorgeous house. It was rough down there. Alligators, if you can imagine. That land wasn't good for much of anything else. The women had to help work cattle.

Old post office on Hynes Bay, Black Jacks.

This area has a lot of history. Lafitte had a camp out on Matagorda. He would pull into these bays, and the Mexican government couldn't get him out. He would come into San Antonio Bay. The people who lived on the island could hear the guns of the Mexican government as they chased him. Every once in a while, we have people come in to see about the legend of Barkantine Lake.

It was during the Mexican War when they had Goliad. Remember, they would bring money into El Copano and take it up to Goliad to pay their soldiers and then on to San Antonio. They hauled it in a barkantine, and it was in September of 1822 or 1823 and a storm came in and blew them into this lake or, actually, way over to where Roger Williams is today. The boat cracked up and they say the Indians got the bullion. The Fagans have the old timber in their house.

Mack Williams says he remembers in the early thirties that one of the Mexican ranch hands lived down in his area, and he would go into Tivoli and he had Spanish gold royals—and quite a bit of it. They asked him where he got it, and he told them, and when they went down to find the Mexican at his house, he was not there. The whole thing and the Mexican were gone, so no one ever knew.

One of the things that impressed me was a story my dad told about when he was a child. His mother would take him to the beach and go off by herself. It was in the spring and there were flowers and he walked around to where she was and she was crying. He picked her some flowers so she would stop crying. She must have

Catherine McDowell on her favorite horse, Punkin', with Francisco in the Black Jacks.

been crying from loneliness. They were so far from anything, and she had grown up around her family in East Texas. Here she was out on the peninsula with nobody.

One of her sons cut himself real badly one time, and she couldn't get to a doctor and the neighbors didn't help her, so she had to put it in coal oil and put it back together. Fortunately, he didn't have a limp or anything. It was a struggle for her.

The ranch headquarters was at Faulkner. Even after Mr. Lucas lost the ranch, this area was still headquarters. Their ranch supplies came by sailboat from Rockport. Every month they went over there to get ranch supplies and groceries and

Martin O'Connor.

such as that. This was a major trip for them. It was a major thing to go from ranch to ranch in those days. It could be a day's trip from one to the other. The Brundretts would have to go from their place to Faulkner to vote, and it would be quite a trip. They would stop off in Carlos City and make a party of it.

The Black Jacks was principally a ranching area. They couldn't grow crops because of the soil, so the one thing they knew was raising cattle. The Brundrett family came in the 1840s. They were a family of ship captains from the Great Lakes. They must have come here because the land was cheap. Most of the other people around the area had grants and land they got for fighting in the Revolution; but they came much later, so cheap land had to be the draw. The land was good for cattle, and when they got ready to ship, they would take them to Rockport by barge and then out from there.

Since my grandfather was foreman for Mr. Lucas, he was given a pretty good boost from Mr. Lucas. When Austin and McDowell came in here and started the land development, Mr. Martin O'Connor started meat markets and things like that and bought up a lot of land going down towards Lamar. They all knew each other and were friends.

The peninsula wasn't the most pleasant place to live because of the mosquitoes and the brush. It really wasn't a lucrative place to make a living. You couldn't farm there. The only thing you could do was fish and raise cattle. There was better grass then than there is now.

Beverly Barber Fletcher

Cowboys at the Black Jacks, now part of the Aransas National Wildlife Refuge.

There were lots of good riders in the Black Jacks—Albert Duke, Jim Williams, the McGrews, Huffs, and the Hutchinsons. They were from around Austwell and Tivoli. This area was settled around 1843.

Reverend Mack Williams

The old community of Black Jacks, the black community, was a schoolhouse and the Huffs' house and the Williams house and the Duke house. Those were the only houses left there when I was comin' up. The church and the school were all the

"Tivoli was a dancing town, and we would dance. We really had some of the big bands here, good bands, and Canales [Barrera's, Reyna's] Restaurant, the whole building, all that back there at one time was one building and that was the auditorium, and that's where we danced."

Viola Emison Barber

same. It was mostly sand down there. That sand would get hot to your feet. You would have to dig down and stand there or the sand would burn your feet up. It was mostly sandy land. There were a lot of gophers. Nobody lives down there no more. They done sold all their property. It broke up way back in the early thirties.

Royal McKinley Williams

Company Towns: Tivoli and Austwell

Tivoli and Austwell were laid out in the early 1900s by Preston R. Austin, a cotton grower and land promoter from Victoria. His partner was Jesse Clark McDowell, a Philadelphia investor whose holdings were later acquired by his son Horace. After losing 40,000 head of cattle in the "Big Freeze" of 1899, Austin formed a partnership with McDowell, the Refugio Land and Irrigation Company, and began accumulating land near San Antonio Bay. Their philosophy was to build up communities in which the company would retain extensive business interests for investment purposes—such as lumberyards, mercantiles, cotton gins, and the like—and subdivide outlying company land into tracts to be purchased by farmers.[7]

The two entrepreneurs first constructed a cotton gin and commissary on Austin's Tivoli Ranch in the early 1900s. Tivoli Ranch had been established in the late 1870s by Colonel Newton Gullett, an old-style planter who ran his ranch more like an antebellum plantation. Tivoli acquired a post office in the 1890s. The property was sold to Austin in 1902.[8] In 1907, the townsite of Tivoli was platted. Austin donated a Catholic church, a school, and even a hotel. In 1911 nearby Austwell was platted on Hynes Bay at the junction of present-day Texas 239 and FR 774. A longtime resident of the area, Lucile Fagan Snider, wrote this account of Austwell's history:

The townsite of Austwell was surveyed and laid out for P. R. Austin, by L. A. Gueringer, civil engineer, in the fall of 1911. The first plat being dated Dec. 20, 1911. It is located on parts of the John Hynes and James Collyer grants on the south shore of Hynes Bay. . . .

The present city of Austwell is not far distant from the site of Old Hynesville or Crescent Village. After these old settlements were abandoned, a post office known as Dubois was established on the Horace McDowell ranch, now owned by J. E. Bauer, of Refugio. The name of Austwell is coined from the first syllable of Austin and the last syllable of McDowell.

Prior to laying off of the townsite, a public school building was erected at the site by Austin-McDowell. At the start of the town, Preston Austin built a wooden church, used as a community church. The Austin interests built a large wooden 2-story hotel on the bayshore, operated under the name of "Leah Hotel." He also built the Austwell Hotel, the first to be built. . . .

Preston Austin designated Austwell to be the metropolis of Refugio County and a port town. Located in the heart of a rich black land farming area, on the shores of Hynes Bay, with rail connections assured and access to the sea a potentiality, the town was well situated.

Austin had a channel dredged through the bay and docks and a loading chute installed. He proposed to interest the government in improving navigation to the

town. The first site of the big gin was on the bayshore, operating under the name of Austwell Milling & Gin Company, near the dock. After the railroad had built in, he had a gin built on trackage property. A branch store of the Tivoli Mercantile Co. was established at Austwell almost immediately. One of the largest and finest cotton seed oil mills in South Texas was established. In addition to their many other enterprises Austin and McDowell had a large cotton warehouse with capacity for storing several thousand bales of cotton.

Several doctors practiced in Austwell, among them Dr. George E. Glover. . . . A hospital for Austwell was being considered by Preston Austin at the time of his death. . . .

Many other businesses flourished, among them, the Austwell Lumber Co., an Austin-McDowell concern, and the planing mill which also handled some lumber and supplies. Several cafes and restaurants, a picture show, drug stores, ice plant and water works, a furniture store, a livery stable, blacksmith shop and many other businesses were established in Austwell.

At any rate Austwell got off to a fine start. A majority of lots were sold and hundreds of settlers moved in.

There were no half-way measures with Austin. He had a water system installed with big cypress mains in every street, with a fire plug on almost every corner. A cement sidewalk was laid around every town block. A telephone system was brought in and he sponsored many local industries.

Bakery in Tivoli during a flood, September 25, 1913.

Austwell too, has seen many changes in the last five decades. The people are a quiet and peace loving people, with a civic pride unexcelled in this area and second only in the state. . . .

[Preston Austin was] a man, who with a vision of the future and a determination to succeed in his ventures, was cut down in the prime of his life, in the middle of his dreams, and had he lived, his visions might have materialized.[9]

The two towns became shipping points for area cotton farmers and ranchers. Tivoli's population in 1990 was 540, Austwell's 189.

The Austin Vision

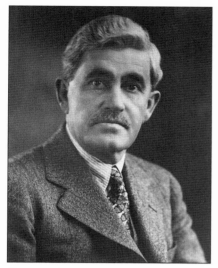

Preston Rose Austin.

Preston Austin is my grandfather. He founded Tivoli and Austwell and his vision was to make Austwell a seaport along the south coast. He formed a partnership with Horace McDowell.

Austwell just dried up in the thirties. It didn't move forward anymore after that. There wasn't a driving force anymore, and it just started withering on the vine. There just wasn't anyone interested in it.

James N. Stofer

Colonel Gullett was an early settler before Preston Austin. He was the one established Tivoli. It is rumored that he had acquired a lot of property through the death of his three or more wives. There were at least three, maybe more.

O'Connor-Swift Store, Tivoli, ca. 1935.

John Hynes owned it before Gullett. It was Spanish land grant way back. Gullett went to Bastrop and got a bunch of German families and imported them down here.

Some people think he was murdered by one of his wives. He was known to have killed a few people. He was supposed to have killed Alonzo Allee and then he had to move to Galveston and got caught in the bad storm.

Carlyn Mernitz Lieb

Austwell sprang full bloom into being out of the prairie. We came here in 1913 or 1914 when I was six years old. My father [John Kinsler] came to work for the Refugio Land and Irrigation Company. He was hired from the Department of Agriculture out of Washington by the RLI to come down here and supervise farming and irrigation and straighten this land up and teach the farmers modern ways. He was a legend in the Department of Agriculture. He still is. When he came down here, they used to hit the planting with a lick and a promise and sit back and wait.

His modern methods were not well received. These people didn't like someone with education and training coming down here and telling them what to do. He finally got it done. They broke the mold when they made my father. He was perfect to me. He was tough. He was the center of the Clemson championship team in 1900. They used to leave eyeballs on the field.

I hated it when we came here. It was real narrow-minded. There were lots of Klansmen also. Those people were real Appalachia. It was pretty wild frontier then. My mother once said there were plantations in the Black Jacks and along the bay.

Preston Austin had a big house down there and he stayed once in a while. He insisted on terracing the land down to the bay, and storms and hurricanes would

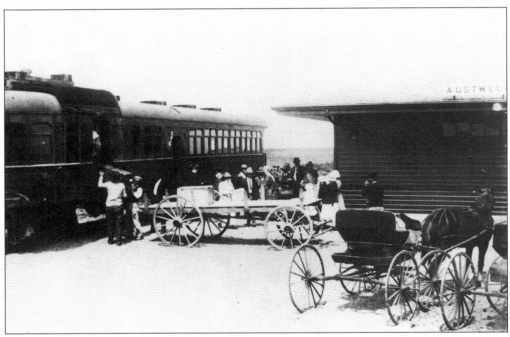

Unloading at the Austwell depot.

wash it away. The '42 storm really finished it. There was no beach left after that. That was a wingding.

Austwell and Tivoli would get together in the old days and the women would do the singing and the men would do the cooking. It was a lot of fun.

Dad bought farming land and continued his work down here after he left the government job. His business was crop breeding, cotton breeding. He developed the Lone Star cotton, the first storm-resistant variety. There was a legend in the Department of Agriculture that said you could put John Kinsler in a chair and blindfold him and hand him a leaf of cotton and he'd roll it in his fingers and tell you the variety, when it was planted and how deep it was planted, how many times it had been cultivated, and on and on.

My father used to say, "If the best part of you is underground, you might as well be a potato." You're supposed to stand on your own two feet and accomplish something. He hammered that into us all the time.

If some of these old-timers were still alive, they'd be getting along today still. They were good men and they stood for what was right. When they spoke, people listened, believe me.

Katharine Kinsler Shaw

Nobody's Business

Preston Austin and Horace McDowell developed this country in 1912. That's when they got the railroad in here. Austin was influential in getting the railroad across

Horace McDowell near Austwell.

that river bottom. He carried a big stick back then. He went to Pennsylvania and got Horace McDowell and they bought a lot of land together. Finally, they split and each one had their own business. They were both promoters and land developers. Finally, McDowell went broke. He had a foreman that padded the payroll. Everybody knew what was happening, but it wasn't anybody's business. People didn't stick their noses in each other's business back then.

Herbert "Buster" Bickford

Railroad Towns: Greta, Inari, Vidauri, Maudelowe

Although the railroad had reached Victoria by 1861, Beeville by 1886, and Goliad by 1890, it was not until 1905 that tracks were laid across Refugio County and the lower San Antonio River area, connecting Refugio and Bay City. With the building of the St. Louis, Brownsville and Mexico Railway, towns sprang up along the line. The depot, cattle pens, warehouses, cotton gin, and other facilities supported the shipping activities. To induce the railroad to route the line through their property, ranchers granted right-of-way through their pastures, set aside land for a townsite, and provided substantial cash incentives.

Greta, Vidauri, and Inari, located along present-day U.S. 77, were all founded during this period. Only Vidauri (pop. 85) has survived. Greta was named for a railroad conductor's niece, and Inari was named for a town in India by A. E. Spohn, an incorporator of the railroad. Vidauri had one of the area's famous mercantiles. It was created from a small section of the Welder ranch and was named in honor of José Jesús Vidaurri, who was land commissioner for the Power-Hewetson Colony and had a land grant in the area. The locals affectionately referred to the store and the settlement as Redlew, which, they explained to me, is Welder spelled backwards. Maudelowe was created when Martin O'Connor arranged for the branch line between Tivoli and Austwell to swing through his ranch. He established a townsite named for his wife and built a general store, a cotton gin, and a hotel.

Reverend Mack Williams at Bethlehem Baptist Church, Inari.

Inari

Inari was near the Marberry Store, just past the Morrows. There were thirteen or so houses. Every one was alike. They was kinfolks. Livin' only around kinfolks created a very different place. Everyone got along great. Of course, there was bickerin' among the kids.

Reverend [Isaiah] Weathers pastored Bethlehem Baptist Church, and the school was in the church. Lucy Bunting [or Bunton] was the teacher. At one time, Miss

Theresa and Miss Beatrice Charleston also taught there.

There was preachin' on the grounds and dinner all day. Everyone spread the wagon sheet out and put the food on it. Pete and Roy Marberry never missed a meetin'. They knew the food was good, and they loved to listen to the music.

The church had no piano and no lights, just Mother Hubbard lamps on the wall. The '42 storm knocked down the bell and cracked it. It knocked down the front of the church and all the windows. At one time, there was only three members left, but I still held services for them. I even held services for Winnie Dunman when she was the only one left in Austwell.

They wanted their services to continue and I liked doin' it. I still like to hold services for the old folks. We lived back then, real life. That was livin'.

Reverend Mack Williams

Víctor Rodríguez and Reverend Mack Williams at the remains of the old Maudelowe Store.

Inari was right there where Highway 77 and 239 cross. It was on the way to Tivoli. There was a church there and Miss Laura Hopkins and Lucy "Babe" Scott lived there. They say Babe Scott was one beautiful woman. They used to have dances down there from time to time.

Lela Edwards Williams

Maudelowe

The Martin O'Connor ranch was where I was born in 1914. Maudelowe was the nearest town, and it was quite a little place. It had a gin, post office in the store, hotel, and a bakery with a mud oven outside.

I was thirteen before I ever went in to Maudelowe. I told my sisters how much candy Mr. Marberry had and they wouldn't believe me. Papa took us all to town the next week. My sisters couldn't believe what they saw. Mr. Marberry gave us Zuzu gingersnaps and candy. You don't get *pilóns* like that anymore. When we moved closer to headquarters, I couldn't believe there were other houses around.

Maudelowe was named for Mrs. Martin O'Connor. She was Maude Lowe before she was married. It was put there mainly because of the railroad. There were shipping pens there. Mr. Marberry ran the store. There was a hotel there, too, for a while. There was a lot of bootleg whiskey in the area. The warehouse was for storing cottonseed and cotton.

When they finished the warehouse, they decided to have a big dance. There

> "Riverdale had a little depot, a telephone operator, and a side rail. There was also a gin, a store, a hotel, and a barber shop. They even had a post office. It was the cutest little town you ever saw. There's not a thing left of it now."
>
> **Allene Pettus Lott**

were wagons all around. I went to that dance with Papa and Mama in the wagon with all the kids. That was the biggest room I ever saw.

Do you remember the mud oven they had down there at Maudelowe? They baked bread in it. It was made out of dirt. I never will forget, I was a little boy and Pete would shout at me. They used a long shovel to bring that bread out. One time, I was a little boy, and I pulled out that bread and Mrs. Marberry shouted at me, "Look out! You might fall in that oven!"

I never will forget all those old houses down there. Right across the street from the store was three houses in a row and then five nearby.

Reverend Mack Williams

That old Maudelowe store is still standing. It is a warehouse now and falling down, but at one time it had a warehouse behind it and we used to go to dances there. Everyone in the area went to dances there. It was a real center for the community.

Katharine Kinsler Shaw, Lucile Fagan Snider

In the twenties, Martin O'Connor had three or four thousand acres in cultivation out there. He had a gin at Maudelowe, and there would be two or three thousand Mexican cotton pickers. The Kinslers and the Hartmans would go down to Laredo or Brownsville and get a passenger train and load it with migrant workers. The workers would come into town and go to the O'Connor-Swift Store and get all the groceries they wanted on credit. Then they would go pick cotton.

That was before the days of fertilizer and they would only be raisin' a bale or a bale and a half to an acre. Itinerant cotton pickers used to come in here. That was before the land was wore out. Cotton wears out the land. In 1919, that storm came and filled the land full of salt and it wasn't any good anymore.

Herbert "Buster" Bickford

George of All Trades: An Interview with George Gould

We performed a lot of services out of this store. If somebody was sick, they'd come in to me and I'd call the doctor and see that they got a ride into town. I'd take care of the bill and the ranch would collect from their check. Sometimes, we'd have to collect for some of their family troubles. Other times, the cowboys would go to town and get drunk and get put in jail. Old Ira Heard would call me up and tell me about it. I'd just tell him to turn them loose and mail me the bill.

The mercantile was started up around 1912 or 1914. It was drawn up between the Power ranch and the Welder ranch. They had a cotton gin there in those days. Judge Linebaugh drew up the original contract. Each ranch put so much money in it.

When Mr. Power died, the Welders took it over. Until I took over the store completely the last seven years, the Welders paid me and I kept all the profits. If there were no profits, I charged ten percent above cost.

I was in the bakery business early on and got tired of it. Mr. Taggert was with the Welder ranch, and he and I got to be friends. He finally talked me into taking over the mercantile on the ranch. When we moved out here, it was way out in the country, not like now. It was a big decision. I refused the offer twice. Finally, the bakery business got so heavy I took the offer. Florence taught school during the week, and on Saturdays she would help me in the store. It really was a two-man job on Saturdays.

James Welder was the one who hired me. He died about a year and a half after I took over the store. He came down here and said, "If you need anything, George, you and your wife, just let us know, we'll try to help you." He fixed up the house real nice. He was a really nice fella.

Especially during the wintertime, people would be all over the place, perched on the counters and around the stove. They would talk about different things, cattle and farming, and kidding each other, mostly. I'd get a lot of kidding, especially about being from England. I had lots more English accent when I first went to the mercantile than I do now.

Thomas Marion [O'Connor II] gave us a lot of business also. Marie and Gloria [O'Connor] and Madeline and Nancy [Fleming] used to come up here a lot. They liked to sit on the counter and chat.

George Gould (left) at the Vidauri Mercantile, ca. 1959.

It was kind of exciting, the thought of coming out here. We knew it would be totally different, not such a rat race. We also had a five-bedroom house and plenty of room to raise chickens, a garden, milk cows, and hogs. It was quite a change from living in the city and working fourteen and fifteen hours a day.

The cowboys were really good hands, real good working men. Most of them were very religious. They had a little church there on the ranch. Those Youngbloods were real good people. They all had nice gardens and raised hogs and chickens. Boo [Terrell] was almost like family to them. He was a really nice man.

Emmaline Youngblood Henderson.

Grandma Welder was a nice person, too. I'd go to the ranch nearly every day and eat breakfast or drink coffee and take orders from Mr. [Eula] Phillips [Sr.].

The war didn't bother us much down here. We raised everything we needed. With the war coming on, it was a wonderful thing, because we had things that other people couldn't get due to the rationing. We raised our own hogs, we had our own cows and our own milk and butter. We had a hundred and some chickens and we supplied ourselves and the store.

Moving to Vidauri couldn't have happened at a better time for us with the war coming on. We didn't feel the effects of it very much. We didn't even hurt too much on gasoline. We used the casing-head gas from some of the wells. It was just as clear as water and you opened up the little petcock and run off a gallon or two. It was very explosive, more like ether. We'd mix it half and half with regular gas.

That was when it all began to change. After the war, the hours the ranchers worked daily got less. Eventually, there was no work on Saturdays and Sundays. Then all these ranches went on to the hourly basis for pay. Their lifestyle changed a lot, too. Most of them got cars. Most of the houses got fitted with bathrooms and electricity. They bought different food than before. Everyone ate a lot more fresh

Hotel Vidauri.

meat, and the sausage and bacon came precut and wrapped. When we went there, rice and beans and stuff were in bins. We'd scoop it out and sell it by the pound. By the time we left, everything was in packages.

We also serviced a ranch down in Duval County, the Duval Ranch. A fella by the name of Hendon was down there, and all the hardware for the ranch came from the Vidauri Mercantile.

Emmaline [Youngblood] Henderson was one of the characters down here. She used to watch TV, everything that come on. Every new soap, soap powder, anything new, I would have to get it for her. Her husband, Mose Henderson, was a good cook. He used to go out with the chuckwagon. After Tom "Ball" Rodgers died, Mose was head guy on the chuckwagon. He had a very dry humor, very comical.

Tom Ball used to tell some outrageous stories about how when they were driving cattle to Kansas, the Indians would try to scalp the colored men, so they would leave him on the Texas side. Nathaniel [Youngblood] was a very good, religious man. Douglas Franklin was a horse breaker for the Welders. He was one of the best men they had.

Reverend Ulysses Johnson would come out from Victoria to have church. There was a little tank between the commissary and the ranch where they used to baptize. It was on the trail from the ranch to the store. Florence and I used to go listen to their services and singing sometime. It was gospel singing, the old-time religious songs.

Postmaster George Gould hanging the mail for the train to catch.

They'd have a big Juneteenth barbecue every year and the ranch would give them a calf and the Shays would give them a goat. They'd invite us all up there. It was really a good feast. They had a big crowd that came from Victoria and all over.

Frank and Aretha Taylor used to have some fights out here. I used to chastize him for the way he talked to her. I tried to tell him no one should talk to a woman that way.

We always had friends down in the oil camps. T. A. Jeffers lived on the O'Connor ranch and we went to see them often. Sophie was a real nice person. She was really humorous.

I really did enjoy these people out here. They were friends and you knew they were there if you needed them. One time, Billy Welder and I were driving around and the pasture caught fire. We finally took off our jackets and started beating out the fire. Your father [Tom O'Connor Jr.] landed in the helicopter and said, "Gould, how do you like ranching?" My face was just black as coal!

We got to understand the different races. We had never been around colored people before. We found out that they were all hard-working people with the same ideas and desires we had. They'd do anything for us and we'd do anything for them. Irie and Bill Nixon would hunt and fish with us. We used to go stay in an old cabin along the river and hunt and fish.

The thoughts of the people who lived in the small communities wasn't much on the outside world. Their thoughts were just in that community and within that county. In fact, some of them had never even been out of the county.

We really never felt lonesome out here. The freight train would stop on the siding and people would come out and get a cold drink and food while they were waiting for another train to come. I remember there was one engineer that used to collect silver dollars and rattlesnake hides. I'd save both for him. He'd make belts out of the rattlesnake skins.

You didn't even think about crime in those days. It was just a very unusual

Dennis Williams, O'Connor Brothers Ranches foreman from 1957 until he retired in 1995.

thing to hear about somebody getting killed. We got a certain amount of news by radio, but we didn't have TV in those days. We did get it earlier than most people. My brother-in-law came from Victoria one time to watch Joe Lewis fight. Just as he walked in the door, Joe Lewis had knocked the fella out. He missed the whole thing.

We used to go to Corpus to do our Christmas shopping. That was a big trip in those days. Once or twice a month we would go to Victoria. There was really no one we could leave to tend things. We never went away on a vacation because of that. Occasionally, we would go to Kansas City and see Mr. Gould, my father. I would walk from the commissary and flag the train down. Train travel was really nice. I enjoyed it.

Even the oilfield workers used to come to the store. Most of the post office business came from Quintana, Exxon, and Standard Oil. The ranch people would come here also and sit around. We always had free coffee, and on rainy days a lot of people stayed around.

When we first came to Vidauri hardly any of the ranch hands had cars, so they couldn't even get as far as Refugio on Saturday. They would come down here on Saturday, all together, and get their checks. After they got their checks and bought their groceries, sometimes the ranch truck would take them to Refugio. Back then, all the work on the ranch was done on horseback. We often would ride twenty miles a day.

We raised our entire family out there. Florence was teaching school at Wood High. When she retired, she was teaching in Mission Valley. Molly Stoner taught out here. Abbie Linam was earlier. Most of the ranch schools were closed after World War II. They started sending the school buses out and bringing the children into town.

We ran the Vidauri Mercantile for thirty-four years. We moved out there in 1941, right at the beginning of the war. That war brought on lots of changes. It was the biggest change in society in this century.

When we moved out here, you might see three cars a day and maybe a couple of trucks on the main highway to Refugio. We'd have more trains than traffic. One would go by about every thirty minutes, freight and passenger both. We would have four passenger trains a day. They'd stop at Vidauri and pick up passengers. There was a small depot here. After the war was over, you would see as many as fifty to one hundred cars a day. By the sixties, the passenger trains had completely quit running.

The big trains with the cattle cars would come by here. I used to help count them. They'd load on that siding and ship them out to Kansas City. They'd put them on the pasture up there for six months and then they'd put them on the Kansas City market. That was when they would raise the big steers. They'd weigh one thousand to fifteen hundred pounds. They were just as wild as the old cowhands used to say.

The old cowhands rode horseback and they'd get up at five in the morning and leave the ranch and come back after dark. We used to keep the commissary open for them on Saturday night until twelve or one o'clock so the ranch hands that got in late could come to the store. On payday, they would often have a crap game on the front porch. Wallace Shay was a little boy then. He would get right in the middle of them.

We'd open at seven o'clock in the morning and, except on Saturday, we would close by six or seven in the evening. We had a gasoline pump, we loaded the mail on the train, we sold and took orders for hardware, windmills, pipe, and barbed wire, nails, staples, drygoods, bolts of cloth. People in those days bought yard goods and made their own clothes. We sold lots of long underwear to the cowboys during the winter.

Tommy O'Connor [Jr.] gave us lots of business in the old days. Dennis Williams did the ordering. Roger Williams used to get a lot of hardware, windmills, pipe, and barbed wire. We shipped it direct from Alamo Ironworks. Dennis came down nearly every morning and drank coffee.

When we went there, the main food was salt bacon, beans, and rice. When we left there, it was regular sliced bacon and smoked bacon. We sold lots of snuff. We sold flour by the twenty-five-pound sack. The sacks were printed.

This brought back memories I never would have thought of ever again.

George Gould with Florence Gould

Roger Williams at the Vidauri Mercantile.

CHAPTER FOUR

Lewis's Bend:
The Old Landmark

"It was the center, the mother of all the rest of the settlements around here. They came from Indianola after that storm [1875] and here's where they settled, in Lewis's Bend. It was the center of everything."

Simmie Rydolph

In some respects, Lewis's Bend was much like the other black settlements that grew up in the region following Emancipation. Yet it was unique in its spirit, energy, and longevity. For decades it was the heart of an entire culture, the vibrant center of the San Antonio River bottom and surrounding area.

Seabourne Lewis

Although the community is easily traced back to the plantation that Seabourne Lewis established on the river in the 1850s, many of the facts surrounding Lewis himself are

Ida Simms, Will Johnson, Addie Simms, and J. W. Farley, Simms Bridge at Lewis's Bend.

obscure, contradictory, or confusing. My cousin Nancy O'Connor and I had spent several years trying to find out who Seabourne Lewis was—but to no avail. About the only thing we knew was that his name was spelled many different ways—Seabron, Seabourn, Seaborne. My grandmother spelled it Seabourne. From old county records we surmised that by 1857 he was operating a ferry from his plantation.[1]

*"They stopped on the San'tone
River and Lewis's Bend and they
sprung out from there."*

Eugene Tillman

Then one night in the mid-eighties, Nancy called me at some un-Christian hour to announce her incredible find. Earlier in the evening, she had gone to visit her father, Thomas Marion O'Connor (II), in search of some book he had in his library. When she pulled the book from the shelf, a very old and faded newspaper clipping fell out. It was the obituary of Seabourne Lewis's granddaughter, Mary Virginia Drake O'Connor, who was Mrs. Dennis M. O'Connor and my great-grandmother. So, as this aged piece of paper revealed, Seabourne Lewis was actually my great-great-great-grandfather. The obituary, which gave Nancy and me our first clue about who Lewis really was, read as follows:

Mrs. Dennis M. O'Connor, 75, was born in Montgomery, Alabama, August 1, 1850. Her maiden name was Virginia Drake. She was the daughter of Washington Drake and Mahaney Lewis Drake. The family came to Texas in 1853, settling in Victoria County on what is now the Sample place along the San Antonio River. Mr. and Mrs. Drake died during Mrs. O'Connor's early childhood and she was reared by her grandfather, Seabron Lewis, who had accompanied her parents from Alabama to Texas.

Mr. Lewis became the owner of one of the largest plantations in the South and possessed many slaves. He was one of the most influential figures in the state during the Civil War period. Mrs. O'Connor became the wife of Dennis M. O'Connor April 16, 1868.

Mrs. O'Connor, like her husband, was of noble lineage. Mr. O'Connor's mother, Mary Fagan O'Connor, was a niece of the Duke of Wellington. Mary Virginia Drake O'Connor was a direct descendant of Sir Frances Drake, whose name and achievements find a prominent place on the pages of England's naval history.[2]

After finding out that Seabourne Lewis was my great-great-great-grandfather, I began to search through my grandmother's papers for mention of him. On the back of an envelope, I found this handwritten notation of hers, titled "Seabourne Lewis, Plantation Owner," which suggested that the Lewis family came to Texas much earlier: "Seabourne Lewis and his wife and family came from Montgomery, Barbour County, Alabama sometime around 1833 or 1834. They settled on the San Antonio River in extreme southwest Victoria County at a place later known as Lewis's Bend. His children, as far as I know were Mahaney, who married Washington F. Drake in Alabama, and Sarah who married a Bickford [Peletiah Bickford]. After the family moved to Texas, Mahaney and her husband died in an epidemic. They had a daughter named Mary Virginia Drake. She and her brother, Tom, were taken in by the James I. Cottingham family at Old St. Mary's where they attended public school in 1860–1862. Her brother, Tom Drake, younger than Mary Virginia, was killed by Dave Odan in the 1870's and is buried in the Fagan cemetery on the Armour Fagan ranch. It is not known to me where Seabourne Lewis is buried."[3]

Probate court records contain this recollection of Seabourne Lewis by a former slave, Dublin Lewis: "I have known Seaborn Lewis ever since my first recollection and up to the time of his death. I was his servant from my earliest recollection up to the time of emancipation in 1865. Seaborn was engaged in merchandise, farming, raising stock, established and carried on a blacksmith shop connected with a wagon makers shop. My employment was wholly in his blacksmith shop and performed and executed myself all the work from the time of his settlement on the San Antonio River in Victoria County, which was to the best of my recollection about the year 1850."[4]

Nancy and I also began interviewing people who might know something about him. My cousin, Virginia Hallinan Tatton, provided some sketchy details, and some of our other interviews yielded information that had been passed down through several generations.

Seabourne Lewis seems to have had a good side and a bad side. Some said Lewis was a large slave holder who could sometimes be a cruel one. Others reported that he was good to the freed slaves and did much to help them establish Lewis's Bend after Emancipation. Not having known of his existence during my grandmother's lifetime, I missed my only chance to find out the truth about him. It seems that he died in Victoria County sometime during the Reconstruction era. Whether his final resting place was somewhere in the San'tone River bottom or a burial site back in Alabama, we may never know. In any event, while his reputation is a matter of debate, he left his mark along the San Antonio River. His name is forever linked with one of the river's most extraordinary and beloved communities.

Old Lewis

The way I understood it, my family took care of Mary Virginia Drake when she was brought down here an orphan by her grandfather Seabourne Lewis. Seabourne Lewis, his second wife, his granddaughter, and her brother, Tom Drake, came from

Kate Rock, Mercy Simms, Marcellus and Kate Talman, Addie Simms, Ada Simms, and C.M. and Ida Simms.

Alabama in a covered wagon in the middle of the 1800s. They settled north of the San Antonio River. Lewis had a plantation down on the San'tone River and had a ferry on the river.

You see, old Lewis had two wives. His first wife was Emma up there at Lewis's Bend. I think there was one child born, named Mahaney, who was Mrs. Dennis O'Connor's mother. I have heard something about a Sarah also.

The way I remember it, Mahaney married Franklin Drake and moved to Alabama. They had Mary Virginia and Tom and then died in some sort of epidemic.

"I like them river bottoms. There was always something to do. River bottoms were our friends. They never let us down."

Herbert "Buster" Bickford

The kids were brought back here and lived with the Cottinghams for a while in Old St. Mary's and then moved down here with Old Man Lewis.

When she lived with her grandfather on his plantation on the San'tone River was when my grandmother started raising her. They were real close friends for many years, but before I was born, something come between them.

Her brother, Tom, was a gambler and lived in Fannin. He made his living any way he could and I think that was kind of an embarrassment to the O'Connors. I think they just kind of excommunicated him. I think they were brother and sister.

Anyway, Old Man Lewis got land, around three or four thousand acres where he raised cotton and had lots of slaves. My grandfather, Peletiah Bickford, married Sarah Lewis, who was the other daughter, after he came back from the Santa Fe Expedition.

So, here's what we got. There was a linkage and a connection at that time when he married the Lewis girl from the first marriage, or at least I think that's the way it was.

Their child was Mary Bickford. Then she married Ed Phelps and this caused a big problem. Something to do with a land feud that wound up in the Supreme Court.

I believe Seabourne Lewis lost everything after the Civil War, and from what I understand, it was because he was on the Confederate side. After the war, durin' Reconstruction, he was considered to be not a citizen of the United States, so them damn carpetbaggers come in and just took it away from him. From what I was told,

Wallace Sevier and Frank Sevier.

he packed up and left and went back to Virginia and was never heard from again. Seems there wasn't none of them left anymore. You take my grandfather. What he told me about Old Man Lewis was, he never talked.

I think the Lewis family all left after the Civil War and went back to Virginia. That's how Lewis's Bend got its name and why all those colored people are up there. Lewis was a slave owner and they took the Lewis name. He freed the slaves after the war and let them settle on the river and take his name. I was there once or twice. We used to squirrel hunt on the Terrell place.

You know, my grandmother took care of the Adlers, too, Dennis and Sam. They had lost their parents.

Herbert "Buster" Bickford

Virginia Hallinan Tatton.

Seabourne Lewis was the grandfather of my grandmother, Mrs. Dennis O'Connor [I]. Seabourne Lewis, his second wife (a step-grandmother), Mrs. Dennis O'Connor, and her brother Franklin Drake came in the middle of the 1800s in a covered wagon from Alabama to north of the San Antonio River. A black slave named Aunt Marthy also came in the wagon to take care of the children. The step-grandmother did not care for the children.

Virginia Hallinan Tatton, granddaughter of Mary V. Drake O'Connor

Old Man Jackson used to talk about Seabourne Lewis. Said he help all the people in Lewis's Bend because them people didn't have no way to make a livin'. Only thing they had to eat is corn, I mean ground corn, take it to the mill. They plant little fields with the corn patch. They didn't know nothin' while they were still slaves.

He took care of them Youngbloods over there. Took care of all them Youngbloods because Old Man Jackson was the father of these young ones.

There was a white family livin' down there named Simms. They had a workin' fella, a old man, to help 'em do everythin' there at the Simms Store. His name was Prudencio Salazar.

Wallace Sevier used to farm over there, was workin' the ranch. He had two daughters. One lived in Refugio. One was named Elizabeth. They used to live at Murphy Ranch, too. It was right across the bridge down in Lewis's Bend.

Jesús Ybarbo

Lewis Plantation

From what I understand, a big part of the river bottom was Lewis Plantation on the north side of the river. It had a board fence that enclosed the whole thing, over a thousand acres. An original wagon road went through the middle of it. Lewis came from Birmingham, England, and had his brother-in-law with him. He raised cotton there and shipped it to New Orleans and Galveston from Mesquite Landing. They hauled it in old cart wagons.

Earl Albrecht

I moved to the San'tone River in 1964 from Lamar County. We bought our property from Texana Matthews. She was from the Fagan and Dubois line. Texana taught me most of what I know about the history of this area. We always talked about history. Texana hung on her grandfather's [Peter Fagan Jr.] bootstrap and listened to stories.

She always said that Lewis Plantation was right down here on the river by us. It was a cotton plantation with a lot of slaves. There was a big old two-story house that was the plantation house. The Sample family wound up living there in later years. Texana didn't say how it was destroyed.

The Sample cemetery was supposedly donated by Seabourne Lewis for slaves off the plantation to be buried. It is much larger than what it shows today. The cattle have destroyed it.

There is an old underground cistern on our property that was supposed to be the Sevier home site, according to Texana. There is a Sevier cemetery in the area. They were an old established family down here.

There was a brick factory where slaves made bricks. This is on some of the Huber lease property. Lewis's Bend and Simms' Settlement were the same place.

Wanda Hood Payne

Down on the river, long time ago, there was a plantation. It was back in slavery times, so they tell me. It was on the San'tone River, across from Shay's [ranch]. The bridge crossed there was called Simms Crossing.

Home of Jacob and Marie Albrecht Dentler.

The Lewises lived in a big two-story house. He was a white man for sure. Eventually, they left there, and other people moved in over the years. They made fields around the river.

Grandma Marthy and Steve Holliman were Lewis slaves and were the oldest people around the area. Marthy was the mother of some of those oldest Terrells, like Bill, Larry, and John.

Milam Thompson

Memories of Lewis's Bend

*"There was nothing better than
that Lewis's Bend."*

Jesús Ybarbo

Everyone I interviewed told colorful stories about Lewis's Bend. Although it was only a small settlement clustered around Mount Zion Baptist Church, it was as lively as many of the area's larger communities. To many, it was as exciting as going to New York City might have been. The wonders of Lewis's Bend have remained always in their minds and hearts.

Just a Lot of Folks

Lewis's Bend was just a lot of folks livin' up there on the river. It was just a big bottom with houses here and there. There was a church house.

They were a fair bunch of folks. There were no rough ones there. They were religious-type folk mostly. There were a few sinners gamblin' and drinkin'. It was a woody area with farmin', churchin', and playin' ball.

The houses were one-by-twelve log houses or board and battin'. They weren't much, but what they had, they kept clean.

The school was in the Mount Zion Church at Lewis's Bend, and Bethlehem [Baptist Church] was in Inari up the road. They were nice places to live. I went to Bethlehem School with Lucy Gibson and Georgie Sommers.

*Congregation at
Mount Zion Baptist
Church, Lewis's Bend.*

Most of us was raised down there in Lewis's Bend. It was nothin' but a river bottom. The schoolhouse was the church house and the church house was the schoolhouse. We went to school in the daytime and church on Sunday. Sometimes we would have revivals and prayer meetin's.

The houses were just straight lumber houses, maybe thirty by forty. There was a lot of people lived out there at one time. They lived maybe a mile or so apart, but that didn't mean nothin'. People walked long distances in those days. They'd come down in a buggy, a wagon, or horseback.

"There is a lot of bottom on the San'tone River."

L. V. Terrell

Further on back, it had been a plantation down there. In slavery times, they had slaves that worked around there. There was a man who had a plantation and he was named Lewis. After Emancipation, a lot of colored people moved to the river. It was called Lewis's Bend. It was a freed slave community.

After lots of people came in from Indianola, it was a boomin' place. Indianola was a big seaport until that storm took it out in 1875. Lewis's Bend was called the San'tone River even though the whole river was named that. If someone said that, you knew they meant Lewis's Bend. It was just about considered the birthplace of the black people in that area.

There are lots of stories out of there. One of them was about the stars fallin'. Grandma Marthy [Perryman] said the stars came out of the sky like a shower, but they didn't reach the ground. They just got to a point and went out. She lived on the north side of the river.

Old Man Crogan Terrell had a likin' to a lot of those people, and after Emancipation they didn't have nowhere to go. That Lewis's Bend area belonged to Terrell and he let them move in there.

By the time we came along, there wasn't no slavery. Everyone was free and had a little farm. If you could farm thirty acres, you was rich.

It was all old raggedy houses. There were a few log houses there, too. The only white people in Lewis's Bend in our time was the Simms. Mrs. Simms had a store. Mamie Lott lived there also. We can just barely remember Mrs. Simms. Everybody went there and bought a little groceries.

Will Johnson, Addie Simms, Ida Simms, and J. W. Farley, Simms' Bridge.

Henry Lott, Toney and J. Y.'s daddy, once owed her for a year's groceries and she wouldn't let him have any more credit. He was gamblin' on gatherin' his crops. He told her if she didn't give him no more food, he would die and couldn't pay her what he owed her already. She let him have more credit.

We had country dances on Saturday night. We'd kill a shoat and barbecue. That's the way the people lived. Get a few things from the store, fish, hunt, and mostly live on that. We didn't make much money, but you didn't need much money then.

The river would overflow and Lewis's Bend would be surrounded by water. They would have to go get wagons to get the people out.

People came to Lewis's Bend from everywhere. There were big baptizin's down there. Some of the deacons would duck people under the water. Reverend Weathers would go out there with you and do it in the Name of the Father, the Son, and the Holy Spirit.

The church services were *hot.* We don't have good church services now. We had good worship then. You could hear us singin' a mile away. Everyone came runnin' when they heard the singin'.

Everyone came to Isaiah Weathers' church on Sunday. We'd have night services, too. He was an awful good preacher. Martin O'Connor was his man. Anything he wanted, Martin would give it to him. Isaiah had a heavy voice you could hear for miles. He knew a lot of history, too. George Macbeth, Elder [D. S.] Sapp, and P. S. Wilkinson were some of the old preachers in the area.

Will Weathers

Aunt Anna Dunman lived around "the curve." Cousin Gert lived over closer to the middle. On Sunday mornin' they all started comin' and driftin' through that river bottom. They would start singin', and you wouldn't believe that sound.

Reverend Mack baptizing in the San Antonio River, 1953.

Some people were born in the woods and some on the prairies. They were very different experiences. It was like two different worlds—that bottom and the prairies.

Reverend Mack Williams

The Tillmans came from Virginia. Andy used to talk about drivin' an oxcart from Indianola to Goliad and then to Mexico. He located in Lewis's Bend around 1870.

Reverend Isaiah Weathers.

He was a slave and so was his mother. They were probably named after their slave master. He seemed to have a lot of privileges for a slave. He was workin' for the freight truckers and he left Indianola after the storm.

The black Lewises were there, and so were the white Simms. Bill Lewis was the one that organized the settlement. He farmed a lot of land down there. The Lotts, the Tillmans, and Youngbloods were big families there. So were the Terrells.

The Lewis slaves were Aunt Dinah, Aunt Martha, John Winn, Andy Tillman, and Steve Holliman. Uncle Steve was a pretty hard man to case. He was funny. He lived more towards Goliad.

Ben Green was a white man who bossed on the River Ranch or Duke Ranch. Aunt Susan was his wife. She was a Stewart and she stayed with him. She was supposed to have taken no trouble from children.

We never heard much about the Lewis that owned that plantation on the river. There were big Juneteenths. Old Steve Holliman was an old-timer. He went up the trail and he used to tell some strange tales.

James Welder, Jim O'Connor, and Tom O'Connor [II] were the big dogs around here. They worked all the Lewis's Bend people on their ranches. The old owners were fine men. Lewis's Bend fed these ranches some of the finest cowboys in the world.

Juneteenth celebration in Refugio, 1895.

Lewis's Bend had changed even by the time I came along. We never really knew it in its prime—not the real old-time Lewis's Bend.

There weren't as many people there when we came along. Paul, Martha, Ellen, Jackson, Garnet Avery, and Aunt Marthy were gone. The Simms twins were gone, too.

The houses were made out of logs from trees. They were called "punchin' houses," made out of board and battin'.

Simmie Rydolph

Memoir of a White Girl in Lewis's Bend

Elizabeth Sevier Haney.

My family fought in the Texas Revolution. They came to this country from France by way of Tennessee. One of my grandfathers died in the Texas Revolution and the other became the governor of Tennessee.

I was born in 1900 in Victoria County. We were sharecroppers. I remember we lived in a tent. My grandfather, Eldridge Sevier, was a bookkeeper for either old Tom O'Connor or his son Dennis. I can't remember which.

We went to Lewis's Bend when I was five or six years old. My father share-cropped for the Fagans. He was in the blizzard of 1899. Cattle dropped and died. He skinned all day for fifty cents a day. He said you could have walked across the river on the carcasses. It was worse than the one in 1924. It was after that so many people died of smallpox.

One of his buddies was an Ybarbo. His cronies were all the blacks and Mexicans. Lots of them still live there. My father went to school on Carlos Ranch. I never went to school in Lewis's Bend.

Janie O'Riley De La Garza was my cousin. She was my special friend. She married Rafael De La Garza. They worked for the O'Connors most of their lives.

All I ever heard it called was Lewis's Bend. The old man built that big house down there himself. He was supposed to have been a rich man. He had two girls

Congregation at St. Anthony's Church.

and owned slaves. I remember my daddy saying Lewis mistreated his slaves.

He was reported to have had fifty thousand dollars worth of gold. I never heard any stories about how he got the money. He buried the gold and money to keep from losing it to the Confederates during the war. I don't know whether he was a cattle raiser or a cotton plantation owner. Must have been raising cotton with all those slaves. I know a lot of slaves came in by boat.

His daughters were much older than me. They say they lived in a big old house. It was two-story and had four big rooms and a little addition where he lived off to

Will Sample Jr.

himself. The kitchen was outside with a big old chimney. The house was still there when we left in 1910. I can remember my aunt telling me the Lewis girls used to make rag dolls for them to play with. Both of them were old then and had their hair in little knots on their head.

Old Will Sample lived in the house and married Emma Sample, the schoolteacher in Lewis's Bend. He was chubby and red-faced.

Young Will found a schoolteacher dead one time. He was so upset he was wild. The rats had eaten her.

Old Man Sample lived in the house after Lewis left. I don't know how he got it. Years later, my aunt used to run to the head of the stairs and shout, "Mr. Lewis, Mr. Lewis, come down and tell me where your gold is!" She said it sounded like someone was coming down the stairs.

We had to call the old people Aunt and Uncle. Betsy Sample was Will's mother. They were sharecroppers like us. I don't know how they got the house, but they were there when we left. Maybe his wife owned the property. Aunt Fannie was one of Aunt Betsy's daughters. The Lewises may have gone busted in the Civil War. I don't know if he ever remarried.

We used to go to the old bridge. The store was about a block north of the river. They kept a few stores there, but when anyone needed lots of groceries, someone went to town. They shopped for everyone. That was the way we did. This happened every three months. It was twenty miles to Victoria.

Holeman's plank house, San Antonio River bottom.

It was nice down there. We lived on the bank of the river when it was still beautiful and clear. We had to carry our water to our house. It was made out of logs and mud and the floor was dirt. The yard was hard dirt, like concrete. It was swept every day.

There were big old pecan trees all around our house. Lots of flying squirrels hung out in those trees. We would play out in the yard at night. We lived in the old Burnet house right next door and then we went to the Lewis house when Old Man Sample died. It was made of planks.

Dick Avery.

Richard Harris.

Will was Old Man Sample's son. Old Man Will was the one married Emma. He and his old man both thought they could play a fiddle.

When it flooded, we would have to go across the river to O'Connor property. They had a little church over there that we went to. That's where my brothers were baptized. We were Catholics, and Father Plana was the priest. When we went to church, we would take a picnic and spend the day. My father absolutely refused to work on Sunday.

There were two old sisters, Martha and Mary. Mary picked cotton for us and Martha was totally blind. Their names were Shorter. They tended the small church with two benches. This wasn't Mount Zion. It was a smaller church than that.

I knew Prince Terrell, Larry Terrell, Bill Terrell. I knew all those people down there. There were black and white Terrells, Bill and Joe Hogan were there, and Fagans, Talmans, and Averys. Dick Avery rode through the yard all the time. There wasn't no fence, nothin' to hold him back. I think he thought he was a big shot.

Richard Harris was around. My father would talk to him all the time. I knew Louis Power also. I just barely remember him. Tom Holliday was half and half. He was supposed to be Old Man Sample's son. Who knows? Some say he was Doc Holliday's son. He was as nice as he could be.

Three of my brothers and sisters died at that Lewis house. They were buried out there on the O'Connor prairie. That was why we left there. All of my family are buried in that cemetery. I think it was the De La Garza cemetery.

I don't remember many funerals, but I loved to hear baptisms. They always drew a good crowd for those. The whites would go down there to see them for entertainment. I remember Mrs. Simms' mother's funeral. She's buried out there on the prairie. There was one newborn baby I remember, too.

My father was a barber. The colored folk came to him on Saturdays. The men had whiskers and fairly long hair. The women never would have dreamed of cutting their hair. It was always long. He cut hair for two bits.

Everyone had to do something extra. Cowboying got them only three or four dollars a month. Lots picked pecans, bones, and soda water bottles for extra money.

The people in Lewis's Bend would have a spasm if anyone offered them a handout. They didn't look for nothin' they hadn't earned. It was peaceful, we all got along just famously. It was just a bunch of good, hard-working people living in peace and harmony and contentment.

This was Lewis's Bend.

Elizabeth Sevier Haney

Good Times in the Bends

Lewis's Bend was down there on the river. Mrs. Cornelius Simms had a store down there. A road went down through there that used to go to Victoria, the county line it was. The Power ranch was right on the hill south of it.

Aunt Becky Lott, Bill Terrell, John Terrell all lived down there. Aunt Becky lived near the road. Uncle Jackson Youngblood had a house there. I remember Larry Terrell, too.

GOOD TIMES AT
Lewis's Bend

One time they were tailin' calves, and Bill Terrell pulled a calf's tail off. He said the tail was rotten. He was too strong. That was a strong man. He would almost crush your hand.

I went down there once in a while. They had a church house down there. Reverend Weathers preached down there. He had to go down there in a buggy. He was wiping his eyes all the time. He stayed with Mrs. Simms when he went down to preach. It was lively down there on Saturday and Sunday night.

They had a ferry boat down there. It belonged to Mrs. Simms and she charged ten cents to go across. When Mrs. Simms' husband died, Mr. Terrell told her she could stay there for life. She ran the store and there was a ferry boat there. The bridge was built around 1898. Will Sample lived down there too.

It was two or three miles from the Terrell ranch to that river. It was dark down there. I don't see how people rode through that bottom at night.

They had lots of suppers and barbecues back then. They dug a hole in the ground and put a cultivator wheel over it and cooked a hog for their dances at night. I remember their Nineteenth of June. Mr. Joe [O'Connor] and Mr. Tom [O'Connor Jr.] and the Powers and the white Terrells would give them a calf. They had a big time there. Those ribs were good, and so was that cow's head.

They would make cowboy stew for everyone. There were lots of people, maybe two or three hundred. There was whites, Spanish, and colored.

Rafael De La Garza

Cowboy stew for everyone down in the river bottom.

The Simms Ferry

Cornelius and Jimmy Simms were from Lewis's Bend. They ran a ferry across the San'tone River down there in the Bend. It was a kind of flat boat on a rope. That was where all these ranches went to Refugio. They had it cut out so you could drive down.

I don't know where they came from. I guess they come from out of that river. They were there always. Sully Simms was the same bunch as the others. I don't know much about Lewis Plantation. I guess he was white. I kind of lived down there. I only knew colored Lewises. Some of the people in the Bend was Terrells, Youngblood, Lewis, Lott, and Page—a white man. The houses in Lewis's Bend were all scattered around. They had a colored school there. The white school was in Anaqua. There were some Tuckers lived down there, too.

"Down in that old river bottom where Grandma lived meant a whole lot to me."

Lela Edwards Williams

Richard Harris

Rollin' Down the River

Everyone there was baptized by Reverend Isaiah Weathers. For Sunday church we sang hymns and patriotic songs like "My Country 'Tis of Thee" and "The Star Spangled Banner." Some people started gettin' ready for church on Saturday. Food was brought in for after church. They would hang it on the porch all night in the cool to be ready for the next day. Fried chicken, *tasso* stew, cobbler, and cake was what everyone brought. There would be Sunday school and then we would have the eleven o'clock prayer meetin' goin' on. After that, everyone went outside and ate.

Everybody sang together. The old songs were sung in long meter and short meter. In the long meter, the word is stretched out. It isn't used very much any

G. O. Stoner, Kemper Williams, Kate O'Connor, Dennis O'Connor (II), Martin O'Connor, and Tom O'Connor (II) at Lewis's Bend.

more. The music was brought in from the old slavery songs. "Steal Away" was one of the old songs they sang in slavery times to let the people know there was a prayer meetin'. "I'll Be So Glad" was another of their songs.

Religion is not the same now. We used to pray until we could see and hear things. Reverend Weathers was old-timey and made us get up and testify. The old-timers would get up and strut the floor, singin' "Ride On, King Jesus." Aunt Becky Lott had on her red tablecloth and would be stridin' around with parched corn fallin' out of her pocket singin' that. We'd get so tickled.

They didn't have no music. All they did was clap their hands and stomp their feet. It be good, honey. It was wonderful. We sing a lot different now.

I came up with the old folks. They started you out at eleven or twelve. There was nothin' else to do in Lewis's Bend. The children would come into church followin' their parents like little ducks and would sit down on the benches. Reverend Weathers would tell lots of things. He would tell of visions and dreams and slavery times. He always told about an old woman bein' saved by God in slavery times and about God answerin' prayers.

Fables were stories told as examples of God's mercy, tellin' you how to change your ways and free yourself from sin. That's all we had to go by. Reverend Weathers had a lot of these stories. All those stories were for us to go by and change our ways. They were scary sometimes.

Reverend Weathers had an amazin' voice. It would ring like everything. He roared like a lion. Reverend Calhoun and Reverend Edwards would come and preach with him at times. They had amazin' voices also. Reverend Weathers said he was taught by the white folks and said he never went to school. He had a beautiful handwritin'. He was a wonderful old man. He loved Joe O'Connor and Ripley Terrell. He wasn't afraid of Ripley like other people were.

Parents sang to children before they went to bed. "Nearer My God to Thee," "I'll Fly Away," and "Going Back to the Old Landmark" were the songs they sang to us in our home. The rhythms had to have come from Africa. The old folks would keep rhythm with sticks and with their hands. I'm sure that's where their rhythm came from.

We played "Ring Around Rosies," "Kiss and Hug Your True Love," "Needle in the Shoe," and all like that. We sang and had ring plays for our entertainment. There were never any dances down there.

Playin' church was one of our favorite games. Sometimes we would mock the old folks while we were playin' church. We especially mocked Reverend Weathers. Katherine Terrell, L. V. Terrell, Samantha Terrell, J. Y. Lott, Norvell Brown, Elsie Terrell, and Birdie Lee Brown were my church-playin' friends. We made up our sermons from the real sermons we heard on Sunday. It was crazy-like, it was our fun.

Tom Ball would never be caught in church, so I would put on a duckin' jacket and play like I was Uncle Tom, and everyone else would try to get me to join the church. Now they only have revivals to convert people. They used to pray to a person to get religion. The old folks made sure we were sincere. They brought us up through strictness.

People would sit on the mourner's bench until they got religion. They would sing "Where You Runnin', Sinner?" to the people sittin' on the bench. They would put their hands on the people on the bench and everybody would be cryin' and slingin' snot. That was the way it used to be.

When I was comin' up, you had to pray and pray and pray until you saw something or felt a change. You had to be convinced you were saved. You had to have dreams and visions to prove you were saved. People don't shout like they used to.

When you would get happy, you would have one of the most glorious times. The women had beautiful voices. There was no music. We did it from our hearts. We sang a lot for entertainment.

Rosie Terrell Jones

Willie Bell: Local Hero

Willie Bell, father of James Harris.

Willie Bell was born and raised in Lewis's Bend. One of the principal entertainments for the children and grownups alike was playing baseball. Willie was good enough to make it to what was the equivalent of the major leagues for black baseball players, the Negro Leagues. Major league baseball and the farm teams associated with it were all white until 1946, when Jackie Robinson was brought into the major leagues to play with the Brooklyn Dodgers, a pioneering move in integrating professional sports.

Some people I interviewed thought Willie Bell was nicknamed "Cool Papa Bell," but "Cool Papa" was an entirely different person. This Willie Bell played for the Kansas City Monarchs.[5] The Monarchs have always been considered the best franchise in black baseball history. From the diamond, the Monarchs fielded scores of legendary players, many of whom are now in the Baseball Hall of Fame. They swept the 1942 Negro League World Series and defeated the Homestead Grays, which had won six consecutive Negro League pennants. The Monarchs' pitching staff was led by Satchel Paige, and the team was managed by Frank Duncan. He sent many players into organized baseball. It was the Monarchs that trained Jackie Robinson. The team moved to Kansas City in 1915. They dropped out of the Negro Leagues in 1931 and until 1937 barnstormed around the country with one of the first portable lighting systems in sports. They began to bring night baseball to America for the first time in 1930.

Before Jackie

There were some outstandin' ballplayers from Lewis's Bend, but of course none of them were ever able to make the majors. Jackie Robinson hadn't come along yet.

We had a well-known person from there. He was Willie Bell. He turned out to be a great pitcher for the Kansas City Monarchs. He was with Satchel Paige.

Will Weathers

The Kansas City Monarchs, 1923 National League champions. Willie Bell is fourth from the left.

I played with Willie Bell at Kansas City from 1925 for the next eight or nine years. I remember Bell as a good man, a fine man with a good solid moral code. He retired to El Campo, and his wife taught school there.

Chet Brewer, former member of the Kansas City Monarchs

Lewis's Bend: 1865–1942

"I always said, 'Lord, if I ever get old enough and big enough, I'm leavin' this place!'"

Penceola Terrell Williams

The decline of Lewis's Bend began with the outbreak of World War II. For most of the old residents, the actual end came when the church was moved up on the San Antonio River Road in the forties. The site of the settlement is now leased ranchland belonging to the Terrell and Matthews families. Aunt Ellen Terrell moved out in 1942.

When the Bends Went Down

Lewis's Bend began to break up around World War II. Most of the younger folk started movin' out. The big ranches were startin' to take men on full time and havin' them live on the ranches, so this helped break it up, too.

Lewis's Bend and Vidauri were closely connected. Many people went from Lewis's Bend to the Welder Vidauri ranch after the Bends went down. For a while lots of them traveled around and cowboyed on all the ranches. Then they went to Welder's and formed a big community down there that was a lot like the one in the Bends.

Some people went to other places, but the biggest group went to the Welder. It

Jim Rose and L. F. Jecker fishing in Michael Stoner's woods, San Antonio River bottom, 1912.

was all still a big community and church group. Everyone intermarried among these little communities.

One time they wanted to have a Christmas celebration. One of the bosses told them to get a big log and celebrate until it burned down. In about two days it burned up and they got wise. The next time, they went out and got them a green log. It burned for a couple of weeks and they finally had to put it out. This was how they got together from time to time after they left Lewis's Bend. They were called log-burnin' parties.

Aunt Ellen Terrell.

The feelin's and attitudes of Lewis's Bend wound up on the Welder ranch. They all felt like kinfolks. This has passed down through the generations. It grew up in the younger folks. They all feel close. They all love to talk about the old days.

After World War II, the scatterin' started. Don't know who moved the church up to the road. Miss Lucy Bunton [Bunting] taught there. Aunt Elvira, the Harrises, a number of people were there. Then they started to leave to go to town. The old folks had to move out from by the river, and lots went to Vidauri.

When they moved the church in Lewis's Bend out on the prairie, the people didn't like it at all. It ruined the feelin' of goin' in those trees for church. Black people love shade trees and the river, and the spirit was lost when they moved out of the bottom.

Nowhere else was like the Bends. Any distance from there was another world. It was the whole world, the top of the world. When someone left there, they always came back. The feelin' in the Grove was strong.

Milam Thompson, L. V. Terrell, Richard Harris, Will Weathers, Alice Youngblood Cook, Monroe "Bailey" Shaw, Simmie Rydolph, Reverend Mack Williams

It seems like the soldiers went to war and so many of them never came back to the ranches. Outside work started openin' up. Families started livin' on a different scale. Life started pickin' up for blacks in the mid-fifties. People had money.

Evelyn Elliot Youngblood

There was quite a few souls when I first went down there. There was schools and churches and houses there. The young people had to pack up and leave. There wasn't nothin' for them to do much but work cattle. Down through the years, everybody had a little farm. They built levees around the bridge. The young people got too many in number and they had to go out to other places and hunt jobs.

When World War II came along, all the young men that were left had to go to war. In high time, the young people found jobs. There's nothin' there anymore. Even the bridge has washed away. A one-room, one-teacher schoolhouse. The teacher had a houseful. She was a good teacher, Miss Emma Sample. The last old person living there was Aunt Ellen [Terrell]. She was moved out just as the war started in 1941 and that was the end of Lewis's Bend.

Milam Thompson

Lots of young people would like to work on these ranches, but there is too little money, too many hours, and the work is too hard for them now. The outside world influences kids a lot. They don't like the tough part of the work now. It really isn't in them now. They don't want to do ranch work.

Alice Youngblood Cook

Eugene Tillman: Money in the Trees

"Walkin' through the bottoms in spring is wonderful. That's when things are in bloom. The haws, dogwoods, and plums are the sweetest things you would ever want to smell."

Althia Lewis Burns Franklin

Back when old Crogan Terrell owned the place, I was born in Lewis's Bend. I was named Eugene and that was 1902. There was a white man named Talman livin' close to my daddy and they always messed up our mail, so he and my daddy got together and changed the one L in our name to two. That solved the problem, and that's how we got our name, Tillman.

My parents were Anderson "Andy" Tillman and Louise Carter. She come out of Virginia, or Mississippi, or Lake Charles. Her grandma was brought to this country with her three daughters. They landed below the Salt Creek near Lamar where the big tree is. That tree was on my grandma's sixty acres. They tell me that some of the really big ranchers took it away from her, so she and her children went back to Indianola. I wasn't acquainted with my grandparents. I don't even know their names.

She got on a ship to go back to Virginia and she had her papers with her as deeds to that land. The smaller people would sell their land, then when the person who had bought it went to town to sell, the big guys would stop them on the road home, kill them, take the money, and buy more land. I don't know if this is true. It's just what they tell me.

Somebody from New Orleans bought that land from my grandmother and started lettin' people come in and look at that tree. It was known as a special tree. It was

The big tree at Lamar, 1931.

the biggest one in the country. It covered almost an acre in its day.

My daddy, Andy, was a slave and they lived in huts on the plantation in Mississippi. The man would go around and notify the slaves they were bein' sold. Then they would be taken to town the next day. Daddy was born around 1827 and probably landed in Texas in 1846 or so. He was nineteen years old.

Each family was put in a pen in the village and the buyers would pick who they wanted and take them to the wagons. This was told to me. Andy's mama was called out and so was Andy and one uncle and one of the younger boys.

Eugene Tillman.

Seems like the white man's name was called Holliday. He was the buyer. Lots of men were buyin' slaves and bringin' them to Texas. Grandpa Andy claimed he walked off lookin' back at his daddy and the rest of his brothers and sisters still in the pen. He said that was the last he ever saw of them.

This was all because these white people were comin' to Texas and wanted to bring slaves with them. He never told me what this colony was about. Papa didn't tell me if the slave market was in the town or where. I never heard anythin' about a man named Lewis from anyone. I don't think daddy and his family were from Africa. They were several generations from Africa, I think.

Those who lived to get here went on plantations on both sides of the river. They made a slow trip here feedin' the cattle and all the animals. I don't know how long it took. He said they broke land anywhere they stopped and would make a crop to eat. There weren't any fences.

My daddy told me they were told they were comin' to Texas where money growed on trees. It was true. They farmed along the river. Pecans, peaches, and grapes were everywhere. There were hackberries, mulberries, and anaqua. The ground had wild greens and wild onions and chinkipins. All this was the money on the trees. Most of this stuff we just ate. We didn't sell much.

That river was important, you see. It was really important. When these people came in here to settle, they had to be near water. You didn't see people out on the prairies and plains. They were near the river for fish, ducks, water, and bathin'.

The river was important to our people. It was important to everyone that ever roamed that country and to every nationality. We drank out of that river. We were raised up that the river purified itself every three miles. Even if there was a dead cow in the river, it would purify itself. Later the big ranches got to diggin' wells and the river wasn't so important anymore. Everythin' is so convenient now. It was so different then.

Papa lived there almost all his life. He moved up to Hall's Point for six years and then he moved back to the low country. I don't know if they were one of the first black families in the area. They had to be one of the first.

Lewis's Bend was a crossin' spot. There was a plantation in the area. The plantation raised cattle, horses, and hogs. The black women worked in the house.

It was many years after he got here before Emancipation. Those government men rode in here tellin' the black people they were free and on their own. They told them they could take four stakes and mark off as much land on these prairies as they wanted to.

I heard my daddy say many times that the darkies all talked it over and said they didn't want to go out on those prairies and starve to death. There was no water, no nothin'. They were used to the boss man tellin' them what to do and givin' them what they needed. They were even given the deeds for the homesteads, but they wouldn't go. They didn't know how to survive.

Some of the slave owners treated their slaves much better than others did. Lots of them had God in them. I always felt that. The bad slave owners would try to act like they treated their slaves better than they did. They would rub their mouths with pork fat so it looked like they were eatin' meat. Even after they were freed, they wouldn't leave. The ranches let them hunt and fish on their land. They said, "He's brought me this far. I'm goin' to stay with him." Many slaves wouldn't leave their masters after freedom.

After Texas got a fence law, the government put a price on the land, two bits an acre. Then the blacks didn't try to get the land because they could have had it free.

When Emancipation caught my daddy, he was cuttin' logs and rails. He was buildin' punchin' houses and fences cut out of the bottom. It was a long time before the freed slaves learned to care for themselves and went out on their own.

There was a lot of mixin' in the river bottom between the blacks and the whites. Lots of blacks had white blood in them. My daddy had two white sisters, Aunt Jane and Aunt Elizabeth. A white man got them by my grandma.

The blacks had to abide by anythin' the white man said. A black child wasn't allowed to pick up any piece of paper. They were afraid they might see a letter and learn to read. They were not allowed to read and write.

They would get stripes on their backs like demerits if they did. There were whippin's if they did do somethin' wrong. It was posted how many stripes you would get for certain things. My daddy said they would put salt in the wounds after the whippin'.

Black women raised the white family. Some of the white ladies were good to the slaves and some were not. The children were often taught the Bible by the white women.

"It was a good life. We enjoyed it. It was a good river bottom."

Rosie Terrell Jones

Julia Edwards Lott.

The white men could do anythin' to the Negro women they wanted to. My daddy said a many a black man was killed for protestin' what the white man was doin' to his women. White women have told me they were sick of their husbands gettin' children on the black women, but there wasn't nothin' they could do about it. The man done enough damage to the woman to keep her scared. It was the same thing he did to the Negro.

White women had no more rights than the blacks. The white women couldn't say anythin' about any of it either. I have had a lot of white women tell me about gettin'

the vote. They would say to us blacks that they were in the same rut we were.

White women were subject to beatin's for things, too. They would tell us to stick with them and we would all get the vote someday. I was pretty young then, but lo and behold, it happened. The white ladies had to break the ice first, but then it happened.

Anybody is scared of dyin'. You gotta lose somethin' to gain somethin'. You don't want to lose your life. I carried myself in this attitude all my life—fear of the white man.

The first church built in Lewis's Bend was built by my daddy. I was pullin' that saw with him. He cut all the logs. It was Mount Zion Free Mission Baptist. It was one big room with a homemade pulpit and benches whittled out of logs. He had all kinds of tools he got from Old Man Holliday. That church was finally torn down.

By the time I came along, there were lots of houses down in the Bends. The church was built and everyone farmed and worked on the ranches. There was a pretty good settlement down there. The bridge was there and so was Aunt Ellen and Jackson Youngblood. There were Sunday meetin's and gamblin' and socializin'. We played cowboys a lot as kids. Jim O'Connor and my uncle John taught me how to cowboy. I learned to ride from my daddy also. He broke wild horses and mules to work in the fields and for buggies and wagons.

I never got to go to school much. I had two sessions of schoolin', then I had to quit when my daddy moved away. Later I went back for two more sessions when I was fourteen. I always did real well in school.

I planned out lots of things in my life but I didn't have any money. If I had just had the money to put my plans to work durin' World War II, I could have done lots. I once designed a cultivator and some men came out from Farmall and watched me and stole my idea. I went to the lawyers but never got anythin' for it. People were always lookin' at it. I had no idea about puttin' anythin' on the record, and it was stolen from me by a bunch of men who kept writin' things down and drawin' things. About eighteen months later, Farmall came out with the same thing. The only thing I ever got out of that was lots of credit at the McFaddin store.

Cowboyin' was the onliest work around in those days. We was important if we was a cowboy. Farmin' was hard work down in the bottom, but we lived good in those days. Ridin' horseback all day was the easiest way. Throwin' calves was the only really hard work. We enjoyed it. It was always jolly. We got a lot of kick out of it. We had fun doin' all that.

O'Brien and O'Connor would hold contests among their cowhands. Tom Green was the best. He was with O'Brien. So was his brother Levy. They all liked that cow work. Both those ranches supplied their boys with brush jackets. They were well taken care of. They gave them their horses and slickers, too.

John Thornton Williams was my papa's half-brother. He taught me how to cook. I cooked for several ranches. I ran a hay rake for fifty cents a day. I've cowboyed and preached. I worked for Jim, Will, and Lawrence [O'Connor] mostly. I was at the Loso [El Oso] Ranch for them and the McNamara, too.

I worked with Matt Jones. He married my sister, Mattie. Charlie Lasso, Pedro Lasso, Ferdinand Heron were with me. Jim Cummings was the boss. Matt Jones was hard to beat. He worked for O'Connor all his life.

We just worked cattle on those ranches. We'd come in, get our food, and sleep on the ground when we were in camp. We had lots of fun then, playin' cards and doin' some singin'. I was born and raised in church, so I never did any card-playin' with them.

They went to church for church in my day. You could hear the singin' all over the river bottom. People would run to church it sounded so good to them. You could sing and pray all you wanted to.

In the spring the river bottom smells mighty good. In the fall it smells different. It smells damp and wet. I appreciated natural nature. That nature, that nature, that nature. I always believed in that nature takin' care. I would rather cook bread than buy it. Bought food is imitation. Many complaints we have now are manmade. Everything is obedient to God and nature except man.

The moon don't miss and the sun don't miss. We used to have signs we could go by. You used to be able to depend on it, but not now. Humanity has messed it up. We can't follow the signs now.

We never used a doctor in that river bottom. We used lots of natural medicines and herbs.

I learned about people and horses and could talk with people and about those things. I learned about people, mostly home folks. I was dumb about gettin' out among other people. I was at home with cowboys, ranches, cook wagons, farmin', and workin' cattle.

I had a pretty good go with white people. I think about so many things I could have done. It bothers me quite a lot. I have done a whole lot of good things, but it doesn't have much power for me. Some of the things I didn't get to do have more power over me.

My dreamin' days are about over with. I always dreamed about being in big churches. I believe that a person can dream dreams that would come true.

Eugene Tillman

CHAPTER FIVE

Kith and Kin

"Down in this river bottom, there is either a linkage or a connection between everybody."

Herbert "Buster" Bickford

Our families came to Texas throughout the nineteenth century in organized groups, as solitary pioneers, or as slaves. At times, we came in great waves and for as many reasons as there were individuals. Religious freedom, economic opportunity, the desire for land, and a yen for adventure always topped the list of reasons for immigrating to the Coastal Bend. The slaves had no choice, of course. They found themselves in the new state of Texas, like it or not.

Some of the ethnic groups have intermarried, while others have married only within their own culture. Many families are related, whether they want to admit it

Terry, Amos, Thelma, Billie, Lula Doughty Roper; Mattie and Hugh Doughty.

or not. The simple act of sorting out who is related to whom is an almost insurmountable task.

Yet regardless of their circumstances, most families in the San Antonio River bottom have remained strong and united, and family ties have been maintained down through the generations. Families needed each other to survive in the early days of settlement, and many have remained close units into the present time.

Rural cultures are under siege from the modern-day world. Our values, our isolation, our lands are endangered by the priorities and attitudes of the more prevalent and numerous urban populations. They do not view the world as we do and far outnumber those of us who live in traditional, nature-oriented communities.

As the world becomes more and more hostile to the rural legacy, these pioneer families of the Coastal Bend continue to support each other for the survival of a way of life that has shaped the Texas Coastal Bend culture for generations.

The River Bottom Families

As the narratives show, a river bottom family formed a tightly knit group. Several generations lived in proximity to one another, so everyone shared the same experiences. The strength and importance of these family ties is a common thread in the narratives.

The Bickford Family

My grandfather, Peletiah Bickford, was a horse raiser who drove them up the trail. His daddy came from Hull, England.

My grandfather on my daddy's side married Sarah Lewis of Lewis's Bend. She was his first wife and the daughter of Seabourne Lewis. The other daughter was Mahaney Lewis that married a Drake.

My uncle Will Bickford went up the trail. He took horses and broke them on the way up. Will died in 1880, and the original old Tom O'Connor died long about then, too. Goin' up the trail was hard work, that's all. My grandfather never talked much. He lived his life on that place until he broke down and I took care of all of them. I bought them all out.

Herbert "Buster" Bickford

The De La Garza Family

My father had a sister, Julia. She was married to Jesús De La Garza. He died when the children were young. One day before he passed away, he sent for my father. He knew he was going to pass away. He called my father to his room. He told him he wanted him to help with his children, especially the boys. He wanted him to teach them how to work.

One of them was Rafael. The others were Charlie, Martin, and Pete. My father was at the Murphys. He taught them what to do.

You know, those boys learned how to work. They were good cowhands. Now we have child labor laws. Kids can't learn how to do jobs properly early enough.

Johnny De La Garza

The Gibson (Gipson) Family

Well, the river bank was about as far as from here to there, and we'd sit up there in the front of the house. I don't know what kind of roof it had. It always leaked

Lola Gibson Adams.

when it rained. You had to put things all on the table when the river would come up. You thought about leavin' when things like that happened, but you'd think of something to do.

Papa wouldn't take us out until the water was slappin' under that bridge. It was dangerous because it could have washed some of those pillars out from under the bridge. Papa would take the wagon across the bridge when the water started comin' and put it where we could get to that West ranch and stay with Aunt Lydie Youngblood. You know, I wonder sometimes how that place looks now.

We would get our water in a wooden bucket and have to let it settle out before you could use it. We would wash our clothes down to the river. We could fish off our porch.

I remember a girl drowned down there in that river. Her name was Shelley. We used to go down there and kind of wade in the shallow part and Shelly got in up to her head until the waves washed her down. Every time she would come up she'd yell, "Help me." We hollered and hollered until the people came down to see what was wrong. Couldn't nobody swim 'cause none of the men were around. The last time she went down we never did see her anymore. She was caught on a piece of branch. That's how they found her.

We had fish fries down there. I was a bigger girl then, 'cause we had moved out of Goliad before that cyclone hit. I don't know what year it was.

Monk Gipson, Alan Benson, and Irving Gipson.

Lots of people used to come out there to visit. Lee Powers, Lula and Della, his mother, Florman and F. Y. My baby brother Leonard had a baby by Eda Riley. His name was Sam Gibson. They wouldn't let him go by Gibson. They made him go by Harris.

Do you remember Ed Harris? He was a half brother to Lee and them, but he was black. His mother was real black. Solomon Cole was one of his boys.

Well, he left home with Jerry Youngblood to find work. My mama raised Howard. His mother died when he was a little bitty baby. He don't know nothin' about his mother. She had "brothledge" or something like you eat. I think that's what killed them all.

Ellen Terrell used to turn the cup over and let it drain and read the signs in the leaves. She could look in your hand and move something in your hand. She could tell you about death. I don't know if she was tellin' the truth, but we believed it. She and Aunt Fannie used to shoot ridin' in the saddle.

There was Julia Weathers, Mazie, and Ceola. Mazie said, "I hear my baby gettin' my daddy's spirit." She's sit there until prayer meetin' was through, and when it was time for the *tasso* to come in, Mazie would walk kind of wobbly and walk, walk. Mazie would get the *tasso* and walk on out, get on out.

Irving Gipson and Reverend Will Heard as a young boy.

Yeah, we'd head on up the river and use those strings to dip up the small fish. We'd clean 'em down there and go back up to the house and fry 'em. We'd cut 'em up in pieces and fry 'em. I think we used to even eat the liver. Fish and cornbread, that was the best. Sometimes they must have been big old fish, 'cause they would smell.

We'd go across that bridge to Aunt Lydie's and get that milk. We'd let it sour and make clabber. They had those old big bulls with humps over there and we'd be barefooted. The bulls would run us and our feet would get full of grassburrs.

They had a school down there. You had the same book for two or three years, the same old book. Our teacher was from Victoria. Her name was Jeanette Wall. I knew her mother before Ethel was born. There was Maggie Collier teachin' here, too, and my brother Buddy went and married her when she was teachin' in Lewis's Bend.

Sunny days, them alligators would come out on the big logs. There were big old trees blowed down on the river bank. I remember we used to chunk 'em off those logs and they'd crawl back in that water. My mama used to tell us not to get close to those river banks 'cause they'd slap you with their tails. I don't know whether that's true or not.

Mama had a buggy and a horse and when we would go to Lewis's Bend at night, the roads were long and crooked. Mama would sit up there and hold the reins. The horse knew where to go. It was black dark, pitch black. That's when I got religion. People would put nickels on their feet and tap time. It sounded like music.

They had a big Nineteenth of June. People used to cook up stuff. I remember Mama had chitlins and she'd cook during this holiday. She had a little trunk and she carried stuff to the picnic grounds. We'd play checkers and dominoes 'cause Mama wouldn't let us play cards.

Monk was the last one left home. He went to the army. I remember he made out his allotment check to me and I remember when I got my first check. Our post office was in Anaqua. I remember I sent my brother younger than Monk to pick it up. I knew what day it was supposed to come. We were out of food at the time.

After Mama and Papa died, we was out there and Lucy was in school. It was just me and my grandmother and Nat and a younger girl. We used to sweep our yard with a broomweed. We kept it clean as a house.

We used a Montgomery Ward catalogue for toilet paper in the outhouse, and we papered our walls with the Sears-Roebuck catalogue. Sally Lamont Threadgill and that farmer, they had a lamp and a big old high stove.

I remember one night I had indigestion, and my throat was closin'. I got me some salt water and taken a sip of it every now and then. I think it was caused by those tamales Granny Davis brought me. That salt water was the way I got rid of that. We didn't have no doctor medicine. We boiled stuff and drank it. Once in a while, Mama would give us Castoria and castor oil. You get a bottle of soda and mix it with that beauty until it get thick and then you can't taste that stuff.

There was Mason Bennett and Mandy. Mason was a fat little creep. We'd all have to sit on the platform durin' church. The pulpit was on a platform and the benches were old wooden benches. Some of them had backs and most of them didn't. The Bennetts had old dogs. When they would get a hog, they'd spread it out for everyone to have some. Sure was a good community at that time.

I remember Mr. Tom Heard used to come to our house. He smoked a pipe, then he'd get up to leave and stay for hours and hours and hours after he got up to leave.

I was raised with Lee and Willie Heron. Violet was the youngest one. She was real fat and dumpy. There was Woodrow and Wilma. There was good times in Lewis's Bend at that time. Uncle Steve, Aunt Violet, Richard Kellogg, I remember all those names. Martha Boulder, she lived in Lewis's Bend . They had a yard full of flowers. A common flower was the zucchini flower. It came in red, yellow, and pink.

You remember Aunt Kate Jones? She had two children named Carrie and Lizzie. Joe Tillman's wife was named Tilde and she was Kate Jones' daughter. Remember, Kate Jones had a boy named Bubba Peach.

You know how she got pregnant by a railroad man and she told it to Cousin Albert. Loads of trouble, and they sent Cousin Albert to the penitentiary for, I think, two years, but he stayed for eighteen months. It was when the train was runnin' through Refugio and on to Houston. Well, this was a worker on that train. This little boy was named Johnny and he was bright with curly hair. Well, anyway, Polly Cole was a half-breed. Raised this little boy and his sister named Dorothy.

After Cousin Albert got out of the jail, he would come to our house and we'd stay up all night with him tellin' us stories and things. Wasn't nothin' but lies, but we thought it was the truth. We were so glad when Cousin Albert said he was comin' up to the house.

Old Mrs. Simms had three girls out there, Kate, Ada, and Addie. The little boy was named Cornelius. Kate moved to Refugio when all those people died.

I wish I had something I could make pictures of all these things out there.

Lola Gibson Adams, collected by S. W. "Toney" Lott

The Lewis Family

"Old Lady Fannie Rice raised my mother, Narcissa Mitchell. She was supposed to be an Indian. My mother died in childbirth. I was always lookin' for her after that."

Lela Edwards Williams

Laura Robinson Lewis was the mother of Charlie Lewis. She had some Indian in her. Charlie Lewis was a slave until he was nine years old. They were slaves to the Lewis Plantation. Charlie was born around Lewis's Bend. His father was probably from Alabama and may have been bought by Seabourne Lewis and brought here to work on the plantation in the river bottom.

Althia Lewis Burns Franklin

The Rice Family

The Rice family was given eighty acres of land by Dennis O'Connor [I]. Henry Rice Sr. worked cattle for the O'Connors. They never were slaves of the O'Connors. As long as there is a Rice, it will belong to them. The land is around Fannin on the San'tone River. The family was always farmers.

Leo Rice

John Alvin, Fannie Rice, and William Hicks Jr. of Fannin, 1890s.

The Rodgers Family

My father's family came from Lewis's Bend. He was Jim Rodgers. My uncle, Tom Rodgers, was always called Tom Ball. There were two men at the Welder ranch named Tom. One was Tom Curly and the other was Tom Rodgers.

Tom Curly had nice hair and kept it combed, and Uncle Tom let his go and it balled up, so that was how he got his name. Uncle Tom was born and reared on the Welder ranch. He lived there most of his life. He was buried at Lewis's Bend in 1953. There was a cemetery there. Reverend U. S. Johnson did the funeral ceremony.

Most of the people down Lewis's Bend way went to Refugio when it broke up after the war and the '42 storm. Uncle Pete Lewis had a house down there that faced the river. There was a slope on the side. It had a cattle pen on the other side of it. It was real close to the river.

We went down there a lot when I was young. Lots of javelinas lived in that river bottom. Tom Ball rode a horse down there all the time. One time he was ridin' a horse out there, and the horse started pitchin' and jumped the fence. When he came down, Uncle Tom was still ridin' him.

I remember Isaiah Weathers and a lot of families down there. The Lewises, Marberrys, Youngbloods, and Averys were some of the people down there. I saw lots of javelinas down there near the river, and I remember Richard Harris. He was with the Murphys for years and years. He and I would have talks about his life on the ranch.

The Welders thought a lot of Uncle Tom. They tried to make him quit ridin', but every chance he got, he would roll up his apron and go out when the young ones couldn't even do it. He was married several times. I don't remember seein' him all that much because he worked the old "can't to can't" for fifty cents a day.

He would often talk about sleepin' out when it was so cold his slicker would stand up. He told all kinds of stories in his time. It was hard for a young one to get a chance to talk to him. Everyone around wanted to talk to Uncle Tom. He told me a story about why only blacks were allowed to work on the Welder ranch.

I worked on a delivery truck all my life. Country people weren't that different. They just worked longer hours. The cowboys were looked up to by the town people. Al McFaddin always had a Christmas party for his people on De León Plaza [in Victoria]. My father worked for McCabe-Carruth Funeral Home for a number of years. It once was the home of Mr. Mitchell, who did work for the government on the fever tick.

Everyone rode horses back and forth from the ranches to town. We could hear

Tom "Ball" Rodgers.

the cattle comin' over the bridge. I always loved the way the cowboys talked to the cattle. They sho' could talk to those cattle.

I would get my mother's broom and stand on the porch and I was a cowboy, too. When I was a kid, I loved to see them, but I was always kind of shy of cattle. Lots of these guys I watched were from a long line of cowboys before them.

There weren't any real race problems here. There has always been good relations between the races here. We had segregation here, but that wasn't anything like blacks had to put up with in other places.

My mother taught me to learn women's work and housework in case I ever needed it. I regret some things back, but I'm proud of what my parents taught me. They taught me to work and be honest. I think I have been.

Tom Rodgers, nephew of Tom "Ball" Rodgers

The Simms Family

Barnes Simms (1822–ca. 1860). Original daguerreotype made in Edgecombe Co., North Carolina, in 1843.

I am a Simms on my mother's side. It was my maternal grandmother that lived in Lewis's Bend. Her name was Mercy Cecilia Rock and she married Julius Marcellus Simms in 1881. He first appeared in the census records of Victoria County in 1850. He died in 1891. They are both buried in the Simms cemetery on Murphy land.

Mercy was left a widow with five children and she ran the ferry and the store in Lewis's Bend after her husband died. Julius had been the ferry operator on the river at Lewis's Bend, called the Simms Ferry. She eventually moved and bought a house in Goliad on Clip Road. She lived there until she died in 1929.

All the Simms men died young. Julius was drowned on the river, supposedly in a flood, but this is only hearsay. They came from North Carolina and can be traced back to 1764.

Ada and Mercy Simms, Marcellus and Kate Talman, Addie Simms, Floyd Simms, and J. W. Farley.

The Terrells and Simms are related. Barnes Simms, Julius's father, married a Terrell woman named Frances Jane, who was a sister to Crogan Terrell, who was Ripley's father.

My grandmother said every black woman that was buried in Lewis's Bend, or married, had on one of her dresses. She sold gunpowder in the store out of the keg. One time Mama Ida Jane Simms burned her face digging gunpowder out of the barrel. An old black woman wiped her face with her apron and spread duck egg over her face. She did not have scar one from that.

Ida Lee Simms, my mother, used to talk all the time about playing with the black kids and playing baptizing in the river. She once beat the tar out of Will Sample with a quirt. She saved up her pecan money and had a little riding outfit and a sidesaddle. When she rode up to the school, Will yelled, "There comes Ida on a terrapin shell." She ran him up a tree and couldn't get to him, but she cut up his legs good. Ida Lee saw him at Skidmore some years later and he still had marks on his legs from that.

Mama and her sister would ride the train all the time to dances in Papalote. She said many a night she would wear the sole out of her shoes. They only had one pair of gloves, and you had to have gloves at a dance. They split the pair and carried a black stocking over the other hand.

Mama was a tough customer. She once dared a man to take her pecans away from her. She made candy at the store and sold it when she was very young.

Grandma Mercy died when I was too young to remember her stories. I wish I could have heard what she had to say.

Lois Farley Jaillet

The Terrell Family

Willie Terrell. *Bell Lott Terrell.* *Herbert Terrell.*

Henry Terrell was born in 1837. He was an N.C. [North Carolina] slave and was sold to the white Terrells in Texas. He married Violet Callan, who was born on the San'tone River in 1845. She was the daughter of Marthie Lewis. This was not the same as Martha Perryman. He lived down in Lewis's Bend. One day he was workin' in the field near Jackson Youngblood's and my daddy, Bill Terrell, was workin' with him. Uncle Henry had buried his money in the field. He started chokin' and died. He has many descendants lived and died in that river bottom. My daddy, Bill Terrell, went to work for the O'Connors after that.

Ben Green.

My family all lived down on the San'tone River 'cause they didn't know where else to go.

Willie "Luck" Terrell

The beginning was from Gallen and Martha. Henry and Violet Terrell worked for the Terrells that was white. That was the way they got the Terrell name. William Terrell was known as Bill. Most of the white people, such as the O'Connors, the Welders, the Fagans, the Murphys, and other white people living in that area, called him Uncle Bill. He farmed for Mr. and Mrs. Terrell and worked on the Terrell. By the way, in the black family there was twelve children. The oldest was named Harold Terrell. His wife was named Ellen.

Lee Anna Terrell Young

My parents were ranchers and I married one. My daddy was Larry Terrell and he was foreman for the West ranch. My mama, Elvira Steward Terrell, was their cook. I was born on that ranch in 1912.

The Jacksons, my grandmother on my mother's side, came from Louisiana and were the Terrells' slaves. On my daddy's side, they were Burns, but they took the name of Terrell when they bought them in slavery times. My daddy, Henry Terrell's grandfather was Larry Galloway.

Tom Steward and Melinda Steward, my grandparents on my mother's side, ranched for Old Man Dennis O'Connor [I] and the O'Briens. Tom Steward used to say, "As long as the O'Connors have horses and cattle, I don't need to buy a home." The O'Briens owned him first, then he went to the O'Connors.

Some of the Stewards were also called O'Brien. Stewards and Greens are also the same people lots of the time. It causes lots of confusion tryin' to figure it out. The reason for that is that Susan Steward lived with a white boss named Ben Green on the Duke Ranch. Her children went by Steward because she wasn't married to him. This was all around the turn of the century.

My husband told me there was a man lived in the Black Jacks. He was a Dukes and he lived there so long, when he died they named the ranch after him. Albert Dukes was one of them lived there. I don't know if this was true, but that has been the story all along. I'm only tellin' what I've been told.

I was schooled in Lewis's Bend. I think everyone went to school down there. Emma Tillman, Gussie Phillips, Pearlie Rydolph, and then Emma Sample were the teachers.

My father said some people came in there named Simms and settled. Old Lady Simms and her husband, Shelly Simms, owned a store there. Different people came in and settled.

Jackson Youngblood and Aunt Ellen Terrell were the big dogs down there. Grandma Marthy [Perryman] lived there, too. She was also related to the Youngbloods. The Terrells were related to Youngbloods also. Jackson Youngblood wound up livin' in her house right on those river banks.

Alice Terrell married Jackson Youngblood. It was an old log house. She was way up in her hundreds. They had a big funeral for her in Lewis's Bend and buried her in the Sample cemetery.

All the old families had cemetery plots in the river bottom.

Rosie Terrell Jones

"We knew everyone down there. We were like a family."

Milton Thomas

Uncle Bill Terrell worked for the white Terrells. He and his family were once their slaves. He often told stories to Willie Terrell. He knew the legendary Ripley Terrell and told all the stories about him. The Terrells were feuding with the Fagans at that time and this created lots of tales.

Willie "Luck" Terrell said the old Terrell house was haunted by Uncle Bill Terrell. He was often seen on the staircase. The house was destroyed by the '42 storm.

James K. "Spec" New

The Weathers Family

Reverend Isaiah Weathers.

I was born down on the San'tone River. My great uncle was the famous old preacher from Lewis's Bend, Isaiah Weathers. I was born in 1905 at Inari, a little ways east of Lewis's Bend.

My mother was Laura Hopkins and my father was Frank Harvey. My mother was an Avery, and on my father's side I'm related to the Harveys and the Rydolphs. Henry Newman, who helped raise those O'Connor boys, was related to me.

I guess I am related to everyone around. Sam Ricks was married to my mother's auntie. He was a famous old cook around these ranches.

The Weathers came from Virginia. I'm related to Henry Charleston, too. He's my brother, my only brother. Mama had two daughters, but they died. My father was killed by Rob Spriggs. He hit him on the head and he died from that lick.

The Olivers, Averys, and Lotts are my people, too. The Terrells were good friends of my family.

The Gibsons were around there, the Scotts, and Aunt Martha Perryman. She was an Avery. She lived to be very old. She sewed for people. She would buy from peddlers that came around. They came through selling cloth, shoes, and household needs.

Ike Dunman, Jake Scott, George Charleston, Alf Harvey, Isaiah Hutchinson, and Tebo Scott were all around there workin' cattle. We had some big roundups.

That's what the folks were doin', farmin' and cowboyin'. They stood out pretty good. They were hard workers, honest, popular men who rode horses. It was cowboyin' or farmin'. I chose cowboyin' until the Lord called me.

Cowboyin' was a job and a sport. It was all we had, so we had fun out of it. I was trained under some good cowhands. We had cowboys then. Now they have cow herders.

Lots of cowboys become preachers. You watch animals and you learn how to handle people. People act like animals in some ways. We know animals and we

Reverend Will Weathers.

learned how to handle, preach, and teach people. Folk who are raised up in town don't know nothin' about animals. I was called to preach even though farmin' and ranchin' was all I knew.

It was necessary for us to have a good reputation in those days. I think I did. At least I made a reputation for ropin' and ridin'.

Will Weathers

The Youngblood Family

My family worked for the Powers and the Welders. I was born on Murphy country in 1921. Dan Youngblood and Jemima Dawson Youngblood were my parents. His father was Jackson Youngblood and he married Alice Terrell. My mother's mother was Ellen Dawson. We moved to the Powers ranch when I was a baby. Much of my family lived in and around Lewis's Bend.

I grew up with Jesse Blanche Wesley and Othello Tisdom, and Helen. They were named Williams then. Jesse Blanche stood with me when I married Spence. Helen died from lockjaw. They waited too long to take her to a doctor.

From left: Barbara Novella Lott Youngblood, Nathaniel Youngblood, Rose E. Youngblood Johnson, Rosie Lee Youngblood Robinson, and (front) Diania Jean Youngblood Jones.

I often wondered how the black people got all mixed up with the light-complected people back there. They got mixed up back there and that is why some of us are real light. Some were forced and some weren't. They taught us not to do this, but somewhere it happened. What they taught us was *it*. If we asked, they would give us a different answer. Lots of things we had to go find out for ourselves. Sometimes parents weren't honest about things.

Alice Youngblood Cook

It's a funny thing about old people. Not many young people got time to fool with the old. They can teach you so much. Jackson Youngblood, George Youngblood, Andy Tillman, Babe Lott (Paul Lott was her daddy), Ellen Terrell. Henry, Boo, Hamp Terrell were all Miss Ellen's sons. Another old man at Fannin was Uncle Steve Williams.

Nathaniel Youngblood

Family Favorites

In the Coastal Bend ranching culture, if you did not have a legendary figure in your family tree, you really were considered a bit low on the totem pole. It was a matter of great pride to have a hero, a town character, even an outlaw in your lineage. The ultimate honor was to be the illegitimate child of someone famous. People always whispered to me with great pride that a certain relative was "born on the wrong side of the sheets" and was supposed to be so-and-so's son or daughter. One is considered a bit of a fool to deny historical facts in regard to strange and wondrous occurrences and people in a family's past.

Tom Ball

My grandfather, Tom Ball, was such an even-tempered, beautiful person. He made that place. All of us kids loved for him to come in. He would take me to the Vidauri store to buy candy, and he let me ride donkeys. He taught me how to shoot a gun. He had been feeding a rattlesnake for years—it was ten, twelve feet at least. Even today, I am not afraid of snakes. My grandfather was a tophand. He never let anyone abuse animals. He would make a mark on the wall like a T—that was a day's work.

I heard he worked with a broken back. He was tall and he carried a watermelon on each side of his saddle. He would let his legs hang down out of the stirrup. He always had goodies for me. We roasted onions and sweet potatoes at night. He was a special treat for me.

I never saw him without a smile on his face. He wouldn't drink coffee unless it stained the cup.

Tom "Ball" Rodgers.
Photo by Dimitri Kessell.

He was a great teacher. He would show you how to do it, not just tell you. He would show you right and wrong. He even showed me cattle that had never seen a human. The only time I ever saw him angry was when I abused a jack one time tryin' to get him to pitch. He was very kindhearted about animals. I've always wanted to own land. Uncle Tom was satisfied with livin' on the land.

I never saw women in the country complain. They seemed to love ranch life. Few people understand my love of the country. I never could understand why they didn't want their own land. They seemed to be satisfied out there. I guess they had the country without having to own it. He was perfectly satisfied.

He talked to us about the Chisholm Trail and about how Indians would attack them. He showed me where the trail started near the ranch. He had swappin' blood in him. He traded all the time. He said the Indians would run them off into waterholes. This was the man. He never said anything bad about anyone. They had a rough life on the trail. There were fights and killin's, but he never talked about those things to me. They worked from sun to sun seven days a week and really enjoyed it. He got home three times a week. He would rather have been in the woods. Everything he did was with horses and cattle. He never did farming. He was a big gambler. He banked in a hollow log. He put his money in a can. He was always scheming how to get more. He smoked a pipe with Brown Mule or Prince Albert. He chewed tobacco, too.

He was very tall, better than six feet, and he was mostly legs. He could tell tales and lies. He kept everyone laughing. He rode barefoot with his feet out of the stirrups. He was slow and a lot of fun. He worked that ranch seventy-five years. He was my hero. He let you know he was living.

Milton Thomas, grandson of Tom "Ball" Rodgers

I was born out there on that ranch, the Welder ranch in 1902. My father was the famous Tom Ball. He was a fine old man. Bosh Heron was my uncle. Uncle Bosh and Daddy were two of the big ones out there. The McGrews and Herons were related. The McGrews were white and the Herons were black. They knew they were related. All this got mixed up in slavery times. The Tuckers were in there somewhere on Mother's side. I am related to the Herons, the McGrews, the Tuckers, and the Tillmans. The Herons were born at Lewis's Bend down on the San'tone River.

I remember Isaiah Weathers, the preacher. He baptized most of my family. We had Association barbecues and church meetings. The Nineteenth of June parties were some of the best.

Daddy was a cook after he was too old to cowboy anymore. He made the best cowboy stew. We lived on the ranches and around the Bends and worked cattle. He was four years old when they freed the slaves. His mother and father were slaves.

He never had his own stock and he didn't have a brand. I don't know why he didn't. He did his figurin' on the wall.

He worked cattle and cooked for the Welders. He made the handle for his old gun. He could whittle wood, and he was a great shot. They didn't buy anything in those days. That gun was off about a quarter of an inch and he learned how to shoot it. He was a fine fella. Boo Terrell's daddy made saddles on the ranch. The Welders gave him a huge funeral.

Everyone knew about him and still do. Everyone still tells tales about him in the area. He told tales about the Chisholm Trail. He told about taking six months to go up and six months to come home.

He could keep a cool temper. I never saw him mad in my life. He raised my sister, but I went to San Antonio when I was seven.

When I went to Victoria to get Daddy's death certificate, the man in the courthouse couldn't talk to me for thirty minutes. He just put his head down and cried. He said Daddy was his best friend in the world and that he had saved his life from drowning one time.

Myrtle Rodgers Penn, daughter of Tom "Ball" Rodgers

One time, Tom Ball had a whole slab of bacon in his bed. When Mr. Welder checked his bed, he said somebody was always tryin' to do a trick on him.

Uncle Tom used to could walk on coals barefooted. He was with the Welders forever. He was a nice old man. We would laugh about that. He cooked most anything. That bastard could cook!

He was a cowboy, too. He could french a calf. Hear tell, he was *bad* on a horse. He was an old man and cookin' when we was coming up.

Dan Youngblood, J. Y. Lott, Nathaniel Youngblood, Ananias Cook

He was stout, a good rider, barefooted. He died at the Welder ranch. Everybody knowed him. He cooked barefooted and stepped on them coals.

Rafael De La Garza

He always had a *morral* tied on his saddle. He be headed for the bottom to hunt something, and my daddy would say, "There's death in that sack." He'd kill anybody's hog or whatever he could get his hands on.

He was cookin' at the Welder ranch, and they was layin' to catch him. Nobody really cared, but they wanted to hooraw him. He had a bucket of lard, and he came by Mr. King and Mr. Jim. They asked him what was in that bucket. He said it was just a little cowboy stew. When they went to open it, he said if it had turned to lard, he couldn't help it.

L. V. Terrell

Uncle Tom was brought up kind of like I was—brought up in the community here and yonder. He was a good rider. He'd steal, but he was a great guy.

Milam Thompson

I can remember when Tom Ball was baptized. He was an old scoundrel at times. Daddy had to hide turkeys to keep him from stealin' them, so everyone was tryin' to get him into church. Daddy used to say Old Tom would never be seen in church unless there was a turkey in there for him to steal.

Rosie Terrell Jones

Will Sample

Will Sample was a fiddler. His father was the white Will Sample. He was awful scary. His favorite song was "Whoa, Mule, Let Me Put the Saddle On." I'd set right down there by him. He played at country dances. I loved to hear that fiddle. His favorite word was "goddang."

Sarah Sample Tillman, Thurman Terrell

Steve Holliman

My grandpa was Steve Holliman. They trained him how to play a fiddle. You see, he was here in slavery times and he had one leg shorter than the other. They didn't put him out in the field to work. Some of the Fagans, he was with them, learned him how to play a fiddle. Whenever they had a dance, they'd send him to make the music. "Rowdy Ho" was his song.

Grandpa used to tell me he'd play that a many a time for the white folks to dance by. Grandpa say he had to walk many miles to go to the dance. He practiced his fiddle at home.

He said one night he walked to a dance. The wolves, they called them lobos, big old things. One night he had been to make the music for the dance, and he was on his way home across the prairie. Bunch of them big lobos got after him. He

Milam Thompson.

broke and ran to one little lone tree. But the tree wasn't high enough for him to get completely out of the reach of them.

Grandpa said they would run around and around when they get after you. Every time they would get where you were, one would jump up to grab you. And then the next one would come up.

Grandpa decided one would finally reach him and thought, "This is the end of my time. I'm gonna play my last time." He put his fiddle under his chin, pulled the bow across, and that fiddle went to makin' a high-pitched sound.

He said them wolves taken off, they run. He said to me, "Son, when they left, I got down and they never did bother me no more." It was a peculiar racket to them. Grandpa said if you can make a peculiar racket when a wild animal get after you that he has never heard, he won't come up to you. He'll run, but it's got to be a peculiar racket. The next thing is, if you can light you a torch or fire, they'll never come up to you if they see that fire.

He lived to be 129 years old. He was a great talker and could tell a lot of tales. Many people would go and talk to him. He had a great laugh. They would tell him tales to hear him laugh. I was his favorite grandson. I liked to hear him talk. He told me lots about slavery times.

He told me a story about one of them old Fagans saved his life. There was some desperados called the Butler boys. They caught him and forced him to stay with them. There was two bunches of them, and they made him the note carrier. They was bad and this was slavery times. Whenever they was gonna rob a store or make a raid, he had to take a note from one to the other about arrangements. Grandpa said he had to drive the wagon. They offered him anything they got out of the store. All he wanted was boots and a hat. He wore those high boots and he got them.

He was a little low man. The Fagans' posse had an idea he was takin' mail between the two. The posse laid for him, and finally one day the posse caught him. He threw the note in his mouth, chewed it up, and swallowed it. The onliest way he could save himself was to swallow it.

They made him strip, was shootin' at his foot, tryin' to make him admit he had a note. He said he didn't. He did, but it was in his stomach. After such a time, the next thing they told him was, "Get on your horse and ride." In those days their way of doin' was to let you ride off, then shoot you. Grandpa said he knowed it meant death, so he didn't hurry. He started off, some threw their guns to shoot him, and Mr. Fagan said, "He wouldn't do nothin' but what he was forced to do. Don't you kill Steve." Grandpa said that man saved his life. I think he said Pete Fagan. He wouldn't let them shoot him and when he died, he died a natural death.

He wasn't from Africa. I think he said he was from Georgia or Mississippi. He was brought in here by a family. He probably took their name. He told me all about the Civil War.

Milam Thompson

Memories of Anderson Tillman

Anderson was brought from Virginia, perhaps through Mississippi, to the Texas Gulf Coast. Then he was brought to the San Antonio River settlement by his owners.

He lived on the banks of the river in the southeast corner of Goliad County. His owners were haulers, and Grandfather said he was the ox driver. He drove from Goliad County to Old Mexico, hauling freight back to Goliad and Indianola.

After the death of his owners, he found out that the forty acres of land they had promised him was not really his. He drifted down to Lewis's Bend, and there he met Dinah and they had three children, Martha, Simmie, and Tommy. In later years, they separated and while living close to the O'Connor ranch, he met one of the Rice girls by the name of Sarah. He married her and had four children, Albert, Clayborn, Amelia, and one whose name we do not know.

Sarah died when Amelia was born, and after a number of years he married Louise Carter and they had fourteen children, Joseph Anderson, Peggy, Nettie, James, Laura, Andrea, a very gifted child who died at the age of eight from tetanus, Mattie, Eugene, Frank, Luter, and two sets of twins who died as infants.

Grandfather was a man who was a carpenter by trade, a marksman by practice, and a physician by knowledge. He built every house and home that he lived in. He also built for other blacks and whites.

He and his boys cut the lumber from the bottoms using hand tools. He taught this skill to his sons, and some of them were good builders. He was a great marksman, very skilled with a gun. He gained much respect for his ability to use a gun. Often the whites would wager on Uncle Andy, as he was so fondly called.

He had the knowledge to use herbs, trees, and other natural medicines. He also

Mt. Zion Baptist Church after it was moved from Lewis's Bend to Victoria.

delivered babies along with his wife Louise. I remember one medicine he used for swelling and one for tuberculosis. He told us of three people the doctors had given up to die and he was called to their bedside. After treating them, they lived, and two of them outlived him.

He also had an incredible memory. He could hear the Scriptures read and could quote it from memory. Grandfather was a charter member and a deacon of the Mount Zion Baptist Church. He served under Reverend D. S. Sapp, Reverend John Nelson, and Reverend I. H. Weathers.

He lived and worked on the West ranch, the Terrell ranch, the Power ranch, and then went back to the Terrells. Old Man Terrell gave Grandfather eighty some odd acres to use and live on until he died. This was right across from the Will Borg ranch in Goliad County.

Grandfather lived a long, healthy, fruitful life. After Grandma Louise passed away on July 29, 1924, he got down and was in bed for four or five days. We had the doctor come out and he said he was just worn out. Grandfather called us four boys to his bed and told us he was going to leave us, and as he was talking, he passed away. What a beautiful way to go. He died September 26, 1924.

Grandpa Tillman was a man of wisdom and many skills. He lived to see his youngest child reach fifteen years old. He loved the Lord and believed in right. God was good to him and to us by giving us such a grand gentleman for our father, grandfather, and great-grandfather. May the Tillman name continue on for many generations, always remembering our roots.

**Eugene Tillman, Rosie Terrell Jones, Simmie Rydolph,
collected by Rosie Tillman Jones Hosey**

Life Ain't Always Fair

Simmie Rydolph.

Well, Grandpa was not too much of a slave. He was real young durin' slavery. When they brought him to Texas, he was free, but he didn't know he was free. He used to haul goods from Mexico to Goliad with an oxcart. He was a marksman. I mean, that old man could shoot a Winchester. That's the reason they would send him to Mexico, because in Mexico nobody would fool with that old man. They knew if they missed him, they were dead. He would haul that freight from there down to Goliad. Grandpa was not really bound, he had a lot of freedom. The only thing that he got gypped out of was some land he owned.

He could go where he wanted to go and come when he wanted to come. Now, I don't know where he got the Tillman, where he got that last name. Because this guy that worked for your people, John Thornton, that was grandfather's brother. John never did go by no Tillman. So I don't know where Grandpa got the Tillman. But they was brothers. Grandpa never did work for the O'Connors. He worked up the river toward Leverity, farmin' and buildin' houses. He was a carpenter. He made his lumber. He went to the woods and cut down trees and hewed it out and polished 'em off. He made the lumber he built houses out of.

Now I'll tell ya, what has me confused is that Old Man Crogan Terrell that owned all that land on the north side of the San Antonio River. He was good to Grandpa in a sense. After Grandpa started gettin' old, he went up to just this side of Boyd's, where Crogan Terrell, he had a strip of land that was down in the bend of the river there—near Hall's Point, a hundred and some odd acres. He went to Victoria and had papers drawn up and gave it to the old man as long as he lived. They lived up to that agreement. Mrs. Terrell lived up to it because Old Man Terrell died before Grandpa did. The minute Grandpa died, Mrs. Terrell kicked Gene Tillman and all those heirs out of that bottom.

Gene didn't want to leave. Gene and Frank and Grandpa's two youngest sons had taken over the property, and they were doin' real good. They made some good cotton crops. They bought 'em a car and had eight or ten head of mules, good teams. I don't think they expected Mrs. Terrell to take it so quick. She had taken that property over and they had to move. She leased it to the Welder so they couldn't farm it no more. I kind of think that Grandpa had some kind of connection with the Terrells, 'cause Terrell owned Lewis's Bend.

Farmin', that's what he did. Grandpa fell out on Mr. Terrell, they tell me. Of course, this is all before I got here. He moved out of Lewis's Bend across the river on the West property. Grandpa didn't get along with ol' man Frank West, so he went back to Mr. Terrell. That's when Mr. Terrell give him that property 'cause he said that he had known him so long, he didn't want him driftin' around. They say he told Grandpa, "I've got five times as much land as West got, so you stay here and I'll give you this land." Terrell give him that land down in the bottom, so that's the only way that he got connected up. Still, it's right back to his name, I don't know how he got Tillman. 'Cause I know nobody else had it.

Mr. Terrell bought Grandpa the lumber for his house. That's the first house that he have ever lived in with bought lumber. Other lumber was made out of the bottom timber. Mr. Terrell had Grandpa build it right close to the river on the north side of the San'tone River, in that bend. Right off, about three or four hundred yards from Boyd's property. Terrell gave that property to Grandpa because Boyd was gettin' all the good out of it. He told the Tillmans to get Boyd's animals out

The Kern boys on a hay wagon.

of there. Gene and them did that. Gene and them raised cotton, and they bought a brand new car, a 1922 or '23. Gene and them were doin' real well. When Grandpa died, to prove that Gene didn't expect Mrs. Terrell to take it, he moved that new house that Mr. Terrell gave Grandpa out of the bottom and up there on the hill. Of course, Mrs. Terrell gave him that house, but he had to get it off the Terrell property.

I don't know what enticed people together there in Lewis's Bend. They built a church down in there. Of course, by being in Victoria County, and no school for blacks, they held school in that buildin'. Victoria County sent out teachers, black teachers, to teach the black children there in Lewis's Bend, in that church house.

Andy Tillman and Steve Holliman were good friends. Grandpa was a peculiar old man. He didn't do a whole lot of jokin'. He was very serious. Steve did a lot of jokin', told a lot of tales, and stuff like that.

I've got worse since I've gotten old. When I go to bed, the first part of the night I go to sleep. The second part of the night, every time I drop off to sleep, I travel, dreamin'. I go back over all that stuff from Steve Holliman and all that, travelin'. All that stuff comes back to me, but it just don't do me no good.

Simmie Rydolph, grandson of Anderson Tillman

Martha Perryman

Author's note: Martha Perryman, fondly called "Aunt Marthy," accompanied my great-grandmother, Mary Virginia Drake O'Connor, to Texas in 1853 as her nursemaid. As a young girl, she witnessed the great meteor shower of 1833, a phenomenon known as "the day the stars fell."[1]

Martha Perryman, mother of twenty-two children.

Grandma Martha Perryman was my great-grandmother. I loved Grandma Marthy. She made the best tea cakes in the world. She was the healthiest person I know of. The day she died, she fed the chickens and gathered eggs at my Aunt Margaret's house. When she came and sat on the porch, Aunt Margaret asked her if she could get her something. She wanted coffee. When Aunt Margaret came back with coffee for her, she was dead in the rockin' chair.

We used to love to go to Goliad to visit her. She was such a loveable person. It is hard to describe her. Mama wouldn't let us bother her too much, but she loved to play with the children. She loved to have us around her, but the elders were afraid we would bother her.

"Aunt Marthy Perryman was an old, old, old lady who said she remembered when the stars fell. It was two o'clock in the afternoon when the stars began to fall. She was about fourteen at the time. I was six years old when she told me this."

Elizabeth Sevier Haney

I loved to go to her house on the river before she moved to Goliad. It was on the high bank and when the river was down, she would let us go near the river, but never in it. I was young then. We moved to Refugio when I was sixteen, but I do remember that river. I was so peaceful there. There was something different down there we weren't acquainted with elsewhere.

She was twelve when the stars fell, so she was born around 1810. She never was married, but her daughter was my Aunt Caroline. Caroline's daughter was my Aunt Margaret. Grandma Marthy came in from Alabama as Mary Virginia Drake's mammy when she came to live with her grandfather in Lewis's Bend. She was around 125 when she died. The paper said she outlived all her children and grandchildren, and only a few of her great-grandchildren were still alive.

Helen Williams Magruder

Sure, I remember Grandma Marthy. I used to go over to her house and cook bread and fried potatoes for her. I cooked it in a fireplace. All she had was an old iron pot and that fireplace. I enjoyed goin' over there. She looked like a little African with her head tied up and wearin' big dresses and aprons.

Rosie Terrell Jones

"We were all out pickin' fruit, and all at once big balls of fiah came fallin' outen the sky. . . . These huge balls of fiah would bust all around us like flashes of lightenin' and then they would hit the ground. We was so scared, we like to died. We busted and run like a yondago. We run for the house and laid undah beds and tables hopin' they would hide us. We laid theah and prayed. Looked like the whole world was comin' to an end. . . . Ain't nobody hurt, though. Stars kept fallin' about a half hour an' then it was like night. Ooee! Sho' was dark for a long time. Weather didn't settle down for three or four days."

Anthony Silas, 115-year-old Spring, Texas, resident, newspaper clipping of May 28, 1931.

I remember her. She was old, way over a hundred. She was still gettin' around then, too. People used to be made of good stuff back then.

Josephine Holliday Durst

Alonso "Lonze" Edwards

Papa used to stay upstairs at the River Ranch. His mother was kilt Christmas mornin' out there in that yard. He was four years old and after she was kilt, Miss Jenny and Mr. Tom O'Connor [I] took Papa and they raised him.

He told me that they said he was four years. They said her brother was foolin'

Alonzo Edwards in the black hat he bought after his wife died.

with a gun on Christmas mornin' and accidentally shot her. Now, that's what he told me, accidentally shot. They raised him, 'cause he told me that. He was baptized in the Catholic church, and he said he used to drive Miss Jenny to church with two oxen when he was a small boy. And he never did go to school. But you couldn't beat him out nary a nickel.

When he sent you to the store to get something, he'd already tell you when you got back, before you hand it to him, just how much change he had comin' back. He learnt that countin' sheeps, cattle, and stuff like that. That's the way he liked to count. But never went to school a day in his life.

He couldn't read. We'd laugh all the time. When we'd go to Mexico in the summertime, we would go down there at Mexico and it would be a Budweiser sign and he would say, "Stop, so I can get me a Budweiser." He'd see the sign, you see. But now he wasn't supposed to could read. I know he could read good enough to understand.

We went to the cotton patch to pick cotton, out there at that ranch. We did everything. We was wantin' a watermelon and Papa said the watermelon wasn't ripe. Me and my two sisters carried us a knife to the field so's we gonna cut them

Lonze Edwards, Elias Jackson, and Sam Ricks.

watermelons open. We gonna get us a watermelon, and hot, too. Right now, if we eat one of them things, I bet we'd have fever. Cut that watermelon open. Eat that watermelon and put that knife in the cultivator seat. When we got ready to come to the house, we always come to the house earlier than he did to cook supper. Got ready to come to the house, I hollered and told Nettie, "Don't forget to get that k-n-i-f-e when you pass by." He say, "Yeah, get that knife." Now, how he knew that, I don't know. And we got scared then. We said he could read. But he couldn't read.

Aunt Mareatt Williams.

I never heard him sing at all, never did hear him sing or nothin'. But he used to get on that cultivator and go from one end to the other, when he was cultivatin' or whatever, and he'd whistle. I don't know what that was he's whistlin'. Every time I would ask him, "Papa, what is that you whistlin'?" He say, "That's the tune the old cow died on." Now, what that was, I don't know, "the tune what the old cow died on." Now I don't know what that meant, but that was all I ever heard him do, was whistle.

Lela Edwards Williams

Aunt Polly Upton

Aunt Polly Upton was one of the black Uptons. There were black and white Uptons down the road between the O'Connor Salt Creek Ranch and their Melon Creek Ranch. She was wonderful and a tough customer.

She would open the gates between her little place and the O'Connor ranch and let the cattle into their place. The grass was gone on the Winsor place. My husband [Merle Winsor] said she rode like an Indian and she would go back at night and let the cattle back into her place. She saved those Winsors and Uptons from starving to death.

She was a beautiful woman who stood so proud. As each member of the family died off, someone else in the family would take Aunt Polly. It was just understood that she had to have a home. No one objected to having to take her in. She just passed from one family member to the other and was loved by all.

Joyce Anderson Winsor

Aunt Mandy Harris

We used to go see Mandy Harris, Richard's mother. She would always say, "I got a misery in my head." We always took her a little pint of something and the misery would go away. She kept her hair tied up. When she died at 103, her hair was absolutely white. You know, when Richard's wife Willie died, she left seven or eight children. Aunt Mandy and Richard raised those children, plus he also wound up with all of the Cook children. He'd been with the Murphys since he was thirteen years old. He never did work with anybody else. When he got older, he got paranoid that Aunt Aggie [Murphy] was going to fire him. I told him he always had a home on Murphy land. He once told me and my mother that he felt like a Murphy.

Marye Murphy Greer, Zilpah Daniel Edwards, Louise Murphy

Seven Degrees of the Same Person: Nicknames

Many river bottom families can trace their lineage back to pre-slavery times, a daunting challenge when you consider that surnames were extremely complicated. A family in slavery times often used the name of their master, with the result that brothers could have different last names. Or they might use the name of the household's matriarch or, in the case of children, the name of the family that raised them. Nicknames in Texas, as in the Old South, are a part of everyone's life. They are terms of affection as well as identification and description.

One day in 1984, Nancy and I were having a terrible time during an interview trying to determine what person the group was talking about. We had heard the name Slim, Toota-Baby, Whang, Little Baby, and an assortment of others, but all seemed to refer to the same person. At least eight people were talking at the top of their voices, and the mayhem was advancing at such a pace that Nancy grabbed a schoolbell and started pounding on it. I had a group of whistles in my purse that I used for my gun dog. After using both of these devices simultaneously, we were able to quell the commotion long enough to determine that Nathaniel Youngblood was the proud owner of this string of nicknames. From that time on, it became easier to unscramble the interviews, for we realized that as many as six or seven names could belong to the same person.

River bottom nicknames always make sense about a person. The names often allude to an event in a person's life, a physical characteristic, or a memory. Nicknames are filled with humor and creativity. They are almost a biography in themselves.

Nathaniel Youngblood, master of nicknames, with Evelyn Elliot Youngblood.

Bird-Eye, Tangle-Eye, Whatever . . .

We never had nicknames in our family. Then I married into this South Texas family. Talk about an education! You would think we came from two different worlds. There was not one member of my husband's family that you knew what their names were. There was Butter, Red, who they sometimes called Abe, and Ting, and Sis, and Pud, and Boy.

One time we went out to dinner and my husband was talking to a man at the next table and kept calling him "Tangle-Eye." I thought that was just awful. When

"And right now, he got every-one of his grandchildren with a nickname. And they answer him by it. I guess he probably wouldn't know what their real name is, gets 'em mixed up. If he hollered at one, they gonna move. They know who he's talking to. The oldest grand-child is twenty-five years old, and he still call her by her nickname."

Evelyn Elliot Youngblood

we left the restaurant, I commented that I thought that was a terrible thing to call someone and Merle replied, "I know it was. His name is 'Bird-Eye.'" This man had been kicked by a mule when he was young and it left his neck crooked and it made him look sideways.

One time Merle's mother was saying that we needed some fences fixed. She told the boys to get "Chili the Rat" to do the job. Finally I asked her what the man's name was and her reply was, "I don't know what his name is. We've always just called him 'Chili the Rat.'"

Joyce Anderson Winsor

The other day I saw a black friend of mine and he was telling me he had just been to "Two Lump's" funeral. I knew exactly who he was talking about. We call our oldest grandson "Bully Gator." There is nothing in the world like the black culture for nicknaming. They have a wonderful discernment for character traits.

They know the people who are kind, they know the phonies, they know who are haughty. You don't fool them. I think this is where I get the funny trait of naming my grandchildren. I grew up around the black culture and everyone had nicknames.

Nicknames were terms of endearment. You never nicknamed someone you didn't like. It really is a very, very Southern thing.

Allene Pettus Lott

A Dialogue about Nicknames

Alice Mae Barefield Williams: My name is Alice, but everyone call me "Miss Mack" or "Sister Mack."

Zearlee Robinson Wesley: When you was growing up, you were "Tildy" and that's all I knew.

Alice: That was my nickname. I got it from one of my grandmothers.

Rachel L. Franklin: They always called me "Nona." That's the last part of Wynona, my middle name.

Zearlee: Well, I never knew what your name was.

Evelyn Elliot Youngblood: They don't know me as Evelyn in Victoria. You call me "Dinkie," then I know who you want. I came up as Dinkie.

Allie Fay Moore Robinson: I had an uncle and an auntie and they called me "Tittle," 'cause everything I'd see, I'd tattle.

Evelyn: My sister calls me "Dinkie" 'cause that's what Daddy always called me.
Althia Lewis Burns Franklin: My uncle always called me "Possie." He said I looked like a possum.

Zearlee: "Hon" was my nickname. When I was a baby, my parents called me "Honey" and then they cut it off to "Hon."

Lela Edwards Williams: My nickname was "Puddin'."

Evelyn: You could get real confused if you weren't up on what everyone's nickname was. Sometimes a person could have a lot more than one nickname.

Althia: "Long Tall Pearl" was Pearl Lott and the little short Pearl was Miss Pearl Tolliver. Short Pearl and Long Pearl, they lived pretty close together, I remember.

Alice Mae Williams.

Zearlee Robinson Wesley.

Rachel Lewis Franklin.

Evelyn Elliot Youngblood.

Allie Fay Moore Robinson.

Althia Lewis Franklin.

Rachel: My daughter was workin' on our family outfit for the Lewis reunion. She was tryin' to figure all this out. She said she found a Jack Lewis somewhere, and she was wonderin', was that any of Grandpa's folks? I told her if it was Grandpa Danny, he would be a Youngblood. She was gonna try to find out when Grandpa and them died and where he was born and all that.

Evelyn: I tried to work on mine here about two or three years ago, but I got so far and couldn't go any farther. For my children, I've left my records in the Bible. A lot of 'em has passed, but they will know who some of their relatives are.

Nathaniel Youngblood, a.k.a.
"Whang"
"Indian"
"Little Baby"
"Toota-Baby"
"Slim"
etc.

Althia: Do you remember whether Uncle Jackson knew his mother or father?

Zearlee: I remember Daddy sayin' that Uncle Jackson's grandma was an Indian woman. He used to tell us what tribe she belonged to. And June said she remembered Aunt Abby tellin' her what tribe that was. But it's gone from me now.

Althia: Now Cousin Mack Williams might know, 'cause Aunt Francis would be from that same one. I know we were from the Watusi on the African side. That's where we get that height from. But the Indian side . . .

Zearlee: Well, that would help June if she could find out. Jack wouldn't be a Lewis. He'd have to be a Youngblood.

Althia: I don't know where he got the Youngblood name from, but Uncle Jackson had that Youngblood name. Grandpa and a few of 'em had the Lewis name. I figured he got it from a Youngblood if you trace it back. It had to come from some kind of slave owner, 'cause when they come over, we don't know what they were. You can look at Grandpa's picture, he's made up just like an old Indian man. He looks very much Indian.

Alice Youngblood Cook: Where they switched those names, I don't know.

Althia: See, Daddy was named Charlie and he was supposed to been "Bug." I don't know what Uncle Elmo did—they called him "Doc." And Doad—now why Jonas had to be Doad, I don't know. But Kim they could have shortened, it was Camilla.

Alice C.: Uncle Johnny had everybody nicknamed. He called my mother "Catfish" 'cause she loved to fish. I was "Grapes" 'cause he say I looked sour all the time. Lucille was "Nightingale."

Nettie Harris: Somebody was called "Pig" 'cause they ate so much.

Alice C.: Uncle Joe was "Titanic" 'cause he loved to have the hood up on the car, messin' with it.

Althia: They called Aunt Ida "Dip." Grandpa was very stern about things, and one time he was fixin' a chimney. He put whatever he had up there and said for nobody to fool with it. Dip fooled around and stepped in it. Grandma tried to save Dip's hide, so she smeared it out.

Alice C.: Brother was "Tea Cakes" 'cause he loved tea cakes.

Nettie: His name is Nathaniel, but they called him "Whang."

Evelyn: As a little baby, they used to call him so many nicknames. He got a friend in Victoria that call him "Indian" 'cause Nathaniel got so much Indian in him.

Alice C.: Well, Lucille and Uncle Johnny used to call me "Tuto" all the time 'cause they didn't want me to tell on 'em. They used to get those young turkeys of Mama's and they'd say, "Now don't you tell Mama, Tuto, don't you tell it." When I'd see Mama comin' from work, there I'd go, trottin' down the road. "If you tell it, we gonna whip you when Mama go back to work." "I'm not goin' to tell it." So I go and meet Mama and say, "Lucille and Uncle Johnny got one of your turkeys and they got it hid at such-and-such a place till you go back to work." I'd tell it every time.

Another Conversation with Reverend Mack

My parents were Butler Williams and Emma Weathers Williams. They worked on the Peach Mott Ranch all their lives. Her parents were Isaiah Weathers and Frances Youngblood Weathers. Daddy's parents were Thornton Williams and Fannie Williams, who was half Cherokee. I don't know what her Indian name was. She was an herb doctor for the O'Connors and the Welders. She made medicines out of herbs and roots. She was heap big medicine. The Indians tried to steal her back. She had to be guarded when she went to gather her herbs.

Grandpa Thornton [John Thornton Williams] was a slave. He worked for Old Man Tom O'Connor (I) and his son Dennis and was freed by one of them before Emancipation. My granddaddy had his freedom papers. He died at the age of

Mack Williams, Andrés Villareal, Román Chávez, and Johnny Parson. The horses are Old Dick and Old Pearl.

ninety-four in 1914. He was born in 1820. He came to this country through England. He was French and African.

He and Grandma Fannie met up in the country and got married. I don't know if they were legally married or if it was an "Indian wedding." There are no records about that. My Aunt Fannie said she came out of "them there hills." She always said everything was a long time ago. I really got interested when she talked.

I don't have much information about where Isaiah Weathers came from, but he did come to this country with his parents to the Blue Grass country. Many old-

Thornton Williams.

timers didn't know when they were born, and I don't think Grandpa Isaiah knew his age. They were from the Watusi tribe in Africa. That was the big, tall African tribe. They were aristocratic herdsmen from central Africa.

Frances Youngblood was from the Blue Grass country. She was blonde and half white. Her father was Charles Dolley from the Dolley plantation. They had many slaves and often sold them. She was twelve years old when they come down from the North. She knew she was born in "tater-pickin' time"—and that was in November, probably around 1853.

They hid food from the Yankees in the cisterns and they would lower her into the well with the food. After she got it all fixed, they filled it with dirt and you couldn't tell where any of it was stored and hidden. They had potato kilns [root cellars] for normal storage, but the cisterns and wells was where they hid food durin' the war.

When slaves were brought down from the North and other places, they were headquartered in Wharton, Texas. Most of them came there from Maryland.

Grandpa ended up in Lewis's Bend after he married Grandma. He worked on the ranches around, and they gave him a piece of land down on the river because he was a preacher. He was pastor of Mount Zion Baptist Church in Lewis's Bend for fifty-two years. His sons worked around the ranches, but he mostly preached. He did a little bit of cotton pickin' and pecan and corn pullin', but that was about all.

Mack Williams (left) with "Lucky Boy," ca. 1953.

He had one day of schoolin'. He would sit down at night and write on a slate board. He had handwritin' that surpassed all others. His girls all went to school in Lewis's Bend. The teacher was old Professor Belt. He was the teacher before Emma Sample.

My people settled in Lewis's Bend. It was all one family, but a big family. Lots of men married into the families. It was settled by the white Lewises. It was a cotton plantation, and he owned a lot of slaves.

The [black] Youngbloods and the Lewises were the same family. Some kept the

Aus Avery.

Lewis name and some kept the Youngblood name from their last slave owner. They were brought from Wharton and settled down here. There was no slave tradin' in Indianola. Wharton was the biggest slave-tradin' area. They were all bought by Lewis and all came down together. Isaiah married into this Youngblood-Lewis family.

This was all unsettled land. Indians were still raidin' Mr. O'Connor and Mr. Fagan's horses. They kept Mr. O'Connor's horses because his cowboys wouldn't give them a beef. They let Mr. Fagan's go. I guess he gave them meat. This was goin' on even in Thornton's time.

Terrells, Averys, Lotts, Youngbloods, Lewises, the Rices, and the Ricks were some of the families that settled in the Bends. Just about all of these settlers were freed slaves from the Lewis plantation.

Uncle Steve Holliman and Grandma Martha Perryman lived so long they saw the stars fall. She lived to be 108 years old, and Uncle Steve was over 120. Uncle Steve was so old when I remember him he had to be lifted on a wagon to make his speeches on the Nineteenth of June. He always said, "Don't let me fall!"

To go on, I went to school in Tivoli. I started when I was thirteen years old. I grew up on the Peach Mott Ranch. There is an oak mott on the Peach Mott Ranch that is called Butler's Mott after my daddy. We were born there and lived there until we were older. He was a cook.

I've been rattlesnake-bit twice and never been to a doctor. I lay for ten days as sick as any old dog you ever saw. In the old days, we helped each other. That's the way folks lived. Everyone took care of each other and did the other one's work when somethin' like this happened.

The marriages worked out fine. The men were always out on the cow crowd. We didn't see too much of Papa. The wives always stayed home. The women did most of the raisin' of the kids, but the men helped when someone was sick. The women were strong. They could do anything. They were adapted to it. It was an outdoor life.

Papa stayed at Anaqua, and Grandpa Isaiah was at Lewis's Bend. He lived in a dog-run house. Mama was at home there with him at the time, not being married. Mama was sweepin' the dog-run one day.

Papa was older than Mama, and that's why Isaiah didn't want her to marry him. Papa whistled and she went in the house. He rode up to the window and she crawled out on the saddle behind him. The old horse started jumpin' and went across the dog-run and across the fence.

The horse was runnin' fast. Papa had stole her away. Grandpa Isaiah was chasin' 'em. His eyes were red and he was mad. Papa and Grandpa squared off. Papa had the skinnin' knife and a .44. Two days later they were havin' dinner together.

My Grandpa Thornton rode Indian-style. That was hunched over. He was a real horseman. He was a small fella, but they say he could ride. Papa rode stiff-legged.

My wife, Alice Mae, was a midwife for a while. The midwife was something special. She was called "Granny." Everyone had godmothers and godfathers, and the kids were baptized in the church. That was a serious job. They were yours to raise if anything happened to the parents.

It was a lot different back in those days. The ranches were more hospitable then. Anyone came around a ranch were asked to stay and eat or rest. Now they are all business. That's the way it is. I guess they have to be. The owners and the workers were closer in those days, too.

I went to school one day and because I couldn't speak English, they made fun of me. So I quit and came home. Every time I'd go, I'd get in a fight and come home. I'd get whipped for gettin' in a fight, so why not go back where I understood things? Ranch Spanish and proper Spanish are real different. The Texas version of Spanish is all its own.

I spoke Spanish growin' up. I was twenty-eight before I learned English. I was raised up with mostly Spanish people. Just a few whites and three blacks. Papa and my brothers spoke good Spanish, and so did almost everybody else, so I didn't have to speak English. There were ten of us. Everyone had big families. When you have ten kids, there is always something to do.

I talked to the cotton pickers when they came into the store in Maudelowe. That made me go back to my Spanish. You never forget it. I still talk Spanish when I am around people that speak it.

Uncle Pete Holliday would sometimes tell how hard it was durin' slavery. Grandma Frances Weathers talked about it, and Steve Holliman talked about bein' sold as a slave and about owners sellin' off families and splittin' 'em up. They always wound up sayin' it wasn't really that tough. They were treated good when they got here.

They never said very much about how they felt about bein' slaves. I think they got vexed about not bein' able to move around when they wanted to. Religion was important to these people. They felt like God freed them. They had prayed so long for deliverance.

Papa and Mr. Martin [O'Connor] were raised up together. They were good friends all their lives. They would fuss and fight like a couple of old women. Mr. Martin was always attached to me, I think, because of my papa. He and I used to laugh a lot about things they did together in their lives. Mr. Martin loved to hear me laugh. Grandpa Thornton raised all of those O'Connor boys. They knew their employers well and they knew how to handle them.

We were the only colored people livin' out at the ranch for many years. Then the Smith family moved out there. One of the daughters was Iwilla, Milam Thompson's second wife.

Papa sent us over there to speak to Mr. Smith and his new family, so me and my brother rode over there. The mama, Annie Smith, come out and we spoke. She weighed about three hundred and a half. She was big! She was a midwife.

The other children came out and we spoke. Their names were Iwilla, Savannah, Jess Jr., and Lawrence. Then out came Lawrence. Good Lord Almighty, he was big! He just reached down and hit me on the head he was so big. Large, I mean he was *large.*

Then Mr. Smith come out and we said hello. Mrs. Smith and everyone called him Daddy. He was a slender fella, had handlebars on him. He asked my name and before I could answer "Mank" [for Manchen], my brother said, "Teet." That was my nickname.

I went back home and Mama said she would ask them over, but Mrs. Smith was too big to fit through our door. Mama had already seen her and knew how really big she was, but she said she could get out of *her* door, so why couldn't she get in *our* door? All the houses were built the same, anyway. That lady was big. Oh, Lord, she was big. She was huge. Those were good old people. The only one left now is Irelant. That was the baby boy.

Now, we can head down to the O'Connor Negro cemetery and I will tell you all about the people buried there. The Rays were the in-laws of the Smiths. Tommy Ray was a brother to Will Ray and they were all from Goliad. They came out to Mr. Martin's ranch. Eliza was Will Ray's wife. She was a hefty one, too.

Felipe and Old Man Sliding are buried close together here. I don't know Felipe's name or Sliding's first name. All I know is that Old Man Sliding was a slave and he was the oldest black person here. He may even have been with Old Tom O'Connor [I].

The Stewards are here. Some of them still work for you. Those Stewards come from Goliad out there on the prairie. Some of the Stewards are called Green. They all had the same mother, but some of them were by a white man she lived with named Ben Green.

All the Weathers—Frances, Isaiah, Wilson, Nessie, and Mazie—are all my family. Gussie was Isaiah's daughter-in-law. She was married to Uncle Sips. Henry Dunman and Soapie Hayes were her brother and sister. Wootie and Ruby are buried here, too. That is a nickname that was given to that boy. He drowned right down here on the river. Ruby was Uncle Sips' oldest daughter.

A. V. Weathers Dunman was one of Isaiah's grandsons. Aceola Weathers was his mother and Isaiah's daughter. All them Dunmans was brothers. Joe, Ike, Henry, and Sophie were family. Ike was the one killed by a horse kick. Sophie was the last to marry, and she married Old Man Hayes. That's the only name I know for him. He had six fingers on each hand. That extra finger was just like the regular fingers. He was a tall fella.

Lela and B. T. Edwards.

The Averys had a little piece of land up there where Leo Scott lives. They all worked right here on the ranches, but they lived on their own land by the river. They worked for the O'Connors. You always hear about the Welders having so many colored people workin' for them. Well, the O'Connors had more colored people than any of them.

All the Weathers were buried out here on the O'Connor cemetery. Everyone but Ollie, that is. He was buried out in California.

Lots of the blacks in this area have lots of white blood in them. Many of them to this day don't want to talk about it because they are still afraid they will get in trouble for it. They don't understand the times have changed and the white man is more likely to get in trouble than them now.

Uncle Sam Ricks and Grandma Frances Williams were slave kids together. That was way up there in Tennessee or somewhere. Grandma Dolley was Mama's mother. Frances was part white and when she sat down, her hair was just as gold. Everybody wanted to comb her hair. She would always say to comb it now, but she wouldn't have any after a while. It was just way down here and it was blonde.

She was real light-skinned. The onliest ones takin' light skin after her was Aunt

Aceola and my mama. Grandma Frances would say she could remember seein' Uncle Sam tied to a wood horse and whipped. He got whipped for lyin'. One time he passed by the window in those old-fashioned kitchens and swiped a piece of cornbread off the window and went on and ate it. Someone saw him and they let him go on and eat it and waited to see what he would say. When they asked him, he denied takin' the cornbread and even after they whipped him, he stuck to that—that he didn't get the bread. He said he got whipped because he acted against what he was taught.

Then they came to this part of the country. They were brought here by Old Seabourne Lewis. Grandma Frances and Sam Ricks all came at the same time. They would take different names for different reasons. Youngblood and Lewis were white and they were brothers, and they came here to settle on the river on a plantation. The blacks took the name of whichever one they belonged to, even though they were all brothers and sisters. Later, these families would intermarry because they didn't know they were related.

Now, Grandma's real family was Dolley and they were from Tennessee. They belonged to the Dolleys and her father worked for the Dolleys who were white. My grandmother and her family all played with the white Dolley children. They were all kids together. Then this white Dolley girl come up with this black baby and they didn't do nothin' about it. They sold my family off and sent a mammy along with the baby to take care of her. They lived far apart, but when they visited, they could see the baby. So that's the way it was.

Grandma was a Dolley and the stable boy was her father. They were sold down to this part of the country from one place to another. The Lewises bought them and brought them down to this part of the country where they had heard there was good land and water. The further they came this way, the better the land got. Old Man Lewis lived there also. After Emancipation, it was named Lewis's Bend. The Lewises and the Dolleys were connected, and the Youngbloods are offshoots of the Lewises. White Lewis and Youngblood fathered most of the black people bearin' their names, and that's why they gave them Lewis's Bend.

My grandfather, Isaiah, pastored that church they built down there for fifty-two years. He was called to preach the day his oldest son, Ollie, was born and he wouldn't go. The members got in a stir and they were gonna get another preacher. Old Man Shorter, the one I told you about, got wind of it. He didn't belong to nobody's church, but he wanted to know who said that.

When the men would take their wives to church, they would go down in the Grove and gamble. They were talkin' about firin' Elder Weathers, and Shorter said he better go stop that. Someone reminded him he wasn't a member of the church and he said, "I am a member of the family."

He went to Mount Zion and stuck his head in the window and called everybody to attention. He said, "This is Henry Shorter, and I heard you was gonna get rid of Parson Weathers. If you try, you got me to answer to." He walked on off and went back down to gamble, and Grandpa stayed there fifty-two years.

Sometimes me and Toney [Lott] get to talkin' about those old folks back there and we nearly laugh till we cry. If you did something like that now, you would be put in jail.

When Uncle Sam came here, he started livin' with Aunt Ann Dunman. They had a big supper somewhere at someone's place. A big fight started. A fella hit Uncle Sam right up here with a cane and cut his eye. They all went down there and

Original part of O'Connor family cemetery.

told Grandpa Weathers. Grandpa got his rifle and refused to put it up even though he was a preacher. He told everybody to shut up or he would put a bullet in their head. Everybody shut up.

The sheriff came from Refugio and put Grandpa in the peace barn. Told Grandpa if he had to come back over this way, he was gonna put him in jail. Now, Grandpa's house was sittin' on the slant. The house was low in the front and up on high stilts in the back to make it level. The next mornin' came and Grandpa was sittin' on the front porch drinkin' his coffee.

The sheriff came out from under the house. Now I remember, his name was Ben Moss. He said, "Weathers, you got another cup?" Moss had slept under the house that night. He came up on the porch and handed Grandpa a piece of paper. That was the end of that. They sat there and laughed and talked. Moss even got Grandpa to plant that two-span corn. It's real high corn. You almost got to be on a horse to pull it.

There are Averys all over this place also—George, Mary, Lucy Latin. She was Leo's [Scott] grandmother. The Scotts and the Averys are related, and the Williamses are related to both. There was also William, Eddie, Willie, Mitchell, Jim, Louie, George, and Jack. That's all the same family. There was Jim Avery Sr. and Jim Avery Jr. The old man was the one that rode the horse through the church.

People used to gather at the church house and have dinner on the ground, they call it. Jim went to get that horse and the horse was breakin' from him. Then it started pitchin', and some people ran from the side of the house to see what was happenin'. The horse was gettin' rammed up against the church and left only one place to go—and that was in the church house.

Uncle Jim, he was a little short man, and he started hittin' him with those spurs. He kept sayin', "Don't worry, don't worry, he just actin' a fool." He went straight through that church house.

Lucy Avery and Laura Hopkins were sisters. She's still got a headstone in the cemetery. She was Laura Avery Hopkins. Before that, she was married to a Charleston. Her son was Henry Charleston from that marriage. Then she married Oliver Hopkins.

The name Bennie McCullough showed up around here. He was a brakeman on the railroad. He came from Refugio or farther down south. He was a mean fella, you betcha. He got in a bog one time when he was drivin' some ladies. He had them to get out and push him, and then he just drove off and left 'em. He drove off and left 'em standin' there.

Out here at the cemetery, the '42 storm took away all those stones. Uncle Sam Lott and a bunch of them built a fence and brought it in a lot. There are lots of people outside the fence on that north side. I think they washed off down the river.

Aunt Ink was Laura Hopkins and Lucy Scott's aunt. Shepphard Haller was a old, old black lady that used to sing the Old One Hundreds.

All the Loves were brought in here as slaves. Alice Mae's grandfather was John Summers. Her father was a white man in Mission Valley. The Summers and the Loves are related, and so are the Harveys. They aren't the same Harvey that live in Bloomington, though. No relation at all.

Papa and Mama were rightfully married, but Papa stole Mama. Papa was down here breakin' horses for Mr. Sitterle at the O'Connor. He rode by Grandpa and Grandma Weather's house and Mama just came out of the window and got on his horse and off they rode. She was the last of the girls to leave home.

When Grandpa came home, he asked where Emma was and Grandma had to tell him that she was not here. She had run off with Butler Williams. Papa was twenty years older than Mama. He lived just up the hill from Grandpa. Grandpa got his rifle, and Grandma told him to put it up. He put it up and went up there to Papa's, and you talk about raisin' sand! Aunt Ellen lived a ways farther down and they come a-runnin' because of all the fuss.

Aunt Guss lived down and around the corner back of Grandpa's. She come walkin' up to the house. She and Grandpa were fussin' and Grandma and Grandpa were fussin'.

So Grandpa went to Papa's and told his daughter, my mother, to come on home with him. Papa say, *"No!"* and Grandpa say, *"Yes!"* Everyone thought Grandpa and Grandma were gonna get in a big one, but they didn't. Grandpa didn't want Mama to marry anyone because she was so good at breakin' mules.

Papa say, "She's my wife now." Grandpa reminded him that they weren't married yet. So the next day, they went and got their license and come on home and Grandpa married them. It sure was shaky in that river bottom for a while until all that was settled.

I want to tell you about Brown Clark and Uncle Sip. There was a little colored colony over by where Leo Scott is. There was always somethin' funny goin' on wherever colored folks gathered. They had lots of humor. Anyway, they had one of these Saturday-night suppers and dances. Somebody pulled a gun and everybody started jumpin' out of windows and runnin'. People just scattered everywhere. Those old people would just naturally shoot you, so when someone pulls a gun like that, people run.

Old Man Brown Clark was runnin' and Uncle Sip was runnin'. Clark got hung up in some rolled-up wire and was just scratchin' and diggin'. Uncle Sip had caught up with him and as he went by, Old Clark hollered, "That you, Sip? What you runnin' for?" Uncle Sip said, "'Cause *you* runnin', fool!"

Everybody was just runnin' and nobody knew why. Funny things like that happened all the time. Our lives could be humorous.

Reverend Mack Williams

CHAPTER SIX

Livin' Off the Fat of the Land

"We lived out of that bottom and we lived out of that river."

Herbert "Buster" Bickford

There is a spirit that guides life along a river, and it is all nature-based. Survival laws are strong. Many people lived by the grace of God, the skin of their teeth, and the river.

The earliest visitors to this region described its lushness and fertility in glowing terms, and even during the upheaval of the Civil War, there was adequate food.

The Murphy family and a mess of squirrels.

No one went hungry. In her research notes, my grandmother says that the San Antonio River bottom provided much of the food in the region during these years, feeding inhabitants as well as the Confederate troops. Food was scarce outside this area.

Except for items like kerosene, coffee, and similar staples, river bottom inhabitants lived almost exclusively off the land. Like the Karankawas, they used survival skills that had been passed down through generations of living in close contact with the natural world. Their entire existence depended on the land, and from that land they raised, gathered, preserved, and hunted the food that ensured survival and sustained them in hard times.

The Gifts of the River Bottom

When that river was on a rise, the fish would come out and get caught in the wolfweeds. You could just walk along and take your hand and catch 'em and put 'em in a sack. Then you would have your fresh, fresh fish. We would get soft-shell turtles also. You had to be careful or they would catch you! People would have to get out of there when the river was on a rise.

Ulysses "Tommy" Cook

"We lived like good neighbors. Everybody lived neighborly and we knew each other. We knew if anybody needed anything and we cared about each other. It was Christlike down there. Being Christlike is sharing everything in life. There wasn't plenty back there, but we lived good."

Josephine Holiday Durst

Native pecan grove at Goliad.

The river gave us many gifts in our childhood. We still love that wild food. We had plover, curlew, and the wild onions were wonderful. The whole river bottom was filled with pecan trees. Some people would know them by name. They could look at a pecan and tell which tree it came from. We were livin' with nature and livin' off the land. The river was a great provider. It was special. You was at home. That's where all the activity was.

Georgine Terrell Levigne, Nathaniel Youngblood, Evelyn Elliot Youngblood, Vivian Lott McKnight, Josephine Holliman Terrell

Georgia Lee Swickheimer, deer hunting, 1952.

We hunted and gathered pecans. Everybody shared food then. They didn't throw anything away. That's how cowboy stew got started. Everybody would bring what they had.

I was baptized in that San'tone River. That was for the people who lived on it. It was very, very important to the people. It was water for drinkin' and baptizin'. It was for daily life and spiritual life.

Rosie Terrell Jones

There were all kinds of wild food out there. Anaquas was part of my living. Hackberries and mulberries and red haws, I've eat a many a one of 'em. Wild apples are little bitty things grow on a bush and they're good, too. Dewberries were a real treat when they come in. There was no kind of freezin' or refrigeratin'. We had all kind of ways to preserve food. We didn't never lose no food then.

Milam Thompson

The Wild Foods of the River Bottom

Agarita berries

Anaqua (knockaway) berries

Hackberries

Horse mint

Mulberries

Peppermint weed

Persimmons

Red haws

Sage tea

Sour grass

Toronjil

Wild currants

Trees did much for us. We shouldn't think of them as old, but think what they did for us. So many of the old trees are not around now. There are more useless trees than when we were kids. People have forgotten how much they provided for humans in our day. There is a spirit in the trees.

Zearlee Robinson Wesley, Nathaniel Youngblood, Troy Robinson

We named the pecan trees for special people. Mama would send us for pecans and we knew which tree she was talkin' about. We were always partial to pecan trees.

Helen Williams Magruder

The ancient pecan trees and oaks are finally going up for sale. Some people were down here buying up the old ones for paneling for houses. They were harvesting the old ones that don't produce anymore. These trees were always valuable to man, and now, when they aren't, they are still being used to help people.

Jeanne Houghton Marks

There were so many trees down here. People were walkin' around and locusts were singin'. You were always walkin' by trees with moss hangin' down on them. The trees were so special, they had names. Trees give life, healin', food, and shade. Some people see all this stuff and some don't. It's like puttin' someone in a herd of cattle. Either they get it or they don't. We knew the trees well. We knew what each one did. We didn't have to plant trees then, they just came up on their own.

Milam Thompson, S. W. "Toney" Lott

When you kill the trees, you kill your food and air. Look how long they stay alive. If you watch the trees, if you live with the trees, you will notice their bodies and limbs change. Some look like they have gotten younger, and some look like they have gotten older. They are just like people. I have been under a tree when it have rained only under that tree and nowheres else.

Rachel Wynona Lewis Franklin

Down here we owe the land everything. We sprang from this land. Every cell of our bodies came from that ground. In our family we are fortunate to know that we are going back into that land when we died. We will turn back into that land.

Tom O'Connor Jr. (III)

Everybody lived on the river long ago. It's the best grazin', huntin', and fishin'. There were swimmin' meets down here on Sundays. It gave us wood, too. You could even tighten up a wagon wheel by soakin' it in the river. It flooded and silted the land, and we baptized in it.

River bottoms are so valuable in dry times. There is always food down there. Pecans are everywhere. We lived out of the river and the bottom. All the food down there is unbelievable. It afforded us many things.

Women washed clothes in the river. We would see them a lot when we were down there as kids. We would fish and hunt rabbits and then start a little fire and cook them. We would carry salt and pepper in our pockets. We ate a lot of alligator gars. There was lots of food in those bottoms.

None of us much ever went on the river in a boat, we just walked along the river and smoked a lot of grapevine. There used to be a mule-foot hog down here. Their hooves were smooth like a mule's. Don't see them anymore.

Anybody raised on the San'tone River was called "river cats," and that was different from the "river rats." High water was the only thing we were afraid of. There isn't much danger in the bottom. Even a rattlesnake won't bother you if you leave him alone. Night down here can be spooky. Those old hoot owls called out and it could raise the hair on your neck.

We were raised to respect ourselves and each other. If you were brought up on

"My daddy was a farmer. He wanted me to farm. I said, 'No. No cotton, no corn, just cowboyin'.' I'll do anything but pick cotton. I never did like cotton pickin'."

Alejandro De La Garza

this river, you behaved. We had motherwit, too.

When we were growin' up, you didn't have nobody to bother you. Used to be at night, it looked like a town in that bottom. Everywhere you looked there was a light. People were huntin'. We never damaged nothin'. We used horses, not cars. The cars destroy a lot.

River bottoms have a different atmosphere. They are different in climate and different in feelin'. There is no breeze in the bottom. On the prairie, you can smell a long way off. Swamp land has a different smell. Voices even sound different than on the prairie. A little sound in the woods you could hear no tellin' how far. River bottoms change sounds.

In the spring you could smell wild onions and greens and we would pick berries. In the winter, we would go into the bottoms to cut the wind off us. We harvested and cut wood, fished and hunted.

Times are rollin' so fast now. Towns make people go haywire. Down here we were taught the right things by our parents. Now people don't live their lives—they buy them.

Anywhere we hung our hat down here was our favorite place. It was all pleasure. That's what it gave us.

Nathaniel Youngblood

Barthelms and son hauling wood in the river bottom.

Fishin'

Fishing has always been a popular pastime along the San Antonio River, but up until the last half of this century, it was also a mainstay of survival. Fish was a basic component in the diet of the river bottom's inhabitants. Among the edible species of fish in the river are the blue and yellow catfish, species for which the San Antonio River has long been noted because of its muddy bottom.

In 1855, a New York physician visiting the San Antonio River area reported this conversation with a man who was no doubt a slave from one of the nearby ranches: "A negro came down with two fish-lines, with enormous hooks, and after baiting them with the entrails of a fowl, he drove the sharpened ends of the poles into the bank, and sat down to wait the result. 'What sort of fish do you catch here?' I asked. 'Cat, sah . . . [and] buffalo-fish, but dem we don't catch.' Soon the fellow drew out a cat-fish, weighing about six pounds, of a species he called the yellow cat, and soon after I helped him with the other line to another of smaller size, which he called the blue-cat. The river abounded, he said, in gars and alligators, and no one dared to bathe in it."

Farther upriver, he encountered other specimens of river life: "I found here some very large unios, the shells of which will weigh, at least, a pound. They lie imbedded in mud . . . . There is a fine fish of the perch family found in all the streams that unite with the San Antonio and Guadaloupe—it is improperly called here trout; it sometimes attains the size of five or six pounds. There is, also, another of the same family very similar to the little pumpkin-seed or sun-fish."[1]

A former resident of the little community of Riverdale recalled a time in the early part of this century when the river flooded and threatened to wash away her brother's boat: "When the river subsided, he found his boat still tied, but overturned, with a 60-pound catfish trapped inside the boat."[2]

Alejandro and Mary Luz Pérez De La Garza. She was world champion catfisher. He never did outfish her.

The buffalo was another edible species. I have never been able to determine whether this was the buffalo carp or another species, but I am told it was excellent when rolled in cornmeal and fried in bacon grease. Those who had access to the inland bays of the area found many additional varieties of fish, including redfish, trout, drum, flounder, and sheepshead.

Fishin' Tips

When you're fishin', pick a good spot. Summer fish like the shade. Be quiet and put a line in a deep place. He'll bite it there. The bay will get soft mud, but the river runs all the time and keeps a hard bottom. Get a sufficient amount of bait. A fish likes a mouthful when he bites. Keep a tight line and leave bait about three feet off the bottom. Nobody ever teaches their young 'uns how to make bait. You gotta do this yourself.

Henry Charleston

To catch fish in the river or a pond, you set two or three lines in the river. When the fish bites, it will pull 'til it gets tired. When you start movin' on the banks of the river, the fish will hear. Maybe that is why sometimes when you have a lot of company, you don't catch nothin'.

The fish like logs and deep water. You have to look for them. The moon makes a lot of difference. They won't bite on a full moon. Weather doesn't have much to

"The other day John Freeman found a recipe for bait. It's made out of cheese and cotton and I don't know what all. It lives in the refrigerator door. I'm careful not to take it for mayonnaise."

Allene Pettus Lott

do with it. I believe when they gonna bite, they gonna bite. Maybe they won't bite for three or four days. When you lucky, they bite for three or four days. If it's real cold weather, a worm will catch a fish. If it's too cold, they won't bite.

Alejandro De La Garza

We used hoop nets in the river with cottonseed-cake bait. Everyone wanted fish on Fridays, so it was a way for us to make money. The hoop nets were like a trap. It was open on one end and closed on the other. It was made out of fishin' line. You put cottonseed cake in there for bait, and you would put it in the river so the smell would wash downstream. We usually caught buffalo fish or cats. You could put the bait on a hook, too.

Reverend Mack Williams

Huntin'

For people who lived along the San Antonio River, hunting was another important activity for putting food on the table. Ducks, geese, quail, doves, wild turkey, prairie

J. O. Linney hunting at Salt Creek, January 1943.

chicken, squirrel, and other small mammals—and occasionally rattlesnake—were harvested for their meat.

Hunting at night, usually with hound dogs, was a means of collecting animals such as raccoons, possums, skunks, armadillos, bobcats, and other nocturnal mammals that were plentiful in the bottoms. Their meat was used as food, and their hides were sold to fur and hide buyers for cash that could be used to buy provisions at the grocery stores and mercantiles.

Getting Your Ducks in a Row

"That river bottom was my home. It was the onliest place I knew. The people were friendly. They shared meat and they shared food."

Lola Gibson Adams

My brother-in-law, Merle Winsor, and I always used to talk about hunting and birds. We were both interested in things like that. He liked to teach me about things like that as we rode along. He knew so much about wildlife. There used to be lots of eagles in the low brush. He could stand in the stirrups and look into the eagle's nests to see what they were feeding their babies. We would ride our horses along the shoreline [prickly] pear flats where the pelicans used to roost.

Back then, there wasn't as much brush, it was more grasslands. Merle would tell how they used to get in a horse and buggy and find a bush. Then they would circle the bush with the wagon and move in closer and closer until they were right up on the bush. They would shoot their shotgun at the base of the cactus where the quail were and just get out and sack 'em up.

Merle and Scrub Kelly would work all week to get a quarter to buy five shotgun shells. They'd go out and take turns shooting dove. They never shot unless there were three or more dove on a line. They would line 'em all up and shoot.

They would hunt in certain areas and end up at a duck pond that always had ducks on it. They would always try to get whoever was with them to shoot at something else so it would be your turn at the pond. That pond was always a good shot.

Gertrude "Gertie" Keeran, 1913. She obviously had her "ducks in a row."

Merle always said, "Get your ducks in a row." He never could understand shooting at a single bird. His father always told him never to shoot at a bird that was by himself. That meant there was something wrong with him.

He always said there were no ducks and geese in the country compared to when he was young. Merle's father said in his day there were swans here in this country. They would wake you up at night when they came in.

Luther Bennet Paul

Keep Them Gun Barrels Straight Up

Martin O'Connor was one of my best friends. We would go out there wolf huntin'. I used to have to run Joe [O'Connor] down when he got on a tear. I did that for Martin a lot. He was about six feet tall and a heavy-set man. He knew the cattle business, that was for sure. He would come out here on the train from Victoria to pay his hands. I would pick him up and take him out to the ranch. He would let me hunt and go anywhere on his ranch. Everybody loved Mr. Martin O'Connor. I never saw him on a horse. I hunted with him on the ranch. He and Mr. Swift would take me with them. Mr. Martin always said to keep them gun barrels straight up.

Herbert "Buster" Bickford

Open Season

Long time ago, you could go out and kill a duck or a deer anytime you wanted. There was no season on those animals, for us anyway, except salt and pepper. Quail, if we wanted quail, we just hauled off and shot 'em. We could catch all the

Clyde Bauer (center front) and ranch hands keeping their gun barrels up, quail hunting on the Traylor ranch, ca. 1950.

fish we wanted. We ate what we caught. There weren't no iceboxes to keep them in. We never shot for sport. We didn't like that.

Johnny Robinson, Troy Robinson, K. J. Oliver

My daddy bought a shotgun in 1917, during World War I. The boy that had it sold it to Daddy because he was going into the service. He paid forty-five dollars for it,

C. F. Bego.

and that was a lot of money back then. I come home one evening and stopped in front of the house and saw something looked like blackbird season. I went in the house, came back out, and made two shots. I got twenty-eight doves. I killed a many a goose with that gun, too. It helped me feed us for a lot of years.

Henry Sievers Jr.

José Serrata's Record

One time I took Tommy O'Connor Jr. deer huntin' in 1935 with me. We were sittin' in the brush when we spotted some deer. We took some old cow bones and rattled 'em. This lured the deer close to where we were. Soon a buck was right up on us. Tommy took the gun and shot the deer between the Shelley and Eustacio fence.

Tommy told me to put the deer in front of my horse. Tommy was ridin' Mike, and I rode the Heard sire. I'll never forget that day. The deer's horns touched my horse's shoulder and that horse threw me. When I hit the ground, Tommy asked me what had happened. I told him that nothin' had happened, I just lost my horse.

The horns from Tommy's deer are mounted in the dinin' room at the bunkhouse.

José Ángel Serrata

Confessions of a Hound Dog Man

I had hound dogs all my life. At one time, I had twenty-three hound dogs. That was before you could buy feed. I had to cook in a washpot for them, and I did.

I never will forget. I fell after a rain one time and skinned my knee and Mother was smart enough to think it might be malignant, so we went to Old Dr. Burns. He splits it open with a hammer and a chisel, and chiseled that knot off that shin bone.

It was benign, but I couldn't walk for a month or two. I was in bed in the *garçonnière.* Mr. Koenig, the blacksmith in Riverdale, had a blue tick bitch that had puppies. I wanted a pair of those puppies so bad. I was around ten or twelve years old, and Dad knew how bad I wanted these puppies. He got them for me, and if he had given me a million dollars, I couldn't have been happier.

I remember the first coon they treed, and I know the tree right now. I can pick it out for you. It's a burr oak down on the river right there at Rock Ford. It's still livin'. I know exactly where it is to this day.

A hound dog is a trailin' dog. He tracks and trails. A bird dog uses his nose alright, but it's more body scent than it is a footprint. They keep quiet and run with their head up.

A hound is smellin' the trail on the ground, the track of the whatever he's trailin'. I've pulled off a many a hound with a coon up a tree, and glad he got away because he put up such a good race.

I'd let him go. It's not the kill. It's all about each dog havin' a certain job. One always has a start dog, a trailin' dog, a tree dog, and a pack dog. The rest of the dogs do the work until they get it goin', then the pack dog falls back into the pack and makes more music. Like old Joe Rufus said, "Doesn't make any difference how they sound, they all run to the music."

I had a pack of cat dogs one time. I hunted from my pickup. That's called road huntin'—you don't walk with them anymore. I hunted with these dogs, and they were so smart you could ride down a sendero in low gear and the dogs would lope in front of the car huntin' in the lights. We'd come to a cross sendero, and they would wait for me to see which one I was goin' down. The minute I'd turn, they would go to huntin' again.

That's a hound dog man. He can train his dogs to hunt with him and he doesn't have to hunt for them or wonder the next mornin' where they've gone. When one barked, you knew what he was after immediately. Mine were so trained I'd toot the horn, drop the tailgate, open the dog crate, blow the horn twice, and they'd just come jump in that crate like popcorn.

Hound dogs are an addiction, just like dope.

John Freeman Lott

"Years ago you could go fish at Black's Bayou, shoot a doe for food, and bring in a bunch of quail if you needed 'em. We would travel around these fields with a rubber shooter and sling shot. All that's past now."

Troy Robinson
Johnny Robinson
K. J. Oliver

The Woods Child

John Freeman's roots are so deep on this San Antonio River, I don't know how his mother survived. He was a little wandering boy, a woods child. He lived in the

Clarence Preiss Sr., 1927.

woods, a little hound dog boy. He was a free spirit. The boy was just like Huck Finn and Tom Sawyer rolled into one. He was just a little spook, he was. You know, he'd build a little man in his bed to fool his mother and take off hunting at night. Grandmother never knew where he was. One time they had been in town, and he'd been down on that river while they were gone. They had let him have a gun when he was real little. Well, I don't think you ever "let" John Freeman—he just "did."

We went to the river right down here and got in the boat and I said, "John Freeman, how did your mother live with you comin' up?" He said, "I don't know."

Baggin' a bobcat.

We passed a little sandbar and he said, "I remember the time when I would have slept right there on that sandbar and run my lines all night long." And I said, "You wouldn't have told your mother, would you?" "No." I said, "How thoughtless." He said, "I wasn't thinking about Mother. I was thinking about these fish."

One time we went to San Antonio shopping and stayed at the Menger. We were out on the balcony. I said, "Isn't this a gorgeous night." John Freeman said, "Lord, I wish I was in the woods to hear old Blue bark." If that won't kill romance, I don't know what will! This type of man needs freedom.

Allene Pettus Lott

Dogs and Other Critters

One time Papa made us stay in the wagon until they could settle the cows. We all slept in a wagon, a chuck wagon. That was my brother and I and my daddy. And, of course, the black man. He had a little old shed there, and we liked to froze to death layin' in a wagon for a bed. We'd a' been better on the ground.

Long about then I had a black dog. Every time it would thunder, he would come out of his pen. I had a chain made with a strap on his shoulder. When it thundered, he got loose. He wouldn't stay there. He couldn't stand the thunder, and he

Pete Fagan (left) and Father Henderson "campin' out."

even got away with that strap on him.

I quit coon huntin' for a while, and I got a greyhound. We were on the river bottom after my wife passed away. That was about '41. We had a black man was the cook. We had a tent in the bottom and stayed there for a week. This cook would go out and shoot coons. I had my greyhound with me and he would get in bed with me. Just couldn't stand the shots. We ran rabbits with him. He was beautiful.

My brother had some stag hounds, and we used to go over at the Duke Ranch when Louis Power was there. He'd catch rattlesnakes and wolves out there. They were fast dogs. They could catch a coyote. Greyhounds would catch something and throw it. Those stag hounds have a mouth that big, and they could catch a coyote high on the open country. I can tell you something. When those dogs would throw that coyote, he'd get a dog by the foot or in the nose with his mouth. You'd have to kill that son of a gun before he'd turn him loose.

Ralph Bego

There was a big freeze in '51. I didn't get to work in those days, but I could see the men feed hay, and my dad and Henry, my brother, had to stay at the Hollow feedin' the Lake Pasture. The ranch had a wagon and a team of mules we could use to haul wood. I remember we borrowed it to go get wood for us and another family that used to live by us. About four of us young boys went and got the first load and then went back for another. On the second load, we took a bunch of dogs we had, and they had some more, 'cause we had seen some swamp rabbits. When we got to where the wood was, we loaded about half a load and then we went rabbit huntin' with the dogs. We caught some with the dogs and some would go in hollow trees and

Jim Coward and his catch.

we would pull them out. Anyway, there was a rabbit that run right toward the wagon, and the dogs scared the mules and they took off into a tree and tore up the wagon. The mules ran off and we had to chase them. We caught one, and one of the boys, Martín Rodríguez, rode it and drove the other one to the house. We were in trouble when my dad found out.

Julián Tijerina

There was a lot of people huntin' back in those days. You'd get on that old Model T car and go out on the O'Connor prairie. You could see a long ways on a moonlight night. You could see somethin' movin' out there, come up a little further, and it'd be a skunk. You could see 'em out there in the openin', you know, and talk about coyotes!

Back before I was big enough to hunt well, Daddy had a place, had a man workin' for him plowin' in the field. They had a good coon dog. I believe Daddy went the first part of night and come in about midnight and go to bed. Then Barney Kelly, he'd take the dog out and hunt until daylight. Then he would come in, get his breakfast, and go out in the fields and plow. Daddy would have to skin out all those hides. You could make five or six dollars a night takin' hides. Feller workin' for a dollar a day, and you could make four, five, eight, ten dollars if you was lucky that night. Coon hides, ringtail hides, and, heck, a skunk would bring fifty cents or a dollar.

They made coats out of 'em somehow or another and sold 'em, you bet. I was goin' to school many a mornin' with the same boots or shoes on that I had on the night before and they just stunk when you got in a warm room right up against the old coal or wood stove. The scent starts, you smell it, I tell you. It just comes out all over the room.

Alton Curtis

Take What You Need, and Need What You Take

Almost every household in the river bottom had its own plot of cultivated land. Many of the area ranches supplied their workers with small tracts under a tenant-farming or sharecropping arrangement. Families were free to use the land indefinitely, and these little fields and vegetable gardens normally supplied each family with enough food to meet its needs.

To supplement their food supply, river bottom inhabitants gathered native wild plants as well as nuts, berries, and other fruits, which were abundant. Pecans were especially important, not simply as food but as a source of cash. A common practice on the O'Connor ranches was to invite the ranch hands and their families to gather the pecan crop on "halves"—that is, keeping one-half for themselves that they could then sell.[3]

Pecans have always been highly valued in this area. According to an early-day settler, when an 1842 drought destroyed crops and made cattle "too poor to eat," an abundant pecan crop and good pecan prices "prevented famine in the land."[4] Pecans were exported as early as the era of the Republic and possibly earlier.

As the narratives make clear, this way of life encouraged the conservation and sharing of resources. Good times and bad times affected everyone equally, so there was a sense that "we're all in this together." They tended to gather what they needed

Working the fields, Frank Dusek farm on Warburton Road. Left to right: Helen Dusek Walker, Annie Marie Dusek Cribb, and Sally (Slofka) Vanek Podehl.

and nothing more. A family with more than enough for their own use would usually share among their friends and neighbors. It was necessary to consume food supplies quickly, or preserve them when gathered, especially before the advent of iceboxes.

More important, sharing was simply what good neighbors did. Often this sharing took place communally, at a gathering at someone's house or after the church services on Sunday. It was customary to take no more than they could use individually or as a group. They did not overtax nature's ability to resupply them, so year after year they were able to survive from nature's bounty.

The Bottom Fields

Everybody down there mostly farmed, maybe a little side ranchin'. They'd do their own farmin' on thirds, fourths, halfsies. They'd job around and chop and pick cotton.

Will Weathers

They would also pick up pecans. Lot of people lived on pecans. Every year there was a big crop. Didn't get much for them, but it was enough for that time. Things were so cheap then.

Ten or fifteen cents a pound was good back at that time. A hundred pounds of pecans would bring ten dollars. That was big money back in them days. You was rich then.

At one time there was a bottom field there, and in them days several people would have a patch or patches they worked in them big fields.

Milam Thompson, L. V. Terrell, Richard Harris

I grew up on the O'Connor ranch with my daddy [Lonze Edwards]. I worked in the

Two-span corn. Kind of like "tall cotton."

fields, my sister Nettie [Shaw] and me. Papa would plant the cotton and we would roll it. We had a horse hitched to the roller named Old Rock. We loved to roll back and forth and we would fight over who got to do it. We'd go up to the field carryin' a can of water. One day, somebody turned over the water can and Rhodie had to go back to the ranch to get more water. Old Mike, the mule, was trouble. He would hump up his back and pitch. Well, Rhodie got on him and whipped him until he quit and went to trottin'. She got to the windmill and brought us some water back. She had gotten that mule in control.

From a child up, Daddy worked on the ranch. Then he got married and he still worked on the ranch. After he had all these children, he farmed and we all worked on the farm. When you lived on the ranch, you got a small farm to work.

Lela Edwards Williams

Alonso "Lonze" Edwards.

Every spring a man named José and his wife Manuela would come into the river bottom and make themselves a house out of trees and palmettos. They would fix it up real nice and lodge there for the summer. They would work the crops, and then they would leave like the birds when winter came. You couldn't just light on people's land like that now, but you could then. It was kind of odd to us that they would come just in the spring.

Rachel Wynona Lewis Franklin

The people were down there and they were all together. Whatever one had, everyone had. It was just like a small town. You could hear singin', whistlin', talkin', and

Palmetto hut of Antonio Rodríguez.

everything that was goin' on out there. Long Tall Pearl [Lott] would share everything with the others. That's the way they did.

Alice Youngblood Cook, Althia Lewis Burns Franklin

There were ducks and turkeys everywhere. That was our livin'. We'd sell them in the fall of the year. In the evenings you would have to go get them and bring them

Driving turkey from Ander to Cuero, ca. 1910.

in. Findin' where they were nestin' could be a real pain. We traded the eggs for things we needed at the store. There was lots of activity around those old houses all the time, lots of life goin' on.

Althia Lewis Burns Franklin, Gussie Marshall Richardson,
Rachel Wynona Lewis Franklin

Porfirio Urbano (right), wild hog huntin', McFaddin ranch.

The first nickel I ever got was given to me by my brother-in-law when I was about four years old. I wanted to buy corn with my first nickel, so someone bought it for me. The place to plant corn is where outdoor toilets used to be or old sites where animals and people live. I planted that corn and we had roastin' ears that year, and that's how I spent my first nickel.

Buckeye land is not sand or caliche, and it's not blackland either. It's soft and reminds you of ashes. It's easy to dig in, but it's not right on the surface. You have to go down a little ways. I can remember when I was a kid, armadillos dug deep in

Tom O'Connor Jr. (III) playing with an armadillo.

buckeye land because it's soft. It is good to plant corn in. It's kind of special.

I'd get me some corn and put them in hot ashes and parch it. It wasn't really popped, but it was good. I'd put the parched corn in my pocket and eat out of my pocket as I went along. You could roast acorns also. They was good.

I raised a family and cared for a mother on four dollars a month. I made a deal with Mrs. Hanley at her store for credit, and Mr. Fagan stood behind me to get groceries for four dollars a month. I'd get sugar, bakin' powder, maybe some rice, flour, coffee. I raised my own lard from hogs, got my own honey, took corn to the mill and got cornmeal made out of it. I raised my own beans and all kind of peas, pumpkins, and potatoes.

Wild onions was growin' in the bottom. I'd cook them in cans over the fire while I kept my eyes on those hogs. They all had names—Longtail, Swayback, Longears, Shortnose—every one had a name. I could tell you if 'ary a one was missing.

All this went on in the thirties. I was married in '28. Sugar was seven cents a pound, flour was a dollar and a half for fifty pounds. Everything was cheap then. Coffee was sold by whole beans. You put it in the stove and parched it. It was all two bits of this and ten cents of that.

Milam Thompson

Honeybees—Easy as Cattle

I've had a beehive ever since I was a young man. You have to keep boxes ready for bees in the spring. You need frames and supers and you put your dividers betwixt your supers and your bottoms so only the worker bee can get there and put honey. They fill it up after May. They suck the flowers and they get pollen on their legs that they take around to other flowers and plants. They don't work no more than fifteen miles from their hive. They love mountain laurel, but they work all kinds of flowers—any kind of flower they can get dippin'.

In June and July, they'll be hustlin' around, cappin' it with wax. The honey at the top will be the ripe stuff. Don't never rob the bottom of the hive. Always leave that for the bees for winter. They live off that honey in the winter. Your bottoms have to be changed out so they won't get rotten.

They love cake. They'll suck all the sugar out and take it back to the hive. They're death on that cake. The bees will also eat peppermint candy you put in there and get used to the scent.

Sometimes they'll swarm if there's two queens in the box. There ain't but one can stay in it. She's like the big boss. She's the one gonna give out the orders. If you get two queens, you gonna have to get one outta there. If you don't get them outta there, they gonna fight. The young one's gonna put the old one out, and she'll take those young bees and go.

I like bees. I like them better than anything—you know, just to be foolin' my time off when I ain't got too much to do. I like to work 'em. I like to have 'em jam up.

Monroe "Bailey" Shaw.

You can't put a queen in a hive natural. They'll kill her. They don't want her there. You've got to put her in a thimble.

They live for thirty days, work bees, that is. They work themselves to death, but she's cumulatin', so you never run out. You double your hives every year, but you have to keep extras and watch out for webworms. They'll get in there and run the bees off. Watch for ants, too. Put oily rags around the legs of your racks what you got 'em on. Brush your boxes to keep spiders away. Never let spiders hang around. They kill 'em, too.

They ain't no trouble. They take care of themselves. I wish I had children like that, I'd raise a thousand. They make their own livin'. When they born, they ain't a bit of trouble, as easy as cattle. If you get too many or you want to quit raising 'em, you just let 'em swarm and they'll go find a hollow in a tree somewhere.

Bees ain't dangerous to you unless they don't like your scent, then look out! I smoke my bees out when I want to gather the honey. Spanish bees will fight you when you rob 'em, but they make real good honey. They won't come out and attack you, but if you go in there and they ain't used to you, and you go to hittin' at 'em, you're in trouble!

Cotton pickin', Austwell, August 1937.

You just take it easy. They put a seal on it when it's ready. Unless honey is capped, it's green. Green honey will give you a stomach trouble. When it's ripe, you put comb and all in a jar. A hive will make about a gallon and somethin', maybe two gallons sometime. You can sell for around ten dollars a gallon.

You lease land to set your hives on if you don't have your own. There really ain't nothin' to it.

Monroe "Bailey" Shaw

Pecans for the Widow Women

Zilpah Daniel Edwards.

People used to come from Mexico to pick cotton, and they camped there at the ranch by where the water trough is. The women used to take their clothes to the river to wash. They carried the clothes on their heads.

Simon Dykes, the son of Charlie Dykes, who got killed in the bottom, told me this: Mr. Dennis [O'Connor I] was sitting on the porch and told Simon Dykes to go see if those poor people had enough money to buy groceries. Simon went over there and came back and said they might need something. Mr. Dennis gave them a note for the store. When they came back through later, they paid Mr. Dennis.

We used to make troughs out of elm trees for Mr. Dennis. He would tell us to cut trees, but don't cut no pecan trees. The pecan trees are for the widow women. He used to fill a wagon with groceries and drive them around to the hands' families at Christmas.

Rafael De La Garza

I remember that thing with Grandma tellin' us about pickin' pecans. In the wintertime, you had choice pecans, those great big ones on some of those old trees. You could fill a grass sack and set it in the kitchen until you got ready to take it to Victoria.

The most money we had was during pecan-pickin' time. We'd sell the pecans. Otherwise, they picked cotton. The people lived good. They had plenty to eat, they had clothes to wear, and out of that little bit of money they got from pecans.

Josephine Holliday Durst

My Grandfather Stoner owned that plantation that was originally the Rose plantation. It was where DuPont is now. Every fall, I had to go with my mother to pick pecans on the plantation. The trees down in that river bottom were beautiful. She loved pecans and fall was pecan time.

Zilpah Daniel Edwards

Everything on this earth is good for something. There was a day when we lived off the trees and could sell pecans for a price.

Trees are just like people. They have life just like human beings. They just can't talk. It's natural in a person's body to like trees. It produces nuts, berries, and shade. It's a valuable plant.

Johnny Robinson, Nathaniel Youngblood

"Trees were faithful to me in fur-nishin' me food. Pecans fed me. I knew certain trees well. I kept up with them like friends."

Milam Thompson

This is a story I've got to tell you. We was fishin' on that river, just the three of us, my daddy, my neighbor, and myself. Daddy took corn and had it soaked for a couple of days so we could use it for buffalo bait. This neighbor and myself, we each had one. Mine was in a cotton sack, a satchel, I called it. The neighbor's was in a bucket.

We walked across Hall's Point where it makes a curve around. We camped over there and walked across and put our lines out in that curve. We stayed there two nights, I think. We didn't have no iceboxes in them days, just homemade ones. But anyway, we kept the fish alive in the river, what we caught. So the last time, we picked up our lines.

It was during pecan times in the fall of the year. We picked up a few pecans to eat while we was walkin' around to pick up our lines. We had a sack full of fish and when we got to the car, there was a man in a big sombrero with a pistol and a scabbard, sittin' on a horse. He couldn't talk English hardly and Daddy couldn't talk Spanish, see. He did say, "Where the pecans?" I took that sack off and said, "Ain't got no pecans." Poured out the bucket and said, "Ain't got no pecans." Pulled out my pocket and I had two in my pocket.

It was on the Terrell ranch. He was a ranch foreman. He was a pretty old man. There was people in there pickin' pecans, and I guess they reported us to him. That's why he came to us. We didn't bother the pecans. That's one thing we never carried.

We went fishin' years and years on that river—all the way from Riverdale, up above Goliad, down to the Simms Bridge. Nobody ever bothered us. We didn't take no gun along. All we done was fished. We didn't bother anybody. Takin' pecans was serious business in those days.

Henry Sievers Jr.

Listenin' to the Animals: The Recollections of Henry Charleston

My mama's daddy bought land around the river after he came out of slavery. His name was Bill Avery. They were all slaves that came in through Indianola. They mostly worked for themselves on the farm. My daddy, George Charleston, farmed and worked for the O'Connors and the Fagans sometimes when he needed money.

I came along in 1910. I mostly grew up here as a child and spent a lot of years in Houston. When I was out here, I didn't have much company. I did some schoolin' at Bethlehem School in Inari.

I made snuff-bottle trains and got in a sand track and ran them. I kept old pieces of machinery and made lots of things out of it. I made child-size wagons for myself. I'd get way up on those hills and turn it loose.

I played cowboy all the time when I had a break from chores. We didn't have much play time. They always taught us in those days, if you wanted to eat, you had to pay for it.

You could get lost out on that Big Field of the O'Connors. I hunted a lot and hung around the river bottom. I killed lots of huge bullfrogs on that river. That's better eatin' than chicken.

I used to pick up my gun and go before these smart fellas came into this country. We were taught as kids it was wrong to take other people's things. We never did this and stopped anyone else who tried to. Smart people, city people not wise to country ways, don't understand that. I never liked Refugio too well, so I worked on the railroad in Houston.

It was wide-open, wild country in those days. Everybody was neighborly. You left your doors open. City folks comin' here made it smart. They don't have any idea about the country. They don't know how to hunt or walk in the woods. They just mess up everythin' in the woods.

They drag their feet, and when you break a stick, it can be heard a long ways. Watch your feet, pick them up, and set them down solid. You gotta watch the trees and take your time. If you see somethin' move, you stop until you can make out what it is.

I remember all the old guys that were out here. Joby Wallace played music out here when they had dances. He lived down under the hill here. They'd come and get him, he was so popular. He played "The Buckin' Wing." I stuck a splinter in my foot doin' that one time. They had soda water with a balloon on the top of the bottle. It was usually lemon or sarsaparilla.

Henry Charleston.

I can call a squirrel. You look on the ground, and if you see green cuts on the ground, you know a squirrel is around. I ate knockaways all the time, just like the squirrels.

There is a bird goin' in the woods that makes a sound. He is a pimp to the other animals. As long as he makes noise, you won't find nothin'. You have to either kill him or get him out of your path. That bird does it for all the other animals, too.

Cows and horses talk their own language, likewise. If you have a cow and don't treat her right, she'll tell the other cows. If you treat her good and give her plenty of feed, she'll also tell them that. The next night you'll wonder where all them cows come from.

Cows will have conversations among themselves about whether they like you or not. When you do somethin' they don't like, they will look at the other cows. Eventually, you'll be wonderin' why those cows don't come around you much. It will be because they don't like your setup. They will try to go your way, but if they ever once get to the place where they are scared of you, they won't be bothered with you.

I got a cow at the house comes in with a low that is real heavy. She's callin' the rest of them, "Come on, I'm goin' to get my food." I have three cows. They used to be alright. Now they have one extra cow out there. They will go into a seeney-bean thicket and she won't follow. Now, she come up to the house and make noise so I will feed her. She will start to eatin' then. I give her somethin' to hush her mouth. Then she will call to the others to come on.

Animals were my playmates. I'd get a calf and talk baby talk to him. He'd come up to me and remember me. He will always know you if you do that. I could say some of those baby-talk words I said to him as a calf and he would remember them.

The river used to get low enough so you could just walk across it with shoes on. It happened soon after all those fish were found dead. Now it never goes down very much.

"In that bottom, I was raised up huntin' all kinds of animals. I could look at an eye with a spotlight and tell you what it was. I know a deer eye from any other kind of eye."

Quinn Love

The old river makes a bend way back in there. It is a good area for squirrels. There used to be coons down in there almost as big as I am. Papa killed a many a coon was bigger than I was as a kid. There was game here all year around. There never was no law down here because nobody ever killed over a mess of game. A rabbit was the best meal they had.

The river bottom was real important to people. It had plenty of trees and wood in it and plenty of pecans. There were sweet gum trees and lots of other ones. We ate a lot of tree berries also. They were sweet when we couldn't have candy.

There was a lot of huntin' there. I gets a lot of joy out of huntin'. I like bein' by myself. I begged Mama not to sell it all, but they did it anyway. As a boy, I didn't have no playmates, just once in a way. Sol, A. V., and Booker T. were my friends.

Snakes came in here with the flood in 1913. They were everywhere, even on the animals' backs. I had an uncle got drownded in a quicksand bed on the back of Weathers' land. His name was Taylor Avery.

Victoria used to be a day's travel there and a day's travel back in a horse and wagon, so we socialized around here. Cities, to my mind, are out of plumb. They are not run like they used to be. That's why I came back. You can live a certain way down here that you can't in the city.

Herd of O'Connor cattle in the river bottom.

I knew Will Upton. He and Adeline married while I was here. I knew Lonze Edwards. I tried to marry one of his daughters. I knew Nettie and wanted to marry her. Bud Lias [Elias Jackson] was another one of the old-timers.

Joe Guadalupe was a pasture rider around here. They were friendly people, those pasture riders. They stopped and talked to you and gave you an idea where game wardens were. They fixed things as they went along. I thought they was great men. For them, a bull didn't get too bad and a cow didn't get too wild. They were real cowboys. Sometimes there would be a herd three miles long comin' by here.

They were carryin' 'em to Fort Worth.

Animal buyers and sellers would come around this country and deal animals. The market used to send a man out every weekend. He was steady buyin' meat. He'd cut that meat up and put it in a wagon and put cloth all around it like a mosquito bar.

Food kept back then. It didn't spoil. The feed they feed now has too much water and fertilizer in it. It makes animals grow ahead of themselves and it won't keep. It's the fault of the food they feed the animals. We made jerky and it kept forever.

The trouble with a lot of folks is they don't pay attention in the woods and outdoors. I have done pretty good out in the woods. I have seen a whole lot of stuff. You have to watch every little tree. Sometimes I just sit down and watch squirrels.

A lot of times a fella don't want to be bothered with nobody. You just want to go off and think in the woods. You go away back in there.

I once had a place back in there where a tree was cut off. It looked like a chair, and I would just go and sit on it and wait. I just go back there and look around. I learned a lot from that. I learned that the quieter you are, the more game you would get. Mostly I liked to travel by myself.

There are a lot of wild hogs down here now, but there didn't used to be. They are steady comin' from the ranches. Tame hogs get out and go wild.

I was pretty busy and that kept me from gettin' lonesome. I stayed out here two years one time and I didn't receive one penny. That was after Mama died when I moved down here. Everyone thought I wasn't goin' to make it, but I did.

If you keep busy doin' somethin', everythin' will be alright. Some people are so jealous-hearted, they don't want you to do well. Some are jealous-hearted if you get ahead of them.

I take anythin' comes along as long as it is eatable. Coons, squirrels, and rabbits are my favorite. I have killed coons in the daytime. I find their nests and wait them out. I noticed how the nest was, real heavy, and shot into it. I was afraid it might be a snake, but it was a coon. He fell right in my lap.

For squirrels I look for cut-up green stuff and seeds. I watch them and find out how they act in the woods. They will go where wild fruit is. Rabbits, you surprise them. If one jumps up, you whistle and he will sit down like a dog.

A .22 is the best gun if you use blunt-nose hollow points. I've done pretty good for myself. I fished, hunted, and looked for bullfrogs. To catch a bullfrog, you walk slowly by a pond, and he will look at you. Shoot him in the head and don't touch him. Bring him to the bank quick, or he'll go to the bottom.

I've hunted snakes. I didn't eat them, I only killed them. One time a snake was fourteen years old and I killed him. I knew it was a snake-infested place. You gotta look close. Take your time and walk slowly. I got him. He stayed there until the buzzards ate him up.

I killed a goose with a long shot. He was the first one I ever killed. He got way high and circled. He lit in a small pond. He looked up and craned his neck and I took a shot at him and turned him a flip. He sure was good eatin'.

I eat lots of plants. Whenever high water come, right down in that muddy part is a plant has a lot of iron in it. You boil 'em and pour the first water off and eat 'em like greens. It has lots of iron. They have it domesticated now in house gardens. They call it Swiss chard and Japanese kohlrabi.

There was a lot of stuff out on the prairie, too. There was camomile for typhoid and malaria. You made a tea and bathed in it and then you drank some that you reserved. It would knock that fever out.

Animals are kind of like people. You have to have long patience with them. You got to be very gentle with them. People don't understand all this, especially if they are from the city. People who grow up in the city all their lives are half ignorant. They don't know nothin'. They don't pay attention to what is goin' on around them. In the country, your lifeline depends on it a whole lot. All the country people know there's food and medicine out there, but you got to know what you are doin'. You can get killed in the country just like you can in the city.

I had a little old Airdale dog one time. An armadillo came up one night late when I was asleep. I heard her growlin' and having a conversation with that 'dillo. The dog was crazy about armadillo shells for some reason. The armadillo was after him for killin' too many of his people.

He told him too many of his people had died. All the hides that were skinned around this house must have been the dog's fault. The dog was so scared, she couldn't move. I had to run the 'dillo off from there. Eventually, I had to kill that armadillo before my dog was scared to death.

A dog and a cow will talk to each other. If you notice them real close, you can understand them. A dog will bark a certain bark when somethin' ain't just right. He will die tryin' to protect you if you are good to him.

Clearing the fields on the Traylor ranch near Bloomington—this takes "long patience."

Animals talk to each other. They know if you say somethin' about them. Different animals will talk to one another, too. Animals will talk to another among themselves just like people do. If they are havin' a conversation about you, they will look at you.

When you hear coyotes howlin' out there at night, they are talkin' about eatin'. That's all they got to talk about. I run up on one, I was real close. He was so busy he didn't hear me. I thought he was a dog at first. Eventually, he looked around and saw I was a man, and I don't know where that coyote went. He moved fast.

One time I went down to the pecan grove. I was goin' to get me a deer that day. There were vines you could lay down in. When that deer come out, he moved so fast I couldn't get him. Animals know when it is huntin' season. They recognize guns and they just have a feelin'. Squirrels will go to town when the season comes. Don't think they don't know a gun.

I have almost stepped on a snake before, and when he saw the gun, he started wigglin' sideways until he was out of my sight. I just had to watch that. I let the snake go so I could watch what he did. He was there for a fight, but when I picked up that gun, he moved. A cat will make a snake move. If a cat gets a chance, that snake is his.

Animals will warn each other. Just like that wren I told you about that pimped off on anyone in the woods that might kill them. He makes a funny noise, and the other animals move. They obey one another. Anytime you go out in the woods, you will see one.

I had lots of kinfolks up in Lewis's Bend. The Tillmans are kin to me. Lewis's Bend was as important as the San'tone River was to me. There were trees, woods, and a whole lotta people livin' here and there. They put clean clothes on to go to church. The trees are what made it Lewis's Bend.

There used to be a dance down there about every weekend. Different ones will have a dance. Back then, your neighbor would look out for you and your place. It was better in the old days. The children were watched by all. You had to walk the chalk line then. It was better for everybody. This loose society will get us someday.

I remember Old Man I. H. Weathers. He had a car, but he couldn't drive it, so I drove for him sometimes. I sang in the church sometimes, too. He was so tall. He would come to your house early in the mornin' on Old Cora. He'd holler, "Got any coffee?" He'd talk and talk and talk.

I lived back in my part of the river. It was important to me because I knew every spot where you could kill somethin' for food. There were spots where you never would kill anythin'.

You should eat what you crave and you will be healthy. If you pay attention to your body, it will tell you exactly what it needs.

Don't never let an animal smell you. Always stay upwind. If an animal smells you, he is very wise to that and he will move. An injured animal would rather die in the open and let another animal get him than a human. I guess that's because they are wild. I have never really understood that.

Animals will make different noises when certain animals are around. When a dog trees an animal, there is a special way he will bark. If he runs up on a snake, he will use a keen voice. If it is a rabbit, he will make a runnin' voice. If you know a dog, you can tell. If a dog trees somethin', you better get up and see about it, or you will ruin him.

The minute you find out you are lost, sit down and let things come to you. Hear a sound and listen to where it's comin' from and go to that sound. You never know a sound until you get up on it. It isn't scary if you know what to do. One animal will use another animal's call, so you got to be knowledgeable.

We were told to stay away from the bank of that river. It was treacherous in some places. There were sinkholes all along the way. We could have drownded in them. The scariest night I ever had was with a panther. That was much scarier than the river.

Some of the problem around here is that the old-timers didn't teach the young ones what they knew about nature—how to catch fish and all that. They used to know how to make buffalo bait, and they would come home with a buffalo fish as big as an elephant. Nobody knows how they knew what to do.

Horses are pretty smart. They're smarter than cattle. Their nickerin' is talkin'. They talk a little tune. I've never been close enough to them to learn what they talk about. Cows like to eat.

Horses and cows like each other to a certain extent. A horse knows where to bite a cow, and a cow knows how to stay out of their way. You can train a horse and he will be company to you. Cattle won't do that.

A fella who lives in the country knows what he eats and what he don't eat. When he gets on the ranch, he raises his own food and he has enough to give to others.

Oil changed things a lot. Long years ago, if anyone killed a hog, you got a piece. Now they give them vinegar [wine] so they won't squeal, and nobody will know, and you don't have to give any away. That ain't the way it used to be.

Settle your mind down and do what you gotta do, and do just that. I've had a rough go for it. I sleep anywhere I feel. The oyster is my birthmark. I'm supposed to eat all the oysters I can. I was a water man growin' up. I liked water. Dreamin' comes accordin' to what you do and what you want to do. Pay attention to your dreams. Dreams can tell you how to accomplish that.

I don't have much of a dream. I just wanted to get my house like I want it, and I'd be satisfied, and that's what I'm workin' on now.

Henry Charleston

Tom O'Connor (II, third from right) and a group of friends sport fishing on Mission Bay.

CHAPTER SEVEN

The Darker Side

"There are a lot of mysteries along that river. Probably years ago when they first came, there was a lot of stuff going on."

Víctor Rodríguez

It's all too easy to present only the good side of a place, as if it were all a utopia. This river bottom, in spite of its beauty and friendly nature, harbored people who committed ugly deeds and engaged in unlawful activities. I have spent much time interviewing people who knew the story of its darker side.

Feuds and Killin's

Along the San Antonio River, there have been occasional outbursts of feuding over the decades. Some of these prolonged quarrels ended in violence. Many of these darker deeds have become incorporated into the folklore of the San Antonio River culture. These stories flesh out our understanding of this culture and add to the colorful tapestry it truly is.

Gamblin'. Frank, Floyd, and Marcellus Talman and J. W. Farley.

The Shorter-Cook Feud

"This river bottom was outlaw."

Beverly Barber Fletcher

One time they had a big dance up there on the Duke Ranch. It was at one of them houses that folks was livin' in out there. There were houses all over out there.

Old Man Henry Shorter, he was out there gamblin'. They would get cotton sacks or anything and spread them on the ground, one here and one over yonder. They were playin' poker, dice, and what not.

Henry's nephew, Timmy, got shot out there while Henry was out there gamblin' and someone came up and told him that had happened. He went over to where his nephew was and asked him who had shot him. Timmy was layin' on the ground and when Henry asked him that, he said, "Cook." But he didn't say which Cook. He couldn't get it out because he was dyin'.

Then Henry asked Timmy if he had a gun and Timmy said he did, but that it only had two shells in it. Henry said, "That's okay, I don't need but one." He rolled Timmy over and got that gun. He walked on off over to the house and met this boy comin' around the house. He asked him what his name was and the boy said, "Cook. I'm Old Man Jim Cook's boy."

So Henry said, "Where's your gun?" He said, "I ain't got no gun, haven't had one all evenin'." Henry said, "You shudda had one." Pow! He shot him before he could get the information from the boy. He shot that boy down. That boy was only about nineteen, he was young. Poor Cook ran all the way around the house back to where he was shot and fell dead. That boy was not the one who did the shootin'.

The Cook family. Ananias Cook is second from right, front.

Henry went and got a horse. This is where Wilson Lott come in. Someone say, "Hey, Will." Now, Wilson talked gruffer than Toney [Lott]. They say, "Someone got your horse." Wilson say, "He can have that sorry old horse if he want it. I'm not gonna run up on Shorter in the dark."

Henry rode on to Goliad and woke up some fella there and got himself a quart of whiskey. Henry was sittin' on the step when the jailer came. The jailer say, "Shorter, what you doing here?" Henry said, "Well, I kilt a man last night." "You did?" Say, "Yeah." So the jailer said, "What are you doin' sittin' out here?" Henry said, "I was just sittin' here waitin' for you to lock me up." "I'll have to take your whiskey." "Well, let me get another drink out of it." Henry got another drink out of that bottle and they took him on off to jail and locked him up. So they had court, and they gave him sixty years.

Mr. Will O'Connor said, "Henry, we gotta fight it some more." Shorter say, "Oh, don't bother with it, let it go." They did fight it some more and they got it down to seven years. Mr. Will say, "We gonna fight it again." Shorter say, "Don't fight it, don't fight it, don't fight it. Let it go and don't fight it."

Now, Mr. Will told him that seven years was a long time, but he went to the pen. After he got out, he used to tell us that all you had in the pen was that shirttail and a pair of pants. He had one mule, a walkin' plow, and one line to the mule. He'd tell it and I'd listen to that old man talk about it. I would say to myself I never wanted to go to that place.

I'd say, "How about when it was cold, Mr. Shorter? Did they give you a coat?" He say, "No, you had the same thing summer and winter. That's all you had." He stayed the full seven years and when he came back, he came to Refugio and he said they gave him a seven-dollar suit when he got out of the pen. He said it looked like the suit had been slept in about forty years.

They say he walked down the street there and the first person saw him say, "Well, I'll be dawg, here's old Henry Shorter." That was Bob Bunton [also Bunting] said that. Then someone else saw him and said, "There old Henry Shorter, he kilt my uncle." Henry said, "Yeah, if there's anymore Cooks that want to stir something up, let 'em come on." He didn't know if Mr. Shorter had a gun or not.

The Cooks just cleared out of there after that.

Reverend Mack Williams

I knew a man named Henry Shorter. He was always talkin' about the murders they had out on the prairie. I don't remember who killed who, it was such a long time ago. I used to hear Willie and them talk. There were dances out on the prairie, too. It seemed like they would last for two days. One time they got to shootin' and this man got killed. There were people runnin' everywhere. Mr. Will Sample got on his horse and tried to run away, but his horse was still tied. There was stuff goin' on out on that prairie, too.

Althia Lewis Burns Franklin

The Terrell-Boyd Feud

Mr. Terrell didn't like Boyd after Hennon Carlos [or Collins] killed that black boy. Hennon Carlos killed this man that was farmin' this land that Mr. Terrell give Grandpa. Boyd's hogs were goin' over the fence into the fields and eatin' the corn. Him and Carlos claimed that this man was siccin' the dogs on Boyd's hogs. Of course, I don't think that Mr. Boyd's words, well, it could be true, I don't think he really meant for him to go kill him. I think it was just an old sayin'. Him and Carlos were workin' for Mr. Boyd, hangin' around there. Boyd just said to Carlos, "Kill the so-and-so."

That's the way it was. He went down and caught this man on Hall's Point

Road, comin' down toward the O'Connor ranch. He just rode up and shot him. Had a little boy in the wagon, and they say that the mule ran off with the wagon and throwed the little boy out and turned it over. Terrell had a house up there on the hill just before you get to Boyd. The people in that house seen the mule lyin' off and turned the wagon over. They went down and got the child.

Simmie Rydolph

The Fagan Cemetery Incident

The O'Connor family used to use the same cemetery as the Fagans, their relatives. Mary Fagan O'Connor was buried in the Fagan cemetery as she had died quite young. She was the wife of Tom O'Connor [I] and had several children by him before her death.

When one of these children, James, died, Tom O'Connor took him to the Fagan cemetery to be buried. Legend has it that O'Connor and the second-generation Fagan boys were feuding over a woman.

When Tom O'Connor arrived at the cemetery to bury his son, the Fagans were sitting in the grave with guns on their knees and refused to allow the burial. Mad, Tom O'Connor went back to his ranch with his son's body and buried him under some huge oak trees. He then brought Mary Fagan's body back to the ranch and buried it nearby.

This was the beginning of the O'Connor cemetery.

Osee "O. C." Matthews

Mausoleum, Fagan cemetery.

The Drake-Martin Feud

There were some feuds down here, too. There was one in Raisin one time between Taylor Drake and Monroe Martin. Martin shot Drake—the Drake and Martin shoot-out. It was in the early twenties. Rosie Willemin's brother saw it. It happened on a Sunday. It was upstairs, and mother made us get out. It started with hogs.

Miss Monroe's daddy and Drake were neighbors. Whenever Drake's hog got out, Mr. Martin would herd them back home. When the conflict started, it was over Mr. Martin's turkeys. His turkeys went into Drake's yard, and Drake and his brother-in-law were liquored up and they just target-practiced on them and killed all the turkeys. Mr. Martin came over and complained, and they caught him and beat him until he was nearly dead. He never got over it. He finally died from the beatin' he got.

The young Martin boy was only twelve, maybe fourteen at the time. The boy was an only child, and it put the burden of taking care of his mother and the place

*"There were spooky things goin'
on all the time. I have had a
many scare in my time. Bein' out
on these ranches by yourself can
be scary."*

Reverend Mack Williams

on him. He swore he'd kill Taylor Drake for what he did. It took a few years before
he could accomplish his deed. Anyway, when the time came, he got hold of a
German Luger pistol and rode over to Drake's place. Why, he just called him by
name, "Mr. Drake." When he looked around, he just blowed him away.

**Charley Adams, Constance Kohl Roell, Victor Heibel, Rosie Hornstein Willemin,
Orville Gaugler, Martin Huber**

The Anton Beck Murder

Does anyone know Anton Beck? Well, there was a mystery about that—whether he
took his own life or somebody shot him. They never did find out. That was way
back yonder and they kind of suspected who did it, but they couldn't say it. It was
back over in the [Reeves] Thicket somewhere back in the thirties. They said he went
off to shoot some birds or something early in the morning and they found him dead
out there. Don't know whether he took his own life or what. Nobody knows.

Rosie Hornstein Willemin, Constance Kohl Roell

Once there was a feud down in the bottom between the McFaddin ranch and a squatter.
Those squatters were surrounded by the big ranch and couldn't get in or out because
they could not cross someone else's land because they couldn't get permission. One of
the squatters was afraid they would all die of starvation, so he sent his daughter to
Anaqua with my father. Her name was Miss Pearlie and she was tall and slender.
Unhappy occurrences like that could have left a mystery down there.

Reverend Mack Williams

The Legend of Amos Green

I stayed with Juan García the night he got killed. They were stealin' pecans from
Amos Green. Juan was a bad Meskin. Everyone had a part of the bottom for the
pecans. Amos gambled all the time. That Sunday mornin' when he went down into
the bottom to pick some pecans, somebody had already gotten them, like they had
been doin' for a while.

Juan García had a man up a tree beatin' down pecans and he was still in the tree.
Amos rode down that mornin' and Juan was sittin' there with a Winchester under his
leg and a .45, too. He didn't think Amos had a gun, but he did.

García was mean and tough and he told him someone had been stealin' his
pecans. García said, "Don't you like it?" Amos said he didn't. So then García said
he would take his Winchester and whip his brains out.

Amos told him he thought he was a damned liar. Amos said he let him get
that gun almost out of that scabbard, then he come out with that .45. García said
to wait a minute, but Amos said it was too late. He shot him five times. The man
in the tree begged him so hard not to shoot him that he left him there and rode
back and went on to Goliad and give up.

The next Meskin he killed up there was gamblin' and he went to the peniten-

L. V. Terrell and Little Biscuit.

tiary for fifteen years. Five others had him clear to the ground, but he never would turn that pistol loose. He had a scar on his head 'til he died. Milam's cousin, Lanch Robinson, was the only one would help him when they had him down.

Lanch was tryin' to keep another man off of Amos. The man had a dirk. He broke and ran and when he came by the tree, Amos took a shot at him. He hid behind a tree. Amos was in an old Model T with a pistol under his leg. Amos hit him in the arm, and then he broke and run.

Some of them told him to let him go. He ran through those bloodweeds and wolfweeds until he got another shot at him. He shot and broke his neck and then walked up to him and shot him again.

When he came back to the car, Lanch told him he should have let him go 'cause he was a coward. Amos said, "Then that's one less I have to look out for."

He went to the penitentiary. Doc Haynes was the high sheriff in Goliad. Amos always wore boots. It was kind of wet and there were tracks from the gun to the dead man. He could have let him go but he didn't. This one he killed was a first cousin to the first one he killed, Juan García.

In court, Lanch didn't want to go against Uncle Amos, but he didn't want to lie. They asked him if the man was runnin' when Amos shot him. Lanch said, "No sir, he wasn't exactly runnin', he was halfway trottin'."

The judge would ask him why he couldn't remember anything. Norvell Brown kept tellin' him to tell the truth, but Lanch couldn't remember anything.

When Amos came from the penitentiary, we was out at my sister Violet's place to get some turkeys. It was close to Thanksgivin'. The Garcías hadn't seen him since he went off. He was only gone for eight or nine years. We met him goin' through the Murphy bottom. Uncle Amos would have shot if they gave him any trouble, but they just kept on goin'.

Amos rode backwards all the way out of the bottom.

L. V. Terrell

There were killin's and bootleggers in the bottom. Everybody carried pistols with them. Amos Green killed Juan García over pecans, and Ripley Terrell was everywhere down here with his carryin's on. Tom Dinkey was a bootlegger. He was a white man.

Amos Green was a murderer. He killed two men. I went to the courthouse because my father was a witness.

The first time he killed, was a young boy down by Duke's Bridge. It was a Sunday and they were gamblin'. Amos Green was drunk. The boy ran for the woods and Amos followed him and killed him.

Then he killed Juan García. It was about some pecans. Others say it was about a woman. Who knows? He didn't believe Amos would kill him, but he shot him right off his horse. That's what witnesses say.

Jesús Ybarbo

Just a Good Hand

I met Amos Green one time and decided he would be a good hand. I brought him over to the ranch with his family and put him to work.

Archie Summer was a good friend of mine and we visited with each other about a month later. Archie knew Amos Green well and knew he had killed several men.

Archie asked when I had hired Amos, and I told him about a month ago. He was such a good hand. Archie asked me if I knew what I had here, and I said again that he was just a good hand I had hired.

Archie told me he had killed a lot of men. I didn't know what to do then. I was scared to fire him because I was afraid he would kill me. I let him stay as long as he wanted to.

Earl Ward

Etta Wilkinson Terrell, mother of Ripley Terrell.

"Ripley Terrell was an outlaw. He went around shooting everybody until somebody killed him!"

Louise Murphy

Ripley's Believe It or Not

There were many characters in the river bottom, but none more feared or famous than Ripley Terrell. He was the only surviving child of Crogan and Etta Terrell, who had a ranch on the San Antonio River. His father was much older than his mother and seemed to have been unable to raise Ripley with a strong enough hand. When his father died, Ripley continued his reign of terror on his mother as well as the entire region—and at times beyond.

I grew up with tales of Ripley Terrell, the wild man of the river bottom. From my earliest recollection, any time we were disobedient or acting like spoiled brats, we would be warned that we would "end up like Rip" if we didn't behave. Although he died an unscheduled and violent death, Ripley lived long enough to create a legend, and one in his own time, at that.

One wonders what the problem was. In today's world, he would probably be on Death Row, telling a sob story of some kind as an excuse for his behavior. His epitaph was written by the people who knew him: "He was a mean drunk but basically he was a good old boy at heart."

The Terrells

They came from North Carolina. They arrived here as doctors, but they didn't leave the North Carolina area as doctors.

Timothy Terrell was born in 1782 in North Carolina. His first wife died, then he was married in 1811 in North Carolina to Temperance Barnes, who was born in 1793. Both of them died in Victoria County sometime between 1860 and 1870.

Their daughter was Frances Jane Terrell, who married Barnes Simms. Crogan Ludlow Terrell was their son. He came to Texas in 1846 and was later a Confederate veteran. He married Lauretta Wilkinson of Berclair. Their son was Ripley Ludlow Terrell. They had a daughter who died in infancy.

Rip was separated from his wife and she was with another man. He had two

German shepherds that she took away from him in the divorce just to aggravate him. She shot them and then shot up the house. Highway patrolmen guarded Ripley's grave after the funeral because his ex-wife said she would desecrate his grave.

The man that shot Ripley was the man she was with. That night, he went to a whorehouse and it was closed, so he bought it. Later, he went in on her, and the man shot him dead.

Ripley was spoiled rotten and had everything. Etta, his mother, couldn't control him and neither could his wives.

Texana Matthews once said that she was having a party when she was about fifteen years old. Ripley wanted to come. He didn't have any friends. He was killed at thirty-one.

Etta moved to Berclair when Crogan died. She built a house costing $150,000 dollars in 1937. The chairs belonged to Napoleon, and there were intercoms in every room. She built it when she was old. She wanted a house that wouldn't burn down.

The story goes that Crogan Terrell had to put $10,000 in the bank before Wilkinson would let his daughter, Lauretta, marry him. Crogan met her on the train coming from Berclair. Crogan was a man of good birth and social standing. The Terrells were the ones with the money. She was a big, beautiful blonde at this time.

*Terrell residence,
Berclair.*

When the Wilkinsons arrived for the wedding, the money was in a black box and was presented to Bill Mason to inspect. He was the justice of the peace in Goliad. The money was there, so she kissed him and they got married. Ripley was born a year later.

Etta Wilkinson was born at Saluria on Matagorda Island, the daughter of Robert P. Wilkinson of England and Mary Brown of Indiana.

Lois Farley Jaillet

Armour Fagan.

I was born in 1910. I am related to the Terrells by marriage. Crogan Terrell married Etta Wilkinson, who was my mother's sister. I have no idea where the Terrell land came from, no idea at all.

I think they come from Tennessee or Kentucky. They brought some slaves with them when they came to Texas.

I spent no time at all on the ranch. All during my childhood, it was leased by the Welders. I do know there was a community of blacks down there. The only one I knew was Uncle Bill Terrell.

"Ripley the Terror" was the son of Crogan and Etta Wilkinson Terrell. He was killed in some kind of a scrape. I made a real mistake of not listenin' to my grandmother when I was a kid.

Uncle Bill Terrell once told me there was once kind of a feud with the Fagans. Every time Mr. Terrell rode over there, he would have a gun on his saddle. I don't know if it's true or not.

I can remember hearing that the river overflowed and that church down in the bottom was moved up on the hill. Then they tore it down and moved it away from there. The whole place kind of died after that '42 storm. They just left there. I don't think anybody's living there anymore. The last of those people I knew of was Luck [Terrell]. He worked for Armour Fagan.

That old [Victoria] Terrell house is haunted by Ripley, Crogan's brother. Bill [Terrell] would be down there and it was coming up a storm. He went in the house and went upstairs to close all the shutters and windows up there. When he came down, he said he met Mr. Ripley coming upstairs and he had his little candle. Bill said he said, "How you, Mr. Terrell?" Mr. Terrell said, "Just fine, Bill. How are you?"

Mr. Terrell was long dead when Uncle Bill saw him. Every time he would see you, he would tell stories about the river. Somebody with a long-tailed coat and no head and things like that. He could give you some stories. Uncle Bill was the only one ever told me any stories and I didn't see him very often.

"Oh, he was terrible! I can remember when I was just ten or twelve years old, and somebody would say, 'Here comes Ripley Terrell!' Everybody would run."

Zilpah Daniel Edwards

That house was torn up in the '42 storm and I finished tearing it down. That was the house where Etta and Crogan lived. Etta went to college in Goliad. Used to be a college there.

James K. "Spec" New

The Terrells had two children, a son and a daughter. Their daughter died when she was a young child. She and Mr. Terrell was buried in a small cemetery on the Terrell ranch. Their son died in 1928 in San Antonio. Ripley would take

William Terrell, who was called Billy, with him in his mother's limousine. Rip would insist "his Billy" go into all the restaurants with him. Bill would be frightened almost to death, but Ripley would dare anybody to say anything about it. Most people was afraid of Mr. Ripley Terrell because he carried guns in his car and kept one handy and people knew he wouldn't hesitate in usin' them if anyone bothered him.

Lee Anna Terrell Young

Ripley Terrell.

Who wouldn't remember that boy Ripley? He was the Terrells' only son. He lived fast and he went out fast. He was something else. He shot his mother one time. It hit her corset stay and didn't kill her. He liked to gamble and he drove a car so fast, you better get out of the way. He gambled in Woodsboro. You wouldn't think he came from good people. He was the only child that lived, and he was born with a bolt loose. Nobody could do nothin' with him but my uncle, Simon House. He would mind him.

One time durin' huntin' season, me and Bill O'Riley were huntin' for fur. We were young men then, both ridin' the same horse. Bill was behind me. We started into the bottom and we heard somethin'. We went to see what it was and we liked to got shot.

Ripley was there with [Tom] Dinkins [or Dinkey]. Dinkins kept his still down on the Terrell place called the Black Jacks. He was ready to shoot, but Dinkins wouldn't let him. He thought we was the law or somethin'. He would shoot people just for fun. He didn't care about nothin'. Now, that's the truth.

We stuck with them down there for a while. We were real lucky. Mr. Dinkins told me later Ripley was about that close to shootin' me and Billy. They knew my father since they were small. My father taught Ripley how to ride a horse. He worked for Old Man Terrell.

Ripley and Alex Tom were good friends of my father. My father stopped Ripley from killin' several people. One time my father stopped him from shootin' up a colored gathering.

He drank a lot and drove fast. He couldn't keep a wife. I don't know why he kept on marryin'. Ripley was spoiled.

He shows that you should treat an only child like you had five or six. Being an only is what done that. Old Man Terrell shouldn't have married that much younger woman.

Jesús Ybarbo

"Wild Ripley"

Ripley Terrell was bad medicine. He hit a colored boy in the head with a bat. That was his first one. He killed all together four men, and then he was killed in San Antonio kicking in a door to some woman's room.

Old Man Terrell was the first one to own an automobile. Ripley just hitched his horses to the car and rode around that way. His daddy was bald-headed and he used to have to sit still and let Ripley eat breakfast off his head. Now, that's the God's truth. My father saw that.

He used to steal peaches from us all the time. Nobody ever tried to stop him from doing anything. He even put his car on the railroad track and drove all the way to Refugio. He killed an old Mexican man. He was always called that "Wild Ripley kid."

Elizabeth Sevier Haney

"Etta lived on the ranch the whole time she was married to Crogan. When he died, she moved to Berclair and built that big house. She left her husband, Baby Terrell that died, and Ripley, Crogan's brother, buried on the property. I think 'Ripley the Terror' is buried in Berclair. Don't really know."

James K. "Spec" New

He could shoot quail with a handgun. He was okay in a way. He was good-hearted, generous, mean, crazy, drunk, bad-tempered, and a killer and a lawbreaker, but he was an alright boy in his way. When he got killed in San Antonio, they brought him home on a train. He was shot in the back by someone this woman hired. She was scared of him.

Monroe "Bailey" Shaw

Ripley Terrell was a good man until he started drinkin'. Then he was a rough character. His mother raised him all by herself and let him have his way all his growin'- up time. He'd shoot out the lights in her house. He drove a big convertible. His mother would run and hide from him and go to her uncle's house up the road. The uncle was the only one could handle him when he got on one of his drunks.

They tell me when he was ten, they got a schoolteacher to the house for him. He took a .22 to the teacher and shot him in the hip. Old Man Terrell was cleanin' the chimbley one time and Ripley tried to shoot him down.

We had double gates all down in this country and he never opened them—he just drove through. Willie Terrell drove him all the time in a Packard. He carried him down to Corpus on those narrow roads. Someone side-swiped them, and Ripley got out to see how much damage was done. Ripley started shootin' and he kilt him.

He kilt another Spanish fella down at the McFaddin store. He was rough, but there wasn't nobody you could find no better than Ripley Terrell was. But he'd get to drinkin' and he'd go crazy.

Any time he was going to Houston through Victoria, he'd be doin' ninety miles an hour. They arrested him one time and he paid the sheriff double. The sheriff asked him what the double money was for and Ripley replied, "'Cause I'm comin' back through this S.O.B. just like I went through it this time, and I don't want to have to stop and pay a fine. You're already paid."

He got shot in a whorehouse in San Antonio and got kilt. He had fourteen holes in him when he died, and he kilt several men before they got him. Something about his ex-wife and some big dogs she was with. The house was full of holes from the shootin'.

He was a little fella, but he sho' was mean.

Rafael De La Garza

Rafael de la Garza Sr., 18 years old, ca. 1906.

Ripley wasn't in the outlaw movies, but he should have been. He was Bonnie and Clyde all rolled into one. His name wasn't in the paper much, but he was bad. One

"Rip Terrell's car was the first one I ever saw. When you saw him comin', you better get out of the way."

Lela Edwards Williams

"That rascal sure could shoot."

Simmie Rydolph

Clarence Thurman "T" Terrell.

time, he was comin' from Corpus and had his overhauls on. He hit a Mexican boy and they put him in jail. They thought he was a po'boy.

J. Y. Lott

Damn, he scared me one night. I was comin' home one Saturday night durin' the time Alex Tom was runnin' wild. He and Rip ran together. It was a full moon and I was trottin' down the road on an old dun horse and saw a car near the ditch. There was two men lookin' into the ditch.

Old Rip had his pistol out and throwed it down on me. Said, "Halt, hold up, you didn't pick my hat up down the road, did you?" Rip put his pistol back in his britches and kept lookin' for his hat.

Alex Tom had been in the Spanish-American War. He had been on San Juan Hill, too. He and his brother owned a little place. Alex was one of those fellas had been through all of it and been in the pen. One time, he and Rip got drunk in Victoria and lined everyone up they could find and made them march military style. They was down by the depot, and they took shots at one or two of their prisoners. All the sheriffs and police came out there.

The law sacked the whole thing up and sent Alex back to prison. Of course, Rip got out of it. They were all good men sober, but drunk, they was gonna whip somebody. I'm tellin' you, we had some real characters in Refugio and Victoria. Durin' World War I, Rip would come down to the bridge where they kept an army guard and get him drunk. Always doin' things like that.

This escapade with Alex Tom cost Old Lady Terrell eight thousand acres of land to get him out of it.

Herbert "Buster" Bickford

That was a tough man. He would sit up in his window with his gun. That's the way Ripley lived. He didn't care. He was spoiled and he had a dog named Ace.

My daddy, Bill Terrell, was the only person ever whupped him. Old Man Crogan Terrell couldn't hear good, so he told my daddy to whup him if he needed it.

Rip was tough. He once beat up a man named Hunt who was a desperado. Later, Hunt was in an attic loft in a brothel in San Antonio. Hunt was runnin' and he shot Ripley's fingers off, then he shot him in the stomach. Rip was so tough, he wouldn't die. They trailed him to the hospital in San Antonio by the blood. He died in the hospital.

He was only thirty-two and had killed three men. Miss Etta was about to turn the ranch over to him, but he died. Rip was also goin' to fix up Bill Terrell 'cause he was crazy about him. He promised he was goin' to give him the Black Jacks to raise hogs. Daddy was a great hog man. Ripley was killed before he could give the land to Daddy.

Thurman Terrell

What do you call this "Doc" that walked to town all the time and gave out papers? "Doc" Campbell, that was his name. He put his hat on one way all the time. Ripley

Terrell picked him up one time on the road. He was walking right over by Reeves Thicket where the sand's real heavy. He got in the car with Ripley. We had no highway at that time. After a while, he just throwed his hat up and said, "You just go on. I'll walk." He wouldn't ride with him, got scared. Ripley was drivin' so fast in that sand, he threw his hat off.

He used to come to Fannin to the saloon all the time. Fannin used to be good. Two saloons and everything. He had this old Studebaker with the top down on it. Why, he'd come down that road. Somebody had a load of cotton or something, wouldn't give him the road, he'd just take one wheel off the wagon.

There are some terrible stories on Ripley. He killed people. I can remember one time he had a tutor, shot her. He shot her and went upstairs and shot himself in the mirror and wound up shootin' out all the mirrors.

Old Rip was with Nott Hanley one time and he went on up to Goliad. Nott said, "You know," said, "wasn't nothin' but the windshield up there. Couldn't see the telephone posts. It looked like picket fences." He called my brother, say, "Poodle, stuck my head out behind that windshield." Said, "I like to lost my head. Couldn't get it back in, the wind was blowin' so hard." That was the funniest thing.

Henry "Blue" Albrecht

"Legend has it that Crogan Terrell had to give Etta ten thousand dollars to marry him. She accumulated a lot of money in time. Some of it she got by skinnin' cattle right along with the old man after freezes. She was awful tough."

Ralph Bego
Henry "Blue" Albrecht

"Yeah, but he had the prettiest handwritin'."

Ralph Bego

Ripley would shoot down through the ceiling of the house to where his mother lived. Even the law would hide when Ripley came through. They didn't want no part of him. He was rich. He drove those big, fine, pretty cars with the wire wheels on the side. When he came to town, you knew he was comin'. There was dust flyin' everywhere. He killed a guy in St. Louis, but his mother bought him off. Then he came back here and kept on actin' bad.

This highway used to go from the Mission River to Houston Street. It was a wide sandy road. He come around that curve and the dust would be flyin'. Everyone was yellin'. He just went right on through here.

"He frequented the whorehouses and gambled a lot. He might stay for three or four days. He had women cryin' all over the place. He was a small man with dark brown hair, blue eyes, slender, about five foot eight."

Seward Richardson

They claim he shot his tutor in the leg one time. He almost killed his father another time. The old man got in the car and Rip drove off draggin' him behind. He didn't give him time to get in the car.

Simmie Rydolph, Seward Richardson

Miss Birdie Amery's daddy was old Judge Amery and they lived down by the river at Anaqua. Miss Birdie and Mrs. Terrell were good friends. They both lived close to each other on the San Antonio River Road.

One time, Miss Birdie and some lady friends went to visit Etta Terrell and when they got to the house, all but Miss Birdie hung their hats on the coat tree in the entry. Miss Birdie knew about Ripley and said she knew better than to hang a hat there.

They were in the living room talking and visiting and all of a sudden, they heard this *whap, whap.* Rip was just a little kid and he had come into the house with his blacksnake whip and had cut those hats to ribbons.

He also liked to have killed his mama. She was riding a horse and he hid in the bushes and when she came by, he jumped out and scared the horse. That horse jumped out from under her and bunged her up real bad.

Mother said she would walk to school down the old river lane among the bloodweeds twenty feet high. They would all of a sudden hear this humming and someone would shout, "Get out of the way! Here comes Rip!" She said they would hit the ditch until he went by going as fast as that car would go.

One of Elsie's brothers worked at the bank. His name was Demus Terrell. Ripley liked to have blowed his leg off. He loaded a shotgun with corn and shot him in the leg. He said he didn't know corn would hurt you. I think nowadays somebody would grab him, lock him up, and call him a sociopath. The word wasn't invented then. Everyone thought he was just eccentric, different.

Leroy Taylor Tibiletti

The school in Berclair was just across the street from the Wilkinson house. And when he would come to see his mother, somebody would whisper, "Ripley's here." Well, we'd all be kind of scared. He'd have a big, special-made automobile with a gun rack on it or something and leather upholstery and very fancy stuff.

It sounded to me like he was the poor little rich boy whose mama let him have everything he wanted. There were stories about the Wilkinsons, too. They used to say Mrs. Wilkinson herded sheep around there barefoot.

Ripley killed some Negro on the place, but they didn't do anything about that. Later on, somebody ran him in the ditch or something, and he said, "I have a good mind to kill you," and he did.

His mother and his aunts all lived together in Berclair. They didn't approve of some of his wives, and sometimes that wife would have to sit in the car the whole time he visited.

I guess Mrs. Terrell liked to drive fast, too. She had several people in the car and decided to race. Of course, the roads weren't paved. She was going to race the train and get across it first or something. I don't know if they hit a sandpile or what, but they overturned and the train stopped and picked them up and brought them in.

Ida Jenelle Blackburn Rodgers, Marjorie Albrecht Baecker, Lydia Kern Loest

Poor George

Ripley was living with his mother, and he was coming down the road and he met Andreas, who was half Mexican and half Indian. He knew Andreas loved liquor and so he asked him if he wanted a drink. Andreas just started grinning and he gave him

"Etta once said the best thing ever happened to her was Ripley getting killed, because she worried about him all the time."

James "Rip" Farley

Tom O'Connor Jr. (III).

the bottle and when he started drinking it, Ripley shot him in the leg. Someone finally killed old Rip, but I just thank my heavens alive he never got me.

I can remember my father telling me that he was an only child and a spoiled brat. He would take his pistol and shoot the eyes out of a picture of George Washington his mother had. Then he shot his legs off. It was unbelievable. He must have been a maniac. You know, they talk about things being so bad now. They were just as bad then. There are just more people now. They'd run and hide because they didn't know if he was going to shoot them or not.

Marye Murphy Greer

A Bat Outta Hell

One time Rip was driving along in his father's old Dodge touring car with the old man in the back seat. Old Crogan was well up in age and getting pretty decrepit. Rip was driving like a bat outta hell across the bald open prairie with the old man being thrown all over the back seat. When he arrived back at the house, his mother asked him where his father was, and Ripley's reply was "Hell if I know, Mother. I guess the old son of a bitch fell out." He just got out of the car and walked in the house.

Tom O'Connor Jr. (III)

Left to right: Earnest Landgraf, Pete Marberry, and Martin O'Connor.

River Rats and Monkeys

This river bottom was not a continuum of happy, peaceful souls standing on the river bank and praising the Lord. There were some real characters in residence all along its banks. Bootleggers abounded, and strange people of both sexes occupied territory for many reasons. Often their territory was used for dishonorable or illegal activities. The decent residents of the area knew which people to avoid and where to avoid them. There were many truly dangerous figures up and down the San'tone.

Several of the people I interviewed swore they saw lots of strange animals in the bottom, including monkeys. This is another one of those "who knows? who cares?" situations. They all make great stories. Far be it from me to try to explain or refute the stranger aspects of this unusual and diverse folklore.

"There were some strange animals in the river bottom. I've even seen monkeys down there."

Alfredo Buentello

White Lightnin'

I know Old Man Pete Marberry and Martin O'Connor would get five gallons of whiskey at a time from Old Man Fisher down in the river bottom. It was good whiskey, too. He lived on the north part of the river. It took twelve hours to get him out of those swamps when they caught him.

Old Man Fisher was a character. He had two of his boys rob a train. He told them if they got cold feet, he'd shoot 'em. One of them did, and he shot him in the leg. He finally got twenty years.

You'd honk the horn and he'd come out with the whiskey. We didn't think nothin' about them bootleggers. They were everywhere.

Herbert "Buster" Bickford

Franklin "Bud" Harvey (left) on Big Foot, Sonny Brown, and Pete Brown on Poco Milo, Traylor Ranch, 1945.

It was called rot gut or white lightnin'. Don't throw a match after you drank it or you'd explode. You'd have to throw a keen yell after you drank it. Smoke would blow out your mouth. It would take your breath away. It was nearly gasoline. Most of it came out of East Texas.

They fooled me one time on that stuff. I was goin' to Oklahoma and someone offered me a drink. I had never drunk that stuff before, just real whiskey. I took a drink of that stuff and it seemed like my brains was rattlin'. I got hot and my brain was just jumpin', like it was fixin' to leave outta there. I was crazy all that day. I couldn't take it. It was too much for me. It broke me from drinkin'.

There was an old man came from Oklahoma who was really greedy with his drinkin'. We decided to break him up from it. He got some white lightnin' and took a pull and smoke came out of his mouth. He just fell over tryin' to go home. It was bottled in anything the bootleggers could find.

Doc Hubbard was the old bootlegger around. Old Man Bennett was one, too. Most of them had stills down in the river bottom.

Sonny Brown

One time I was drunk on bootleg wine. Every time I laid down, the bed would come up and meet me. Every time I drank water, I got drunk all over again for a week. That broke me from wine. I was crazy as a lunatic.

Pete Brown

We mostly drank bootleg whiskey and home brew. We didn't have no brands. Somebody in this river bottom was always bootleggin'. Tom Dinkey had a still at the Duke Ranch bottom and one in the West bottom. Joe West used to say that he wouldn't let people go down in his bottom to hunt and fish unless they brought him whiskey. He never did see whiskey get too bad for him to drink.

L. V. Terrell

There were river bosses on all these rivers. They ruled certain parts of the river. People would move on these boats and as long as they were on the water, they were okay. If they moved on the land more than thirty feet, they could be run off. This was goin' on in the thirties. The river fed people and got them through the Depression. It was tough times, but our ranches protected us.

Pete Brown

There were a lot of tiny communities all up and down the San'tone River. There was the Dalton bottom near DuPont. The Linnville boys were bootleggers there. Then there was the Joshua bottom where the Joshuas lived and inside that community was a group of Mexican shacks called "the Palmettos." There was also Sand Bayou and Black Bayou along the river. People were allowed to roam and squat all up and down that river. There are none of them left now. They have vanished as if they never existed.

**Martin Huber, Eunice Huber, David Huber,
Emily Smolik Buckert, Alfredo Buentello**

River Annie

Years ago, there used to be a lot of bootleggin'. River Annie was the boss. They said she was a very dangerous woman. She had just one leg. They tell me she could take a crutch and break a man's back. She was one bad ol' girl.

I would always ride up to the river bridge with Pete Rydolph and see if she had any hides to sell. She would keep Pete informed about everything up and down that river.

I never did know her last name. We just called her River Annie. She was a white woman and she was mean. She made the worst whiskey out of popcorn and she fished, too.

She was about a two-hundred-pounder with big bones and stringy brown hair. I ain't yet seen a man could outcuss her.

I have no idea where she came from. She lived on a houseboat twenty-five or thirty feet long and twelve feet wide. She had only two rooms built on that boat. Her clothesline hung on the side and you could walk around the boat.

She wore pants and a shirt and used cotton rope for a belt. She was the river boss and she knew everything about the river. She would hide men that were runnin' from the law. She was a truly tough customer.

K. J. Oliver

River Annie had a small piece of property on the Rancho Nuevo part of the McFaddin ranch near the Pajaritos bridge. She was a *bruja* and was a good-sized lady. She wore men's clothes and had wild hair. She was of mixed blood and she had a lot of friends because she was a bootlegger. She sometimes took people across the river on her boat.

Reverend Mack Williams

Rustlers and Other Renegades

As well as local outlaws, bootleggers, and other disreputable characters that resided in the area, a number of famous desperados would show up from time to time. It always caused a great stir, and the locals responded to them much as we respond to celebrities in today's world. Rubbing up against the famous made one a bit of a celebrity among one's peers. In an era of full-time isolation and hard work, this type of contact with the famous was particularly intriguing and exciting for all.

Outlaws and Wild Men

We always heard stories about wild men. There was lots of feudin' and fightin' down there at one time. There were desperados all around. The "Wild Bunch" was from Victoria. It was made up of blacks, whites, and Mexicans. They would ride through the saloons on their horses.

My aunt fed Jesse James one time. She said he sure was a good-looking man. She was young at the time and all she could notice was how good-looking he was.

I bought a piece of land from Shanghai Pierce and a friend of mine was a cousin to John Wesley Hardin. My mother would have to take food to him. It was wild and woolly days then.

Elizabeth Sevier Haney

The Huffs were freed slaves and fence builders. They was a bunch of big old muscular colored boys, maybe six or seven of them. Old Wesley Huff told me it was open range down here until the 1870s when Old Man O'Connor [Thomas O'Connor I] built the first fence around here from in the San'tone River clear down to Salt Creek.

Old Sam [Huff] wasn't really an outlaw, but he never did pay a debt. The rest of them got 150 head of cattle off the Hallinan and the San Antonio Loan and Trust. They'd ride down there and go way out into the bay on horseback and come around that fence.

"Wild Man" Hand Shaw (seated right) and his wife, Ann Shaw (seated left).

They finally caught 'em when they killed that fella on Copano Creek. He was a watchman for the machinery there. They came up there to get some gasoline and he stopped them and they shot him. Ira Heard took 'em in and had 'em buildin' fences and corrals for the whole time they were in. I think they got five or ten years.

Herbert "Buster" Bickford

"Well, if you open some of those closets in Victoria, my God, you'd see skeletons hanging from the rafters."

Marye Murphy Greer

There was a lot of gambling in the area. They would all get to drinkin' and fightin' and wind up in jail. Old Man Charlie Fox and Mr. Bickford would be gambling on the side. It was like a pool hall. They would have those calf-head suppers and gamble in the Woodsman Hall. It was worse than a soap opera here. It wasn't all fun and games.

Some Indian fella got killed on the river. He was learning to gamble and he couldn't talk. Somebody shot him. A Bickford was killed also and they never knew who did it. That's why they call it Dead Man's Bayou.

Lucile Fagan Snider, Katharine Kinsler Shaw, Reatha Morley Schultz, Reverend Mack Williams

One of the Lowe boys was a pretty rough character around this area. Frank and Gene would get in the Mission River and they'd harpoon an alligator and let the alligator tow them up and down the river. They were the brothers that shot at each other, too. Finally, one of them was charged with murder. They thought he should have been hung, but they sentenced him to Huntsville for life. Frank was struck by lightning and killed and it gave the whole town an insight as to the will of God. It made some believers.

Luther Bennet Paul

Cattle swimming flooded Coleto Creek below Reeves Thicket Bridge.

Skeletons in the Closet

My father was born right here where I'm livin' now. When the older generation got into all this bad stuff, I think he was about seven or eight years old. He was left to help my grandmother when one lawsuit after another started comin' down.

One deal that John Bickford got into cost us four hundred acres of land. I had a distant relative named Homer Dubois that got into a cow-rustlin' deal and cost my grandmother four hundred acres of land to get him out of jail. It cost Dave Garner a bunch, too. They was all in it together.

The family had a nest egg and lost it because of this outlaw stuff. Homer Dubois died in Tombstone, Arizona, and Will Bickford died in Wichita, Kansas. Those two got clean away, but Dave Garner and John Bickford was prosecuted.

There was a Spanish fella or a colored fella involved. Alcohol had all of them. When they rustled that bunch of cattle, they were all drunk. Didn't know what they were doin' and didn't know where the hell they was goin'.

You know, there are skeletons in all closets, but I got a clear conscience. What my kinpeople did and how they done it, I'm not responsible. But a stigma does exist. The stigma does go on. Back in the older days, if one member of a family pulled something, they were all held responsible for it. The whole damn family was guilty.

Herbert "Buster" Bickford

Wade Reeves (right) with a former slave and other gamblers at old Reeves Ranch.

"The rustlin' of the leaves and the rustlin' of cattle. You always hear that down in those river bottoms."

Herbert "Buster" Bickford

Reeves Thicket

Tobias Reeves came from Ireland to this area. He is my great-grandfather, but I have no idea when he came over here. He came with two brothers named Bud and Murphy. They married into the Murphys here. Murphy Reeves married Annie Murphy. Bud married Day Willemin.

They had cattle and horses and seemed to have been fairly well off. My mother's mother had private tutors and servants. I think the ranch was a Spanish land grant from the late 1700s or early 1800s.

Tobias Reeves was a red-headed Irishman with a full moustache and beard and a temper to go with it. He knew when he was going to die and wanted green grass and a black rosebush on his grave.

The Reeves ranch was a social center for the area. Lynchings and moonshine stories abound.

My mother said, "You are a daughter of the San'tone River and the Reeves Thicket."

Jerri Hall Peyton

The Reeves Thicket was known in the early days of this part of Texas to be the habitat for cattle rustling and outlaws of all types. The Thicket covered approximately three thousand acres of heavy live oak trees and underbrush. It also contained a lake in the center.

There was lots of bootleggin' and smugglin' of all kinds. During the early days

Morris Tobias Reeves (left) and Lee Williams.

the freight wagons were carrying merchandise from Indianola and Victoria to the old town of Perdido. Perdido is located on Road Creek and Sandy Hollow north of Fannin approximately three and a half miles.

The old freight wagon masters were the Stanley brothers, who were my mother's uncles. I can still remember their old stories. Being the first grandchild, and my grandfather being the justice of the peace, it was during this time when outlaws would rob the wagons for whatever they needed for themselves. They stole horses and cattle and murdered people. There were many early settlers and people who were from the famous old seaport of Indianola. They were coming in here to locate a new home, freedom, and become good citizens.

Earl Albrecht

Reeves Thicket is along Highway 59 between Goliad and Victoria. It consisted of an area that went from Fleming Prairie back to Raisin and to Fannin. It was so dense in there, you couldn't see.

There are many stories about this area. Famous outlaws hung out in the Thicket. Any time anybody was on the lam, they headed for Reeves Thicket. A lot of them went in there and never came out. There were a few good sets of bones bleaching in that Thicket.

Outlaws, epidemics, shoot-outs, Indian raids, and Union soldiers have been through here. It was a big bootlegging area also. Tom Dinkins, the famous bootlegger, was around this area. The Reeves loved to drink. Tobe Reeves was the "Law West of the Coleto" for this area.

Dead people were found here more than once. One time a dead woman was found. It was wild back in here, really dangerous. People used to cringe when they had to come through this brush.

It is a fairly infamous place.

Charlie Faupel

Does anybody remember the Linburg-Linn killing out here? That was something awful. They dumped the body right out here on the river road. Linn was a taxi driver. One night he stole some cattle out there on the Fleming Prairie. Linburg had hired Linn to take him to Goliad in his taxi cab. Back in those days, there was some twenty-odd gates you had to open.

We had gone to a dance in a wagon. We were just kids. They were out there stealing cattle and we could hear them. Now, Linn was stealing cattle at that time. When he got Old Man Linburg outside of town, he robbed him and killed him. He got to Reeves Thicket just across the Coleto Creek bridge and killed him. Linn dumped his body in a kind of little slough and covered it up with leaves.

Linn got caught for stealing cattle, and they kind of figured out he had killed Linburg. This happened in the twenties. It was before the highway came through in '29.

Joseph Roell

Reeves Thicket always fascinated me. I went past it once when I was seventeen with Dad and his best friend, Allee Handy, to take a pair of silver Mexican coins to Mr. [Joe] Bianchi for a pair of spurs he was making for Dad. Dad drew my attention to it and remarked that anyone on the run from the law headed for there. It was said it was not easy to get out of there. It caught my attention, it did, and I never pass Reeves Thicket without thinking about Dad talking about the bleached bones in there.

Mary Elizabeth Welder Knight

Earl Albrecht: Hell on the Inside

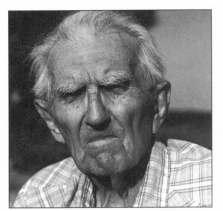

Earl Albrecht.
Photo by Steve Wiener.

My family has been down in this river bottom a long, long time. We came over here when all the others came from Germany. I was born in 1904 in Ander in Goliad County. It was called Hanover early on. My grandfather was with Buffalo Bill when he came to Victoria. He rode around the arena with him on a big white horse.

I grew up with all these people here, the O'Connors, McFaddins, Amerys, Powers, Fagans, Holmans, Marberrys, and Foxes. I went to school in Marianna and was a year old when the railroad came through. In the early days, Marianna was a good business town, and being the railroad center, it had a gin, sawmill, and big mercantile store. During World War I, the old town had everything you wanted.

Even when we lived down there, we used to talk about that river. We were the people who lived our lives on it. It was tough down in this river bottom. Those old men never went out without their guns, and for good reason. It was especially wild durin' cotton time. That was when the gamblin', chicken fights, horse races, and drinkin' bootleg whiskey was in full swing. It was wide open then.

People came here from all over the region. Occasionally someone would come in and try to hijack the locals. They were real surprised when they were lookin' down a bunch of gun barrels. Outlaws would come down that river and wind up at the Cove that was on the McFaddins' place.

The winner! Junior Groll on Blackout in 1947. However, this was legal horse racing.

There was an old wild woman down there named River Annie. She dressed like a man and would "entertain" the cowboys after she got them drunk. She was the river "hostess." There were some bad killin's down there. Dr. Dodson got a lot of them in his hospital.

If a stranger came down here, he had about as much chance of survival as that old snowbird in hell. When you were raised on that San'tone River, you knew what was goin' on. Most people's lives were so damned dull. Very few people had any adventure, but if you wanted it, you hung out in this river bottom.

Lots of people down here were called "river rats." The town people were scared of them. They were altogether a different type of people. They were a real outlaw element that were dangerous even to the more lawless of the locals.

The Negroes down here were good people. They descended from the freed slaves and just stayed after they were freed. You could trust them anywhere. There were some outlaws among them too, but most were good decent people. They were better than the whites as a whole.

One thing I want known is that there was never any serious trouble with the black people. They were some of the best people and neighbors you could know.

Throughout the neighborin' communities along the river bottom and down to the confluence of the San Antonio River and the Guadalupe was an area closely bounded by strong affection, loyalty, and common interest. Whites, blacks, Mexicans all stood together.

When there was any trouble or killin', in general, nobody talked about it. Whatever happened was closed forever. Nobody talked or saw nothin' but the old San Antonio River bottom. These people had integrity. They protected their communities from outlaws and thieves passin' through the area.

We had a many a character like Ripley Terrell. He wasn't crazy or really bad. He was just a spoilt child. His mother was lots younger than his daddy, and he was too old to raise him. He just had and did anything he wanted. His mother, Etta

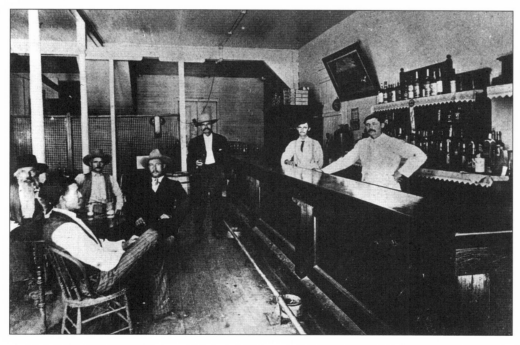

Fossati's in Victoria, ca. 1900.

[Lauretta] Wilkinson, was from Berclair, so she was practically a stranger. Nobody knew her when she arrived down here.

Reeves Thicket was a wild place and Lewis's Bend was on that river, too. Hall's Point and Robinson's Bend were all active communities along the river. All these places had bridges, and bandits would rustle cattle and take them to Karnes City. Those Butlers were in on that. It's still tough country around the Copano area. Imagine what it was like in the old days.

A year or so after Crogan [Terrell] married Etta, a first cousin of his was coming to see him and stay a while. He was met by the handyman from the Terrell ranch, who was a newcomer to the area. After leaving the depot on their way home, they stopped at the old beer parlor and bought some whiskey and beer.

Then they drove down the road towards the San'tone River near Hall's Point. The handyman knew that Mr. Terrell's cousin had a large sum of money in his trunk he was carryin' to the ranch. So the handyman shot the man from Pennsylvania and took the body over to a large bunch of brush on the side of the road near Hall's Point. The outlaw turned the horses loose with the surrey and the horses kept on goin' until they reached the ranch.

Mr. Terrell contacted his neighbors, the Fagans and John Williams. They started out to find his cousin and the handyman. Findin' the body hidden in a thicket, they went looking for the murderer. His footprints were found in the mud leading up to Hall's Point Hollow towards Reeves Thicket on the Coleto Creek. That was approximately ten miles northeast from Hall's Point, the old San Antonio River Road.

Within a few days after the killin', this murderous character was caught in the area of Reeves Thicket. Thereupon, he was killed by the San'tone River "posse."

My grandfather was a part of the posse because of bein' the justice of the peace. He repeated this story many times when he and his family moved to old Marianna. When the murderer was found by the posse, they brought him back to Hall's Point where he was hung by the San'tone River from a live oak tree. Later his remains were put in a cotton sack and left hangin' by the road for six months.

There were some feuds in time among the old ranchers. It was after the Civil War. They had a gathering down there to settle the feud and five men were killed. They all were united against the outside world, but there was a lot of hell on the inside.

There was a big fight at the Anaqua school in Victoria County in 1931. The district had a big barbecue supper and dance. While the dance was goin' on and everybody was full of good barbecue and drinks, the deputy sheriff, who was Rob Williams, got a call from the county sheriff's office in Victoria. They told him to be on guard because the Green boys from Taft were on their way to kill Earl Albrecht. Rob came to me and told me this and I told him I would be ready.

By the time those damn outlaws got there, I had my gang ready also. The big fight started outside on the school grounds. Their gang was composed of three men and two girls. While the fight was goin' on, I got in the middle all alone. Then Leo Urban and my Mexicans gathered on the outside and stood by watchin' the Green gang. When they made a rush for me, I had my .45 pistol with the seven-inch barrel.

Every time I hit one of those SOB's upside the head, I'd pull the trigger. Down he would go. My gang did not use their guns, but they cut those outlaws to pieces.

During the fight, one of the Green gang picked up a large fryin' pan and threw it at the deputy. Old Man Weeks was standin' next to Rob and the fryin' pan hit him in the shoulder and then hit Williams in the head. Deputy Williams lunged forward and turned over the big serving table with all the good eats.

There was a big fight goin' on in the schoolhouse. J. T. Giddin made a pass at my brother, who threw him over some benches and broke his jaw.

After the big gang fight was over, everyone left pronto, all scared to death. I went down to the big barbecue pit and commenced eatin'.

Later Sheriff Sweringer told me the Green boys had beat up the Goliad sheriff, taken his gun, and left for Anaqua to kill me. I didn't even pay a fine. Case dismissed.

There were some famous murders like when Amos Green killed Juan García, the foreman of the Duke Ranch. It was over some mixed-breed woman. Now, they may have been pickin' pecans when it happened, but that wasn't the real reason. There were these two women and they got their lovers into their cars and headed for Refugio and Woodsboro. Some of those men who had been in the fight were in the hospital for several weeks and some of the gang died later. It was later learned they had raped some girls on Mustang Island and killed two of them and buried them in the sand dunes.

Prominent people shot up dance halls and saloons and many a prisoner's body was found on the river banks. These were always out-of-town folk.

Because of the political power along the San Antonio River, if you weren't

Alonis Preiss, Preiss Saloon, Kemper City, 1915.

native, you didn't have a chance in court or otherwise. This particular area has always been a separate political district from any other section of Texas. Remember, these old settlers who made this area as it is today are the political backbone of South Texas, and I am proud to be a part of the original frontiersmen of this famous area of Texas.

My grandfather, Bill Mason, lost two first cousins at the Battle of Fannin. They were later taken and shot by the damn Mexican soldiers and their bodies were burned.

We all knew what happened in these instances, but so what? The old San Antonio River bottom never knows nothin'. I have overheard these old-timers talk about these instances that did happen in the early days along the river. You must keep in mind, these old frontiersmen kept their eyes and ears open and their mouths shut. They were like the three monkeys. The old "gag order" came when these things happened.

Nowadays, the American public can't keep their damn mouths shut. They have to call the police or some damn TV reporter. The average American citizen today doesn't have the guts or courage like these old frontiersmen did. Back in the good old days, when a man gave his word and a real old-time handshake, it was dependable. Those days are gone forever. This is because of deception and trickery by bankers, realtors, and S&L guys.

We were in on a lot of foolishness and practical joking, too. We were always disruptin' the black church meetings. Once we let loose red ants at the Inari church. That broke up the meetin'. Another time, there was a meeting in the old schoolhouse near Duke's Bridge. We put oil of mustard on the seats before they got there. It was a moonlight night. That stuff will set you on fire and they were all washin' it off themselves at the pump well. They thought it was funny later, but not at the time.

Feudin' was going on in the bottom all the time. It was almost impossible to keep score. I don't think it has all been figured out yet. A lot of people have chosen to forget about it.

A lot of treasure hunting went on. Many of the bayous around here had shipwrecks. Goff, Swan, Chocolate, and Hog bayous had ships in them. There were lots of old abandoned missions all around. The Chinese once had a mission in Texas hundreds of years ago. Somebody once found a Buddah.

La Salle was all around the Keeran ranch. They had cannons mounted on donkeys and when they fired off those canons, it turned those donkeys four or five somersaults. Those Indians ran, too.

Travelin' up and down the river all these years, I've heard all the stories and legends. There was once a famous one about the stars fallin'. Those people thought it was the second comin' of Christ. It was a total eclipse of the sun and a meteor shower or two meteors colliding. I don't know which. There were meteor craters all over the place for years. Natural gas would escape and ignite, especially around Shay Lake, and that was the basis for all the jack-o-lantern stories.

I did a lot of huntin' and ridin' in that river bottom when I was a young man. Near McFaddin, I saw a twenty-foot python one time. People brought them in on boats. They liked to live on sandy loam. I wonder if that could have been where the fifteen-foot rattlesnake stories started?

During the Civil War, Yankees came to Victoria. There was a white captain and a large bunch of black soldiers. They had a camp on the river in Victoria near the Riverside Park of today. They raped Dick Peal's girls and some others. The townspeople killed 214 of them, all in one night. People came down for two or three years to find out about this, but no one ever admitted to knowing anything about it. Some of my people were in on it.

Everyone in the area closed in to protect themselves and each other. All knew this story and who was involved in all the killin's. When you crossed the Guadalupe River, you were in San'tone River country and everybody stuck together. They were some tough mothers. A life didn't mean a damn thing.

Back in the frontier days, you had to be tough to survive. The women were as tough as the men. Sometimes they were at home alone with nothing to protect themselves but a double-barreled shotgun. I was raised that way. Lived that way all my life. We all protected each other and kept each other informed.

Purcell was a double-crosser in the Texas Revolution. He crossed everybody. He married into the Albrecht family and was a friend of the Fagans. Old Man Tom O'Connor stole horses and he and great-grandfather Albrecht rode to Purcell's house and shot him. The story has it that the baby in the bed with him almost drowned in his father's blood.

There was always hell to pay in these dance halls. Once a guy threw a firecracker in my girlfriend's lap and burned her. I put him in the Victoria hospital for three and a half months. Later we became friends and I leased some land from him for oil and gas. It was another good fight for Earl Albrecht. Lots of people have tried to run me out of the county, but I'm still going strong at eighty-five.

This area don't belong to the USA. That's the way we lived down here since Revolutionary times. Outsiders were not accepted. After the Civil War, there was a militia down here to control things. That was real tough times. We were a separate nation down here. We were respected. Nobody gave us any trouble. If anyone tried, they just disappeared. The land and the river were friendly, but the people weren't if you were an outsider.

This was the best days of my life, and the best days of the lives of all the people that have passed on. It was a world to itself down there. There were lots of mysteries and a lot of stories on that river.

Earl Albrecht

"And there was old men with beer guts
     and dominoes,
Lyin' 'bout their lives while they'd play."

Guy Clark, "Desperados Waiting for the Train"

CHAPTER EIGHT

Time Has Made a Change

"Time's done made a drastic change."

Troy Robinson

Like many other waterways in Texas, the San Antonio River is today quite different from the crystal-clear stream that first attracted native peoples and immigrants alike to its banks. Enormous quantities of pollutants in the form of urban runoff and bacterial contamination, particularly from the San Antonio area, have turned the river water brown and murky. Agricultural runoff, tainted by pesticides and herbicides, has added to the problem, and erosion from farming has dumped untold amounts of topsoil and silt into the river.

A picnic long ago.

According to hydrologists, the San Antonio is not even a "natural" river anymore. Most of the springs that once fed its headwaters have ceased to flow except after a period of heavy rains. Expanding urban areas deplete the aquifer for drinking water and industrial use. The river's flow is maintained by withdrawals of water from wells in Brackenridge Park, supplemented by precipitation in the watershed.

The effects of human encroachment were noticeable a century ago, when George W. Brackenridge determined to sell off his property containing the headwaters of the San Antonio. The springwater had already suffered from contamination by outhouse seepage and garbage disposal, and Brackenridge believed the recent long droughts were causing the river to die. "I have seen this bold, bubbling, laughing river dwindle and fade away," he said, "and I cannot stay here to see its last gasps. . . . I must go."[1]

Efforts in recent years to control pollution and runoff have somewhat reversed deteriorating water quality, and we can only hope that one day the river will again run pure.

Messin' Up the Land

Landgraf drilled a many an artesian well in this country. The water table has dropped so much now the old wells won't flow anymore. I believe the San Antonio is gonna go dry. They're pullin' too much water out of it. There used to be sandbars everywhere. It used to be real clear. That was fishin' and huntin' country.

Herbert "Buster" Bickford

Herbert Marsh on the Salt Creek Ranch, December 20, 1942.

The city of San Antonio really polluted it starting in the late thirties or early forties. It was terrible. They just polluted it something awful, dead fish floatin' down the river. You could smell the stench all the way up here at the house. Then the water board out

Orion Linney, Jim Coward, and Vincent Fritz, December 20, 1942.

of Austin finally put a big fine on them—around $250,000—for polluting the river. It's gradually getting it cleared back up and it's starting to make a comeback.

John Freeman Lott

A whole lot of things used to be plentiful down in these bottoms. Now you don't see so many anymore. All these farmers using pesticides and stuff now, killin'

Coyote, 1930s.

things off. They think people are killin' the game off with their guns. Well, they're not. They are being killed off with man's poisons.

Johnny Robinson, Troy Robinson, K. J. Oliver

Things have changed in this river bottom. Spanish moss went plumb away with them sprays, and pecans are a lot less now. Now they kill the moss blossoms with the sprays. Some of it's comin' back 'cause they quit them bad sprays. I never used those things much. I don't believe in 'em. It ain't helpin' the land. I don't believe much in farmin' neither. It messes up the land. I ain't much on it.

Richard Harris

Fish, Ice Water, and Salvation

The water was good then. People have ruint the water now. It used to be like ice water. It gave us fish, water, and God's salvation. There were so many different

Cotton-pickin' time, 1940.

things we used the river for. Now it's only used for waste. God had a way of fixin' things so it was comfortable and pleasant to fit man's taste. It didn't do for man to get hold of the earth. Man done messed up everything, and he's still messin' it up. People think they have more sense than God now. People keep tryin' to overpower God, and they keep on fallin'. Everything man needed was right here.

Reverend Albert Wade, Mose Henderson, Nathaniel Youngblood

Changin' Times

"Now? Horses ain't no count. Children ain't no count. There's not much grass and there's too many insects."

Richard Harris

Social and economic changes, as well as physical ones, are occurring in the river bottom areas. The coming of the oil industry, World War II, the building of good roads, better communication, and other forms of "progress" have caused the outside world to penetrate the isolated and self-sufficient sphere of the river bottom.

It was World War II that had the most profound effect on the river bottom communities and eventually led to their demise. When the young men of the region who had been drafted into the war finally returned, they were dissatisfied with the simple life they had once led along the river and on the ranches. Because of their military training, they had more opportunities to find jobs in the urban communities. Soon there was nothing left of the old river bottom settlements. They returned to the wilderness they once were.

With the changing times came changing customs and values. A recurring lament throughout the narratives is that people have somehow changed and the strong sense of community is gone. There is a general feeling that, while the old way of life was harder, it was more humane, more joyful, and more meaningful.

Jeanette Perkins and Aunt Nettie guttin' a deer.

Progress Ain't Always for the Best

You used to be able to navigate that river all the way to Goliad. A man named Marek did it all the time in a small boat he had. We'd go clear up to the T-C Ranch when the river was on a half rise.

Lots has changed on that river, especially the mood and the attitude. It's a hell of a lot different.

It was practically the ends of the earth down there. Everybody was friendly and everybody helped everybody. Now everybody's tryin' to get rich and they don't care how they do it.

Everybody used to associate with everybody else. Now there's a little bunch here and a little bunch there. I've never been partial to any group. I'll associate with any of them if they'll associate. If they don't, just leave them alone. It used to be real isolated out here before the railroad come in 1905. Victoria was the nearest shoppin' place. I sit there in that fillin' station in Tivoli sometimes and watch those women come to the store three times a day just to get one meal fixed. Back when, we had to live out of the river and the bottom. When things change that much, it can't never be the same, and I ain't sure the changes are for the best.

Herbert "Buster" Bickford

"Time sho' passes."

Milam Thompson

Road in the river bottom. Could that be Ripley's car in the distance?

Those Were the Days

Those days were good days because people got together more often. They showed more love and they cared about one another. All of our family lived on different farms, the John Terrells and Uncle Bush. You know, if you didn't see one another in the week, well, Aunt Nettie would say, "John, you better go over there and check on them. Some of them might be sick." Now you can die next door and nobody would know.

Josephine Holliday Durst

What was it like? It wasn't growed up then. There was a road going through there.

People helped each other down there. You felt like you were safe. You weren't afraid to walk at night. You weren't afraid of anything but wild hogs down there.

Life and people are harder now. The old folks stood together. Now people don't go as far out with their sympathy. Life is a lot different now than then. It's a different horse race and a different time now.

Rosie Terrell Jones

Time Has Made a Change

*Time, time, time, time has made a
    change.*
*Oh, time, time, time, time has
    made a change.*
*Oh, Lord, time, time, time, time
    has made a change.*
Oh, time has made a change.

*Oh, the deacons don't pray like
    they used to pray.*
Time has made a change.
    Oh, Lord.
*The deacons don't pray like they
    used to pray.*
Time has made a change.
    Oh, Lord.
*The deacons don't pray like they
    used to pray.*
*Oh, time has made a change,
    made a change, made a
    change, made a change.*

*People don't love like they used
    to love.*
Time has made a change.
    Oh, Lord.
*People don't love like they used
    to love.*
Time has made a change.
    Oh, Lord.
*People don't love like they used
    to love.*
*Oh, time has made a change,
    made a change, made a
    change, made a change.*

*Sisters don't shout like they used
    to shout.*
Time has made a change.
    Oh, Lord.
*Sisters don't shout like they used
    to shout.*
Time has made a change.
    Oh, Lord.
*Sisters don't shout like they used
    to shout.*
Oh, time has made a change.

Time has made a change.

Traditional hymn from slavery times, one of the Old One Hundreds

"It used to be, you got a dime, I got a dime. Now it's, you got a dime, I knock you in the head. We used to live when a dime looked like a dollar."

Nathaniel Youngblood

Change started in the 1920s. Every year the changes started showin' up, but it really came fast after World War II. Even in the twenties, people were startin' to move to town. All this brought us great unhappiness.

The Depression started a lot of this change, too. The farmers couldn't make it and went to town. The young people began sayin' they weren't gettin' enough money. The old people didn't go along with this.

The young ones started the change. Their idea was, if you didn't ask for it, you wouldn't get it.

The old ones looked at the young ones and knew they were the future. They had more contact with the outside world. Everyone was in confusion from this time on. Everyone got lost.

People quit havin' fun workin', and when that happens, life quits being fun because life was mostly work then and still is, really.

Our whole world was gettin' changed. It even began to change on the ranches, and those ranches were our security. We quit feelin' secure when the ranches changed.

We were gettin' more money and then we wanted more money. There was even a strike on the ranch among the young ones.

Jesse Jones.

The old people didn't have nowhere else to go. They didn't want to start trouble. The young ones had more guts 'cause they had other chances. This may have been good for their pocketbooks, but it wasn't good for their souls.

We were educated by the schools, the Lord, and our parents. The youngsters are gettin' it from everyone else now, and we have educated the sense out of people. The WPA and all that Roosevelt stuff really started change. Nobody knew what they wanted to do. Your town jobs were in jeopardy all the time. The bosses there were not our friends like the ranch bosses were. They weren't all that strict on us, but the town bosses didn't care about us.

We quit dependin' on ourselves and were taught the government would take care of us. That's made a real mess of people.

Young people don't want to do for themselves like we did and they don't know how. We didn't have time to be—what do they say?—emotionally messed up.

Sometimes you felt sick and tired, but that would pass away and you were ready to go back to it.

Jesse Jones

Clarence "T" Terrell and Nathaniel Youngblood.

River Bottom Raisin'

We didn't have runnin' water in the "Bends." That river was necessary to our lives. People lived all around that bend. Aunt Ellen Terrell lived right on that river. Every once in a while, the people would have to move up when it flooded. All of us used to go down to the river and carry water.

The old folks used to say that water in that river would purify itself every hundred feet it ran. We drank it and it didn't bother us, so they must have been right. We even drank out of cow tracks.

After a big rain, you used to be able to ride across that prairie and see little perch all in the water puddles. They would rain down. It probably is still doin' it, but nobody pays any attention. A lot of young people laugh at that when you tell them, but it's true.

Charlie Charleston really knew his way around the bays. He lived on them all his life. He was the only one that was good on the bay. The rest of us were scared of that salt water with those stingarees and sharks. Now, the San'tone River didn't scare us. There wasn't anything in it badder than us. It didn't matter how high the river got, we could swim it.

That's why it was fun back in those days. We had lots of things to do. It is a lot of change from then. We even rode turtles in the river.

We lived all them hard days back then. We picked cotton, and there ain't no harder work than that. We worked behind walkin' plows and pulled corn. Runnin' birds off the corn was hard work. They got used to the scarecrows and they wouldn't work anymore. We looked like somethin' else to them.

We talk about it being hot now, but in those days, those heat waves would be goin' across the pastures. We would call those heat waves "horses" and say, "Look at those horses lopin'." You don't see those waves now. We are surrounded by town and we don't pay any attention anymore. We look at somethin' else.

It is the change of time and we have changed with it. The trees have grown up and houses are all around. They cut the view and break up the prairie. The river bottoms were clean with just pecan trees along the river.

"Now ain't better."

Nathaniel Youngblood

We ate when we got through with work. There was no such time as overtime. A day was when the boss said it was, and sugar was sweeter back then.

In those days we were controlled by our parents. They were strict on us and we had to come home and ask their permission to do things. Along about the war time, everything became less civilized. Now nobody asks anybody's permission to do anything, much less their parents. Now people don't raise their children.

Now you can't correct children, either. It's child abuse. We feared our parents. Our fathers had more manhood in them than we ever will. The correction we got from our parents and other grown-ups never hurt any of us. It got us through life. When we were old enough to make our own way, they would turn us loose, not before that. Now the young ones take over the old ones and it's destroyin' our world. We were never allowed to be sassy.

The reason we haven't seen the inside of a jail was because of the things we were taught. The old folks made us take pride in our jobs. Our upbringin' paid off. We were high in experience even if we were low in education. We had horse sense. We kept our hands off other people's things, too. We were trusted by our employers because we were raised right. Our parents were the bosses, and they lived the way they taught us to live. Now too many people have too much education and not enough horse sense.

We all saw these changes comin', but we couldn't do anything about it. Our kids wouldn't listen to us, either. Kids today could use a little bit of this river-bottom raising.

Althia Lewis Burns Franklin, Jesse Jones, Troy Robinson, Johnny Robinson, Nathaniel Youngblood, Zearlee Robinson Wesley, Rachel Wynona Lewis Franklin

Ranch Mad

You didn't have many mad days on the ranch. Going crazy never crossed our minds. We got together and kept each other steady.

Once in a while we would get mad, but the bosses knew it and cared. They always made it right.

When it started changin', we got confused. The ranches started comin' apart from the way we knew them. Oil started comin' in and that made a lot of changes. It made some things easier, like havin' gas in the houses. We didn't have to cut wood no more.

We didn't work together as much anymore. We didn't have to depend on each other as much anymore. People began driftin' away.

We thought we were doin' better then. The government said they were makin' it better for us, but things didn't make sense.

All that we knew was bein' changed, and the new ways were confusin' us. The new stuff didn't make sense. We lived by nature. This new stuff destroyed all that. It commenced to causin' trouble for us.

The new way they educate causes trouble for everyone. I believe in education, but not like it's done now.

We are still confused. Government thinks up somethin' and don't consider the humans involved. We have to challenge the government to get our rights now, and you can't win that one.

Things that made us mad in the old days, we could handle it directly. Now there's nowhere to go, no way to change it. Things like that can drive people crazy.

The mad on the ranches didn't hurt us. It was something we understood.

We were raised to believe in Uncle Sam. He was our friend. Now we know different. We have lost that security and that friend. We have nothin' to believe in anymore.

We give to government and we don't get back nothin' but trouble. At first, we thought the changes were good, but soon we realized better. All we had was our security and our pride on the ranches. We had the respect of others because we worked on the ranches. The new ways took this from us.

Our lives improved as far as more money and easier work, but we lost more valuable stuff like our children and our friends. The government made the ranchers do crazy stuff that confused us, like not lettin' us have calves and killin' cows. They made us burn them. What would you call that but stupid?

Things that crazy happened in farmin', too. All that subsidy stuff, tellin' us what we could do with our own land. We got confused and mad, and we been that way ever since. We didn't have cotton and we didn't have money. They robbed us of everything. They need to be challenged. We feel like our lives are completely out of control. We can't do nothin' about them. We have no say. No matter how right you are, you can't do nothin'.

Wesley Vivion, Bud Garner, Antonio Castillo, Dick Garner, Niño García, and Fred Spriggs on the Welder ranch at Seadrift, 1953.

It was just better back then. We don't believe Uncle Sam or believe in him now.

Some things have been good or alright. Not everything was completely bad, but it hurt more than it helped.

Nobody understands a lot of this stuff. It moves too fast. It's like a train pullin' a bunch of boxcars too fast.

We gotta get back to respect.

Nathaniel Youngblood, Johnny Robinson, Troy Robinson, Jesse Jones

Back to the Old Landmark

Back in 1986, four years after beginning work on this historical project, Nancy and I decided it would be a good idea to take a group of our collaborators back to the Lewis's Bend area for a picnic and taping session. It proved to be an even better idea than we thought. They were all ecstatic at the prospect of seeing "The Bends" again. As soon as we arrived, Toney Lott jumped out of the car, threw himself on his knees, kissed the ground, and started weeping at the sight of the old place. It was a poignant moment, to say the least.

Having grown up in the river bottom, they were initially shocked and upset to see it wild and overgrown with brush. In their day, the beauty and value of the place lay partly in the way the little plots had been cleared and planted. The hand of man was everywhere. Those of us who have had an urban upbringing tend to appreciate the river bottom's undisturbed, natural state. There we can still find some semblance of the wild.

This trip to the river started to unleash the floodgates of memory, and the day was an incredible experience for all of us. Everyone in the group had been friends as children, and even though many had not seen each other for years, they had maintained their shared memories and experiences. What follows is a composite of the day's conversations.

S. W. "Toney" Lott: That's where I got religion down there. That's where I was baptized, right in that old river.

L. V. Terrell: We was all baptized down here.

Milam Thompson: Sho' looks different, doesn't it? It's so growed up now.

S. W. "Toney" Lott

Jesse Jones: The last time I rode through here was when I asked for my wife. It was a pretty good while ago, in 1938.

L. V.: I may never get here again, but I made it here today.

Jesse: I'd be gatherin' horses down here at daybreak and Mr. Welder's boys would already be gone.

Dan Youngblood: I came over that bridge a many a time. One time we lost thirteen hundred steers here. It took two weeks to find 'em.

Nathaniel Youngblood: The last time I was here I was workin' for Mr. Welder.

Willie Brown: There was a little lane went down across here.

All: These banks weren't this steep then. You used to be able to walk right down here. The bank was much lower to the river.

Toney: "I am bound for the promised land." ♪

L. V. Terrell

Dan: I remember Aunt Ellen and Uncle Jackson and Walter Lott livin' down here. The Simms house was near the bridge. They say there was ghosties there.

Jesse: My mother-in-law said they built the dam with mules.

Milam: It was all clean down here, just big trees. There were little lanes all through here comin' off the bridge.

Ulysses "Tommy" Cook: L. V. and I used to get a whippin' for bein' late. Mrs. Sample would get on us for pickin' pecans.

Milam: Welder built the bridge back when it was knocked down one time by crossin' cattle.

Milam Thompson

Jesse: There used to be dances at the Bill Terrells. It was dark in the bottom comin' back from those dances and country suppers.

Dan: We used to dance all night long. Will Sample would get on that fiddle. Chickens were crowin' and it was almost day and we'd still be dancin'.

Jesse: There was the old Simms store by the bridge. You could see the church from there. It just don't look the same.

Dan: It kind of looks the same to me as when I came and stayed with my grandfather. Grandpa Jackson died around 1935 and Aunt Ellen moved out just before the '42 storm.

L. V.: What you doin', tellin' tales?

Jesse: Yeah, tellin' about you ridin' that old roan mare and makin' noises goin' over that bridge. You never saw any cars, just horses and wagons.

Dan: We had some good baseball games in that field over there.

L. V.: We used to walk down here from Johnny Power's ranch.

Nathaniel: We used to have fish fries down below the Simms house. There were some good swimmers in those days. We'd use the seinin' net to catch our fish and have to go underwater to get the net loose.

Tommy: We always sang in school and did dialogues.

Jesse Jones

Dan: I dream about this place. It was good down here. It was more fun than livin' in town. Comin' here was like goin' to Houston, especially on the Nineteenth of June, drinkin' that red soda water. In my dreams, I always take the wrong road and I can't get to church.

Dan Youngblood

L. V.: It was just like a town.

Tommy: The river has changed so much. That's God's work. He can do anything.

Milam: I've got to go down and see this bridge. Maybe I can get straight with myself. The way this place has growed up could confuse anybody.

Nathaniel: We'd walk along here and shoot birds.

Milam: Many a time, I'd come off that bridge and hear the singin' in the church.

Willie: The church was on the rise. Everything else was level. Often we came in a buggy all the way from the Duke Ranch.

Toney: It feels good to be down here again. We lived on Power's ranch over the river.

All: Walter Lott was a good horseman around here. He rode a big gray horse named Iron Gall. He could ride!

Toney: We would have revivals. All the windows would be open. Even the gamblers would come stick their heads in. Porter Johnson gave the revivals.

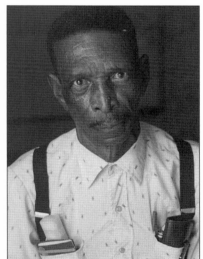

Dan: We didn't have no air-conditionin'. All the windows were open. Air-conditionin' was new style. Everyone used to come to church in those days.

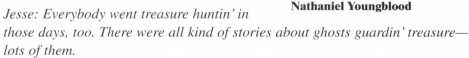

Nathaniel Youngblood

Jesse: Everybody went treasure huntin' in those days, too. There were all kind of stories about ghosts guardin' treasure— lots of them.

Tommy: There were stories about buried money everywhere.

Willie Brown

Nathaniel: Lots of those old people didn't believe in banks. Some of them still don't.

L. V.: Porter Johnson sure could preach and sing. His thought was "Choose Your Own."

Toney: I dreamed about this place a many a time. Simmie and me were baptized here.

Jesse: When I first came here, there weren't any fences and no well pumps.

Nathaniel: You could hear echoes down here when you were young. It seemed like it was runnin' through the trees. There used to be more sound than now. Early in the mornin' around four, you could hear people talkin' all the way from the Duke Ranch.

Jesse: It was dark and you could see jack-o-lanterns, but you never could catch them.

Willie: Milam, do you remember these trees?

Milam: I used to know their names. Funny things can happen in this life. It's been a long time since many of us were here. Little did I know when I baptized here, there would be a bunch of us together again talkin' on tape.

Dan: There's time for business and there's time for pleasure and there's time to think about your soul. This trip down here is about pleasure and your soul.

All: When you were a kid, you just listened to all these things and learned. Now we go back there and just listen and look and try to remember. That's Lewis's Bend and the San'tone River.

Ulysses "Tommy" Cook

Nathaniel Youngblood, L. V. Terrell, Milam Thompson, S. W. "Toney" Lott, Willie Brown, Ulysses "Tommy" Cook, Dan Youngblood, Jesse Jones

Goin' Home

"We learned common sense from our parents and neighbors and the whole community. Now children will sass you out, and their parents will take up for them."

Reverend Mack Williams

We grew up down on that San'tone River not too far from the Lewises. We still have a place down there we call "the camphouse" where our grandmother and grandfather lived and so did our mother and father.

It has a wood stove and wood heater, and we still use them. Whenever my brothers are down there, I go and stay two or three nights. I love it. I just cook and do what we used to do and be what we used to be.

I love to go back there.

Zearlee Robinson Wesley

I go back out there to my homestead almost every other day. I feel so much more comfortable. It seems like I am close to my parents, even if they are dead already. It is so peaceful.

John always asks me why I go out there and stay all day. I just sit on the porch and do a little patchin' up, tryin' to keep the old house together. I tell him that it helps never to forget where you came from. When we were kids comin' up, we didn't know what indoor plumbin' was. Now we have all of these things.

Will Johnson, Addie Simms, J. W. Farley, and Ida Simms, Simms Bridge at Lewis's Bend.

Sometimes you get kind of a big head, so I go back. It reminds me of where I come from. Then I say how blessed I am to have moved up a few steps higher.

Allie Fay Moore Robinson

My daddy was born on the O'Connor [River] Ranch. From a child up, he worked on that ranch. After he had all these children, he farmed and we all worked on the farm.

He grew up back there where that river made a horseshoe bend. Everybody had a little farm down in that bottom. There wasn't no fences, but everyone knew what patch they farmed.

I went back there for the last time, but nothin' wasn't the same, so I couldn't stand to stay. I just had to go back to where we was raised up, but it wasn't like it used to be when my daddy was farmin' it. Then it was so beautiful with cotton and cane and corn growin'. It isn't like that anymore. It's so different.

Lela Edwards Williams, daughter of Alonso "Lonze" Edwards

River bottom, O'Connor River Ranch.

Old Belle was a pecan tree with big old long pecans.

We went down there several years ago. It ain't like it used to be. It just ain't there.

They say when people leave, the trees will die. The spirit has gone out of the place now.

All the people have left and the trees are grievin'. People live with trees and trees live with people.

Georgine Terrell Levigne, Milam Thompson, S. W. "Toney" Lott, Nathaniel Youngblood, Evelyn Elliot Youngblood, Vivian Lott McKnight, Josephine Holliman Terrell

The Music of the Trees: Milam's Story

I was born on St. Patrick's Day. My grandpa told me I wouldn't be able to pass up a wheel because he conquered snakes and he said I would be able to also. I was named after Ben Milam, who was at the Alamo.

My life has been divided into parts. The first three years, I was with my parents. Then my mother went home after her stepdaddy died. When I was three years old, Aunt Fannie died and that put the home without a mother, only my mother. You see, my daddy had three sets of children.

When he married my mother, he was an old man and she was a young girl. She was irresponsible for takin' care of a family. They started a brand new family. He had grandchildren as old as my mother, his last wife. In those days they didn't have welfare and the nearest kin had to take the children. My daddy died when I was nine months old. She did what she was supposed to do and went back to her daddy.

From age four to six, I was in San Antonio with my stepdaddy and my mother. This was after Aunt Fannie died. Naturally, then, I'm livin' like other people lived. But this was another change up, livin' with a stepdaddy, Handy Gray. He was a drunk and a gambler. He used to come home and beat my mama. That hate was buildin' up in me. He had several sick spells from his drinkin'. The doctor told him if he didn't quit drinkin' beer, it was going to kill him. He lived about a year and a half.

On the nineteenth day of June in 1914 in the Rincon Bend, they was havin' a

"Milam lived like John the Baptist in the wilderness. He was a hermit."

Coleman Joshlin

celebration. He was to take us to the celebration. We lived near where I live now [Goliad]. He had to come to town first to get some beer for the party. He drank and made it back to his horse. That's where he fell. Instead of him comin' back, a man came to tell us he was dead. Then my uncle had to take me.

I never thought much about my mother. She wasn't able to care for me and I didn't know nothin' about mother love. I loved her and respected her for my mother.

Right along in there, I had to start to providin' for me. I was with my Uncle Charlie in the San'tone River bottom. I began to hunt for food when I got there.

I never went to school. I learnt myself to read and write. Goin' to Sunday school taught me a lot about readin' and writin'. My uncle put me in school when I was nine years, or at least he enrolled me.

I never had a birth certificate. The school had the record. Once I went to the Minnehulla [Manahuilla] school one year, but only for a little bit. He needed me on the place and always interrupted my schoolin'.

Mrs. Emma Sample, she was a Whitby, taught me when I ran away. That was when I lived in Lewis's Bend with Uncle Jackson Youngblood. After I ran off from Robinson's Bend, I stayed among the Mexicans. I was sent to Berclair to live with Uncle Charlie's brother. He beat me too, and I left there.

Milam Thompson, camp cook, philosopher, preacher, friend.

I ran away lookin' for a job, and the Mexicans were nice to me. That's how I learned to speak Spanish so well. I went to work on the county road with this Mexican fella. I stayed in Fannin with them and stayed away from blacks. Aunt Velma Terrell saw me at Hanley's Store and was nice to me. She was my auntie, and I learned to trust her. A niceness to me is my weakness.

My daddy died when I was nine months old. My mother went home to her daddy. She was a young woman and my daddy was an old man then. That was my first adjustment. I had to adjust to them. Steve Holliman was my grandaddy. He was

Gus Hamilton.

very kind and instructed me in many things. I had no father to instruct me.

My stepgrandmother was sick a long time and when she died I was alone again. I think God may have had some plan for me by designin' my life and misfortunes as He did. I may not have seen God another way. My religion is natural. It came through the spirit.

The clouds will form many things in your mind when you are a boy. They would make me laugh. Sometimes they would look like someone ridin' a horse and they got throwed off.

The moon meant much to me. I would look at the rings around it. Sometimes it looked like the moon was chasin' among the clouds, but it was really the clouds runnin'. That was entertainment to me.

I made a many tracks in this area when I was a kid. I enjoyed old people and they enjoyed me. Gus Hamilton was a special friend of mine. I got my idea of how to love from these old people.

I played with insects. You could go to whistlin' and a prayin' mantis would dance. You can do this with lots of insects. Lamp eels were around after rains. I played with them. They were like tryin' to grab a muddy pig with no tail. I never knew what was poison. I just had to jump in and find out.

I grew up in Refugio, Goliad, and Victoria counties. Nature did teach me, show me, told me in its way. I knew from the design of nature that there had to be a God. It was nature that brought me to God. There was no one for me to take up with but nature.

I believe more in what I did out there than in man. What is revealed to me is more real than what man tells me. I question man, but when I look at nature and see God somewhere about it, I just know it's true.

The trees are my people. You've got to see me as I am. There is a certain amount of play in anything when it's a kid, when it's young. I had no children to play with. I wasn't allowed to go around children, and there weren't any around anyway. Alright then, I looked to nature.

The first thing I guess I played with was a limb. I'd break me off a limb and shape it like I wanted and pull it through the sand. Naturally, it made marks like a harrow. I was plowin' the land. Then I would turn it over and smooth the rows, and I was ready to plant. I was sho' farmin'! The next thing I did was learn to spin around and around and get drunk. That was fun back there to me.

I was in the bottom behind the hogs all day. You just stayed behind them and let them eat and stayed out of people's fields when they were plantin' in the spring. I would climb a tree while I waited on them and see-sawed up and down on a tree limb.

I used to sleep up in them oak trees when I was a boy. If I can lay down, I can lay right there and not fall out.

The next thing I made was a little guitar. My uncle had bees and beehives. Beehives have a frame with honeycomb wire in it. I was lookin' at those wires and I made up my mind I was gonna make me a guitar. Of course, I didn't make me no guitar, I just had wires and limbs, but I could sing pretty good. I'd be just playin' up a fog! No note to it, but it would be a sound.

I'd just make up my little words. I can't even remember 'em. Durin' that war number one, I mostly sung about mother's sons kilt in the war and they wouldn't be comin' back home.

"I don't know where Milam's beginning was. Nobody knows his mama. I just know he was there."

K. J. Oliver

It's amazing how some children have to come up through life. Thoughts can come to them like grown folks, sometimes quicker. They lives in a world, and I had a world of my own, by myself. I never lived in a world with no people. I had to do my own choosin' to live. That's one of my ways.

My beginnin' thoughts about religion started when I was a child. I began to realize there was a God providin' for me. He helped me when I had to steal food as a child. I guess I was about eleven years old. I heard about a revival and I didn't know what it was, so I asked my cousin. She said the preacher was comin' here to get religion to the people. She said it was somethin' God puts in your heart.

I thought it must have been in a little package. I had already started visualizin' religion before that. My ideas from nature were a lot like what it really was.

Milam Thompson and his chuck wagon, ca. 1924.

Thoughts of God came when I was with my uncle. They would threaten to give me a killin' off, and when they got through, it almost was. That gave me thoughts that there must be someone could help me.

Lookin' at nature, I placed it in my mind that God must have made them trees and all those other wonderful things that helped me. Lots of things happened out there that helped me. When it would rain, little fish would collect in the water. I would get them. They were good eatin' to me.

I used to pour water around trees in return for everything they did for me. I thought I was doin' something for the trees. I picturized creation in a tree. I can go to a tree and see God makin' that tree. I can hear the music of the trees from the limbs rubbin' together. The Lord was talkin' to me. It sounded like it was callin' my name. It gave me comfort when I was a little bitty boy. It was entertainment. It was my mother. The comfort was from God, the song was from God.

When I finally got to go to church, the music of the trees was a lot like the old hymns. They were like what my father should have been to me, like a protector or a provider. I often talked to them. I would go to them for certain things. Plants and weeds meant lots to me also. They told me, in my way of thinkin', that there had to be a God. Nature and trees were somethin' I could go to.

You see, at one time in my life, because of the way I was treated by my uncle, I wondered why it had to be this way. It began to get on my nerves. Oh, if my father had lived. In followin' them thoughts, you begin to wish you could die. Until one day, it seemed like every bird, every tree, every flower, the wind, made a racket and talked to me. It just happened.

Everything that God made seemed to get my attention and I realized if God took care of them things, He would take care of me. They were my consolation. They were the kind of things changed my mind from wantin' to die.

I always seemed to notice things in nature that no one else saw. I didn't know I was doin' it, but others did. Like the time I went out in the field when I was three years old to tell them Grandma Fannie was dyin'. I don't know how I knowed that, but something told me, and I walked out there and told them.

In religious thought, I picturized myself as an angel. Heaven was a space that was prepared between the clouds and what was above. I picturized myself flyin' around in a light space. The only thing I could picturize as a soul was something inside me. Hell was where the fire was. It was below the earth. It would have smoke and scorpions in it.

I heard about a revival when I was still with my uncle. I didn't exactly know what church meant, but I had an idea. This was stuff I had to wait to come to me.

Nobody have given me praises. They always thought I was weird. People seemed to reject me and felt like I didn't belong amongst 'em. They thought I was a fool. I've been called fool too many times. I hates that word.

I've been lonely but not lonesome. I've just been by myself. I never needed anyone to play with because nature provided me entertainment. Sometimes people think I'm crazy. I'd be out there bellerin' like a calf and goin' on like a calf. That was fun to me.

I didn't know too much about other races 'cause I wasn't around them. My aunt and uncle spoke real good Spanish. I'd hear them say a Spanish word and I would remember it. When I started to be around Spanish folks, I would ask them what the words meant. That's how I learned to speak Spanish.

My uncle was so cruel, I didn't want to be around no colored people. I thought they were all like that. Back in those days people thought children ought to be treated like that. He never said a plain word of praise to me.

I know how an orphan calf feels. He learns to eat grass on his own. Sometimes they don't know what they are. They might even think they are dogs if they lived with them. I had no one to nurse me—I learned by myself. That's why I can understand that calf.

He doesn't know whether he is a dog, a calf, or a person. He doesn't pay other calves no mind. He isn't like anything else. That may sound simple, but that's the truth. It's the picture of a life of loneliness. That calf was alone, but I don't know if he was lonesome. I know I came through all this, as miserable as it was, with something nobody else has.

Not one time did my uncle ever show me anything. He didn't treat his grandchildren that way. You see, my mother wasn't quite all there, and I had to live with my uncle. They didn't give me but two meals a day. I got some clabber and a pone of cornbread. That was my eats and I'd get hongry. If I got real hongry, I'd go in the watermelon patch. Rain would spoil my tracks out every time. He never did catch me.

Sometimes I'd steal eggs. Uncle Charlie would keep burned logs down in the Swickheimer [Ranch] to use for ash lye. I had to do all the washin' with a rub board. Before I washed, I would have to drip water through the ashes to make washin' powder. I'd put the eggs in the hot ashes and cook them just like a boiled egg.

Studyin' people gave me a gift. I had to pick my way through life, not havin' anybody to train me or teach me. I had to see what was right to take for my own. This cookin' gave me a chance.

This was about the time I was drifted around from one to the other. My mother married again when I was about four. We went to San Antonio again. I was about six when we came back and I went to the Manahuilla school.

When I was a boy, people was more lovin' and more warm to each other. We could depend on each other and would go out to an extreme to help each other. We would suffer long if it called for it to help one another. We would drive for miles to help. If anyone died in the community anywhere around, they would ride for miles around takin' the news.

Everything used to be prairie long time ago. Now it's all brush and fences. Everything was kind of clean. I been payin' attention to how many trees it is now. I wonder if it means there is goin' to be a change. Maybe gasoline and oil will change and man will have to go back to wood. If times last, this privilege of gasoline may wear out and that's why the trees have grown up. There just weren't no trees around here except in the bottom when I was a boy.

I guess I was what they call an abused child now. I was treated critically and different than other children. It made me wonder how it would have been if my father had lived. I would have had protection and somebody to teach me. I wondered, is there a God? I began to look at creation. I began to look at trees and veins in the leaves.

I saw that He made leaves just like He made me. That made me go to wonderin' about God. The wind, the leaves, the trees, everything that God made had a noise that attracted my attention. I knew nothin' about God. Just me by myself, I knew it didn't just happen.

Lightnin' was one thing that really got my attention. I see a tree was struck by lightnin' and just look at it and wonder about the power of God. I could see there was a difference in the power of man and the power of God. How long would it take man to do the same work the lightnin' did in an instant? I could see God's power and might in lightnin' and stuff like that. I was cookin' over at Shay's [ranch] and a bolt of lightnin' came in the kitchen and disappeared. I knew God was a spirit.

My eyes was completely taken off man and turned to nature. That's where I began to see God. When I did finally turn to man, it was cowmen, cowboys, and herdsmen. Cattle people were fun, happy people. They lived by tellin' tales. That was a pleasure to me. My first joy in dealin' with man was in cow camp. It was a pleasure to come into the cow crowd. Cow people seemed to care about a child. They were carin' people.

Havin' enough food is a joy to me. That's why I cook so much. I can't stand to see nobody hongry. I try my best to cook a-plenty. If you don't like this, maybe you will like that. Nobody goes away from my table hongry. I know what it is to be hongry. I can't stand to see anybody without food.

That was the nature of most people in them days. Everybody wanted to help you instead of hurt you. Nobody would do anything deliberately to hurt you. You could depend on your neighbor. If you had animals or anything, your neighbor would look out for your belongin's if you were gone. People would bring your animals plumb back to your house. That's the way people lived in them days, more lovin', more close, more warm to each other. Today it's so different. You're afraid of people today. You don't know who to trust.

I think I was somewhat peculiar. I always want to be to myself. You know, they say God's people is peculiar people. I never did like to sleep with people around in a bunch. I always stayed off to myself. I was raised that way. Many a night I've stayed in that wagon with frost all over me.

The people who raised me didn't pay much attention to me if I was sick or hurt. That's why I had to depend on revelations. I had to do whatever come to me. They paid no attention to me and nobody to teach me. You got to look to something for help.

The way I was brought up was not as fortunate as some people. If you don't have a mother and father to look after you, you got to scramble for yourself.

I lived with the animals and I could make any kind of animal noise. I learnt as I went along. I could mock almost anything I ever heard.

In this life there is many spirits. We can be obsessed with certain spirits. Occasionally that talkin' spirit can get on me. I believe the world is full of spirits. Everything is either spirit or matter, and everything comes from spirit or matter. Everything comes from God or the devil.

God put together matter and spirit and made man. Matter can't stand against time since man disobeyed God. Man is subject to death, sickness, and pain. Then there comes a time when spirit and matter must be separated. The spirit goes back to God.

I am not frightened of death. I am prepared. Wisdom taught me to prepare for death. The whole world is run by vibrations and sounds.

Funny thing, workin' with animals. You learn them and they learn you. Hogs can be taught to lift the lid on a feeder. That's an animal learnin' from you. You can learn them human sense. My experience about animals and learnin' from animals came as a kid. I had to learn from something.

First, you get acquainted with the animal and let him get acquainted with you. Ever since Adam disobeyed God, animals got afraid of man. They looked on him as a dangerous thing. For that reason you got to let him get used to you and learn there is no harm in you and you is his friend. You can learn him whatever you want to. He has to know you love him.

Animals has an instinct some kind of way. After they know you won't hurt them, they will pay attention to you. That's the nature of animals. They watch every

"I went to Victoria once. There was an old white gentleman there at the city square. He walked up to me and asked what the weather was going to do. I told him I didn't know. He said, 'People and the weather are just alike. You can't tell what either is going to do anymore.' You can't depend on people anymore. They are uncertain now. So different than when I was a kid."

Milam Thompson

move you make. I never holler at an animal, I never rebuke them.

I have learned a lot of things from animals. I can see a dog or any kind of animal and tell whether he is sick. I look at the way he moves around. When a goat or a hog is wormy, they will hold their tails down. Deer will do the same thing. Chicken's wings will get droopy.

I was going into town one time to do my tradin' and we passed some cows. I knew one was sick and I said so. No one paid any attention to me, but when we came home the cow was dead. Nobody could figure out how I knew she was sick. They talked about that a long time.

Animals and nature were my life and fun. I never played many games. Other people had parents and other children to play with. I had to turn to nature. Them's the things that taught me about God. I could walk up to a stream of water and stand there lookin' at it forever while it was runnin'. I would throw sticks in the water and name them and see which one won. That was my way of havin' fun.

I'd see God in them things. Lookin' at trees, I'd see each tree is a different shade of green. You can see that God is bound to love greens because he made so many different kinds. I learned to love green because God loved it. Those are the kinds of things entertained me when I was a kid. Even today I do that.

I used to know might near every tree in the Murphy bottom. I knew which pecan trees opened first, and I would go huntin' down there and get lost. Then I'd run up on a tree that I was acquainted with, and I'd know how to get out. You can go in the bottom now and watch the greens change as time goes on. Green means much to man and God, as I see it.

My experience comes direct from revelations. I had to go out there and do the best I could. People who live with nature are different. We have a different experience with nature. In town you have to live with what man made. We see things town people don't see.

You take sounds, different scenes. I was more interested in things like that than I was people. It's not that I'm selfish. I've been called selfish, but I'm not. I'm not stuck up. I don't even know how to act like that.

I have lots of things to guide me. Sounds mean so much to me. The last thing you will witness will be sound—the sound of the trumpet. It will be so loud it will wake up the dead. I want to be somewhere listenin' for that sound.

Trees and wind and stuff like that is where I gets my joy from. I can walk out and listen to the trees. The leaves are shakin' on the trees. I imagined they were singin' a song to me. Bein' brought up by myself, I turned to them things and I leaned on them things.

They give you thoughts and you can see God in things like that. You can see man makin' a bunch of racket and you get bored with that. Dancin' was the only thing brought joy to my body but not my soul, and I turned to that.

I never took a hand to drinkin' and gamblin'. I turned to music because music was a sound. When that sound went out, it got all in my feet. That sound is what stirred me up inside. Sound is a great thing to me. Sound will get anyone's attention.

Sometimes I been walkin' through the woods, through Lewis's Bend a many a time. Sometimes if your heart is just right and your thinkin' is just right, trees can be rubbin' against each other. The sound they are saying is "Lord, have mercy."

You know you get that in your mind and it sounds like those trees are callin' God's name. I've stopped, and the shakin' of the leaves sounds like they are havin' church. That's what comes in your mind when you have a mind like mine. If your mind's not like that, you won't pay it any attention.

I had to pay attention to nature and it has taught me many things. I've cried, I've laughed, I've did everything, listenin' and payin' attention to nature.

Man has gotten away from God. He is obsessed with the wrong spirits. The world is full of all kinds of spirits. We are gettin' away from nature and all that God made. People say, "Look at what I did," not what God did. Our spiritual side appreciates nature, our man side only appreciates what man does. Boastin' and such demons of that kind possess man now. Few people today look to God.

"I just can't forget them hap-penin's, that past. I'll never forget the good and the bad."

Milam Thompson

Nature was all I had to look to. Nature seemed to speak to me. Now, my boys, when I was raisin' them, I would make them things to play with and would try to teach them with these things. I would make them a wheel to push and would tell them if they looked down at that wheel while they were goin' somewhere, they wouldn't step on a snake.

I tried to make work be fun to them. You have to work with a person to kind of test his thoughts and his ideas out to really know how to talk to him. I wouldn't know how to get through to a child in a city.

Nature is the way to teach children. I have seen teachin' that way change children from outlaws to one of the best around. Never teach them no lies, even about Santa Claus or the Easter Bunny. You have to be true to kids. That's one of the best ways to get up to a child. Get him believin' in himself and believin' in you. If he can't trust you, what is he goin' to do with hisself?

As for women, I had no one in life to go along with me. I went out with all I had to find a companion. I married a girl with all I had. I needed her. She was nineteen and I was twenty-one. That lady couldn't resist anything come along.

When we started a family, along came another man's children. I tried to give her another chance, but she didn't take it. She decided to go home to her daddy. Her parents weren't against it at all. I didn't have any idea that a man's trouble began when he got married.

Then I really fell in love with my second wife. She did her bad actin' out in public and told me so. You see, I've been up against it all my life, and that's why I'm afraid of women.

My life has been in the hands of people other than my parents. I have learned a whole lot about people. People thinks differently and will treat you differently. There is good in everybody and a little bad in everybody. You can find something you want to remember in all of them. Even winos may have good in them. He may be the one to save you and your property in some way.

God made us a free agent. He set good and evil in front of us. Man often chooses evil. It is a constant battle. Satan's job is to ruin man. He confuses our signals and misleads us. I have been through some tough things. The story of Job gives me strength. I believe I am beginnin' to be rewarded for my perseverance. The only way you can be free is to speak the truth and know the truth and act the truth.

Only occasionally does someone understand me. My mother was one. Even though she was irresponsible about some things, she understood me. I could go and talk to Mama. When she died, I missed her. She would know what I was goin' to say before I said it.

Her name was Lomie Holliman Gray. She is buried in the Sample cemetery on the San'tone River road. I was split up from her when I was young, but I would go see her from time to time. She wasn't crazy. She had a mind, she just couldn't think for herself. If you told her what to do, she would do it with pleasure. She just couldn't think for herself. My mother was scared of sick people and dead folks. If you got sick around Mama, you was just sick, 'cause she was gone. And you better not die, 'cause she was *sho'* gone.

Fear taught the black man how to humble himself. I have been in spots where I had to stand up for myself. My own people thought I was wrong when I stood up at times. Things I have run into in life made me have to stand up when I thought I was right. The older people would rebuke me at times. When I thought I

"What is revealed to me is more real than what man tells me. I question man, but when I look at nature and see God somewhere about it, I just know it's true."

Milam Thompson

was right, I would not give down.

The answers are not in people. The answers are in God. People disappointed me, the church disappointed me, and marriage disappointed me. I had to come through what I come through. People, the church, and marriage had to fail me so I could depend on God, not man.

People were scared of my knowledge. I think my father was gifted in the way of God. They shunned him also. He would talk about slavery and freedom. He was foolish in their eyes. They said he was actin' a monkey. He used funny words that had more than one meanin'. People felt I was foolish like they thought my father was. There had to be a reason for this. I practice my religion in my own way. To this day, I depends on the Lord, not man. This has caused me many problems, but it brought me to God.

Orphans were picked on in the older days. My life has been rough. I had very little contact with my family in my life. I had lots of half brothers and sisters and one full sister and a brother who died. I still come up by myself, even with all this family.

A lot of time I think if things turned around like they used to be, how many people would survive? I know I could. I can survive anywhere. My thinkers just done got dull and my remembrance done wore out. I think God has begun to bless me now. I thank God every day for being able to tell my story.

I want to be buried on O'Connor land.

Milam Thompson

Author's note: Milam is buried on O'Connor land with a headstone that reads:

MILAM THOMPSON

CAMP COOK, PHILOSOPHER, PREACHER.

1907–1991.

Epilogue

This volume is only the beginning. The origins of the San'tone River culture make a truly fascinating and complicated story. As we progress into the wonders of the folklore and daily life of the river bottom in the next volume, we will see the full complexity and beauty of this culture.

My collaborators have, once again, gone into the depths of their souls and experiences and shared them with all of us. Without their voices, a dying and completely unique culture would have been lost forever.

Thank you once again, my dear friends, for not letting this happen. I thank you for making this project such a joyful process, and the world thanks you for making it so interesting.

Author's study.

Glossary

bad	good
battin'	batten; a thin strip of lumber, used in board-and-batten construction
bright	light-skinned, "high yellow"; used to describe a black person's skin color
brothledge	some kind of ailment or disease; a coined term whose meaning is unclear
bruja	a woman reputed to have special powers; literally, "witch"
Camino Real	the Royal Road or King's Highway, a network of trails that provided the main access to Texas from Mexico in the seventeenth and eighteenth centuries; it connected the East Texas missions with San Antonio and then extended south of the Rio Grande; also known as the San Antonio Road
can't to can't	an expression meaning "from early morning to late at night" (i.e., from when you can't see until you can't see)
case	to figure out, size up
chimbley	chimney
chinkipin	an acorn from the chinquapin oak tree
chiny	a chinaberry tree or its fruit
chitlins	hog intestines prepared as food; tripe
chunk	to throw
cracklin's	the crisp pork skins that remained after the fat was rendered for lard
dirk	a knife
french a calf	to throw a calf down
garçonnière	quarters for adolescent males, usually built apart from the main residence
go-in	a fight or conflict
halfsies	a tenant-farming arrangement whereby the landowner and the tenant split the crop or the profits
hand	cowhand
hooraw	to tease or make fun of
hot	sizzling
huisache	any of several species of trees in the Acacia family
jack	a male, donkey
jack-o-lanterns	fireballs of unknown origin seen at night on the prairie
keen	high-pitched
knockaway	an anaqua tree or a nut from the tree (*Ehretia elliptica*)
labor	177.1 acres
league	4,428.4 acres
light a shuck	to move quickly
light	to settle down or stay in a place for a while
line	rein
littoral league	a league of land along the coast
low	short
Meskin	a crude word for "Mexican"
mess	a meal's worth, an adequate portion of something to eat
morral	a sack made of grass, usually hung on the saddle horn
motherwit	common sense; also a sixth sense, psychic power

mott	a clump of trees on the prairie
night horse	a horse that is kept up at night to round up the remuda in the morning
overhauls	overalls
palmetto	a small native palm tree
peace barn	probably a folk term for "peace bond," possibly "jail"
pilón	something free; the Spanish equivalent of "a baker's dozen" or "lagniappe"
peninsulares	natives of the Iberian Peninsula (Spain)
pimp	spy, informer
pitch	to buck
podnah	a partner, a term of endearment
post	to warn
punching house	a house built with puncheons, split logs or heavy slabs with the face smoothed
remuda	the herd from which the daily work horses are chosen
river bottom	the land along a river
royals	Spanish gold coins; from *reales*
scowl	a low-pitched sound
seeney bean	the pod of the siene (or sienna) bean shrub (*Sesbania* spp.)
sendero	a clearing or trail cut through the brush
shoat	a young pig
smart	"brainy" like a city slicker, having little common sense
step over the fence	to commit miscegenation
susto	fear, fright, a scare
tasso	sun-dried meat, jerky; from *tasajo*
tophand	a skilled cowhand; one who has reached the top of the profession
unshriven	without benefit of confession and absolution
unio	a freshwater shellfish like mussels
up	upper-class
veil	the amniotic sack, as in "born with a veil over the face"
wild apples	the fruit of the plant Turk's cap (*Malvaviscus drummondii*); also known as manzanilla, Mexican apple, Texas mallow

Tellers of the Tales

Adams, Charley (August 3, 1921–March 27, 1995). Itinerant cowhand and trail driver.

Adams, Lola Gibson (1890–1994). Resident of Refugio. Spent a lot of her childhood in the San Antonio River bottom and Lewis's Bend.

Adams, Mary Lucy De La Garza (October 1924–　). Descendant of Texas pioneer rancher Carlos De La Garza.

Albrecht, Earl (October 1902–　) A world adventurer and a member of a pioneer German ranching and farming family in Goliad County.

Albrecht, Henry "Blue" (May 30, 1894–October 22, 1990). Goliad resident, rancher, farmer, and World War I veteran. Saw the Wright Brothers land in Victoria in 1910.

Amador, Ynocente "Tía Minnie" De La Garza (April 27, 1902–January 23, 1997). Member of the Carlos De La Garza family. Her mother inherited the ranch and ran it herself with Ynocente's help as a young girl.

Bade, Lola Sales (February 1920–　). Daughter of a local doctor and wife of a local doctor.

Baecker, Marjorie Albrecht (November 1917–　). Lifelong resident of the Goliad area and its farming community.

Barber, Viola Emison (July 1903–　). Schoolteacher, member of a ranching family of German descent.

Bego, Ralph (August 16, 1905–February 4, 1993). Rancher in the Goliad area.

Bennett, Della May McDow (November 1919–　). Grew up in Goliad. Daughter of George McDow, who drove cattle on the Chisholm Trail.

Bickford, Herbert "Buster" (March 10, 1902–December 14, 1992). Rancher in the Tivoli area and a lifelong resident of the San Antonio River bottom. Member of an old ranching family of the area.

Brewer, Chet (1907–1990). Pitcher for the Kansas City Monarchs and teammate of Willie Bell of Lewis's Bend; later a scout for the Pittsburgh Pirates.

Brown, Pete (September 1920–　). Former cowhand and ranch foreman for the Traylor/Bauer family; deputy sheriff, Victoria County.

Brown, Sonny (May 1935–　). Tophand on the Traylor ranches.

Brown, Willie (October 1929–　). Deputy sheriff of Refugio County.

Buckert, Emily Smolik (November 1924–　). Longtime area resident and food editor for the *Victoria Advocate*.

Buckert, Kai (January 1959–　). Foreman, O'Connor Brothers Ranches (northern division).

Buentello, Alfredo (January 1916–　). Farmer and rancher, resident of Victoria County.

Charleston, Henry (February 6, 1910–19??). Member of an African-American ranching and farming family in the San Antonio River area near the Fagan ranch.

Cook, Alice Youngblood (February 1, 1921–November 17, 1997). Grew up in the Lewis's Bend area. Lived and worked on the Welder Vidauri Ranch and later on the Thomas M. O'Connor Greta Ranch.

Cook, Ananias (1909–1984). Cowhand on the Welder Vidauri Ranch.

Cook, Ulysses "Tommy" (September 1921–　). Hospital orderly at Citizens Memorial Hospital in Victoria for twenty-five years. Grew up in Lewis's Bend.

Curtis, Alton (August 16, 1915–November 13, 1993). Resident of the community of Sarco.

Davenport, Mozelle Roper (July 1933–　). Retired schoolteacher who grew up in Tivoli.

De La Garza, Alejandro (March 1921–). Tophand on the O'Connor Brothers
Ranches. Great-great-grandson of the Texas pioneer rancher Carlos De La Garza.

De La Garza, Elías (August 1930–). Tophand on the O'Connor Brothers
Ranches. Member of the pioneering Carlos De La Garza family.

De La Garza, Johnny (October 1934–). Caretaker of the O'Connor cemetery,
O'Connor Brothers River Ranch. Descendant of pioneer Carlos De La Garza.

De La Garza, Mary Luz Pérez (March 6, 1926–November 20, 1997). Renowned as the
best angler in the region. Daughter of Frank Pérez Sr. and wife of Alejandro De La
Garza. Grew up in the San Antonio River bottom.

De La Garza, Rafael (1888–1988). Cowhand on the O'Connor Brothers Ranches and
lifelong resident of the San Antonio River area. Member of the Carlos De La
Garza family.

DeLeón, Santiago "Jim" (May 1913–). Descendant of the empresario
Martín DeLeón, Victoria's founder.

Duncan, Joe (1917–). Resident of San Antonio who was born and reared in the
St. Paul-Manahuilla area.

Durst, Josephine Holliday (January 19, 1899–July 25, 1994). Grew up in the Lewis's
Bend area. Daughter of Tom Holliday.

Edwards, Ruby Lee Youngblood (August 1929–). Goliad resident who grew
up in the San Antonio River area. Daughter of the cowboy Joe Youngblood.

Edwards, Zilpah Daniel (1905–1997). Grew up in the San Antonio River area. Member
of the Stoner family. Versed in the traditions and lifestyle of the Old South.

Evans, Laura Virginia Lewis (August 1923–). Member of a family of ranchers,
farmers, and sharecroppers. Raised in the Hall's Point community, Goliad County.

Fagan, Freddy (October 1919–). Refugio County rancher.

Farley, James "Rip" (November 1920–). Rancher and owner of part of the
original Farley ranch in Goliad County.

Faupel, Charlie (August 1956–). Rancher and member of the Reeves family
of Goliad County.

Fletcher, Beverly Barber (April 1931–). Daughter of a rancher in the
Tivoli area.

Franklin, Althia Lewis Burns (June 1921–). Daughter of Charlie Lewis.
Spent her childhood on the Parks ranch near Fannin.

Franklin, Rachel Wynona Lewis (December 12, 1926–September 16, 1997). Daughter of
Charlie Lewis, sister of Althia Lewis Burns Franklin.

Gaugler, Orville (January 26, 1927–). Victoria County resident of German descent.
Member of a family of trail drivers.

Gould, Florence (December 1914–). Wife of George Gould and partner in the
management of the Vidauri Mercantile.

Gould, George (February 1912–). Manager of the Vidauri Mercantile of the
Welder Vidauri Ranch.

Greer, Marye Murphy (March 1909–). Grew up on the San Antonio River in
a pioneering ranching family. Operates part of the old Murphy ranch.

Haney, Elizabeth Sevier (April 4, 1900–September 16, 1985). Grew up in Lewis's Bend.
Member of an old family that came to the area during the Texas Revolution.

Harris, Annettie "Nettie" (November 12, 1940–April 13, 1992). Daughter of Richard
Harris.

Harris, Richard (1892–1988). Foreman, Murphy ranch. Grew up in the San Antonio
River area and worked for the Murphys all his life.

Heibel, Victor (September 1912–). Goliad County resident of German
ancestry and member of a farming family.

Henderson, Mose (April 23, 1915–February 3, 1994). Cowhand and cook, Welder Vidauri Ranch.

Hill, Sarah Johnson (1899–   ). Member of the pioneering Winsor family of Refugio County.

Hosey, Rosie Tillman Jones (January 1934–   ). Daughter of Mattie Tillman and granddaughter of Andrew Tillman.

Huber, David (December 1947–   ). Farmer and rancher in the San Antonio River area.

Huber, Eunice (June 1918–   ). Wife of Martin Huber, mother of David Huber.

Huber, Martin (October 1915–   ). Farmer on the San Antonio River Road.

Jacob, Darden (June 1934–   ). Inspector for the Southwest Texas Cattle Raisers Association. Grew up on the Guadalupe and San Antonio rivers. Raises and shows horses.

Jaillet, Lois Farley (August 1927–   ). Member of the Simms family of Lewis's Bend.

Jones, Jesse (May 28, 1917–April 25, 1998). Tophand on the O'Connor Ranches. Son of Matt Jones.

Jones, Rosie Terrell (November 17, 1912–July 28, 1992). Member of the Terrell family of the San Antonio River bottom. Cooked and worked on the O'Connor Brothers Ranches. Wife of Willie Jones, an O'Connor tophand.

Joshlin, Coleman (July 1928–   ). Cowhand on the Welder ranches, preacher.

Knight, Mary Elizabeth Welder (October 1930–   ). Member of several pioneering Texas families. Expert on Irish culture in Texas.

Levigne, Georgine Terrell (February 1938–   ). Daughter of Willie "Luck" Terrell, tophand.

Lieb, Carlyn Mernitz (June 1919–   ). Resident of the Tivoli/Austwell area.

Loest, Lydia Kern (December 1909–   ). Lifelong resident of Goliad County. Daughter of a preacher and expert on German culture.

Lott, Allene Pettus (December 1911–   ). Member of pioneer ranching family of the Goliad area and wife of a local rancher. Expert on Southern traditions and manners.

Lott, J. Y. (January 12, 1913–January 4, 1998). Cowhand on the Welder and O'Connor ranches. Grew up in the Lewis's Bend area.

Lott, John Freeman (February 1913–   ). Local rancher in the Riverdale area. Member of a pioneering family of Goliad County.

Lott, S. W. "Toney" (November 1906–   ). Cowhand on the Welder Vidauri Ranch. Brother of J. Y. Lott. Grew up in the Lewis's Bend area.

Love, Quinn (February 1918–   ). Itinerant tophand. Grew up in the San Antonio River area. Member of the Harvey family.

Mace, Louise De La Garza (October 1928–   ). Daughter of Raphael De La Garza of the pioneering Carlos De La Garza family.

Magruder, Helen Williams (November 27, 1903–June 8, 1995). Grew up in Goliad County on the Thomas M. O'Connor ranch.

Marks, Jeanne Houghton (August 1920–   ). Local rancher.

Martínez, Anita (September 1946–   ). Expert on changes in Mexican culture in present-day Texas. Daughter of San Juana Martínez.

Martínez, San Juana De Los Santos (June 24, 1924–July 14, 1995). Lifelong resident of the area. Expert on Mexican culture.

Matthews, Osee "O. C." (December 9, 1897–February 10, 1971). Husband of Mary Genevieve DuBois, a descendant of pioneer rancher Nicholas Fagan. Her sister, Susanna Texana DuBois, married Osee's twin brother, Roy.

McKnight, Vivian Lott (January 1914–   ). Born and reared on the O'Connor River Ranch in Refugio County.

Morrow, Henry (May 1905–   ).   Member of an early pioneering family in the
    San Antonio River area near the Fagan ranch.
Murphy, Louise (19??–   ).   Wife of James Joseph Murphy Jr., brother of
    Marye Murphy Greer.
Nava, Beatrice De La Garza (September 1929–   ).   Descendant of Texas
    pioneer rancher Carlos De La Garza.
New, James K. "Spec" (January 7, 1910–March 16, 1996).   Member of the Terrell
    family, ranchers in the Berclair area and in Refugio County.
O'Connor, Thomas M., II (1857–1922).   Grandson of Thomas O'Connor I.
O'Connor, Tom, Jr. III (March 6, 1915–August 7, 1996).   Great-grandson of Thomas
    O'Connor I. Rancher, banker, oilman, and superb storyteller.
Oliver, K. J. (December 1914–   ).   Itinerant tophand.
Paul, Luther Bennet (January 1939–   ).   Commercial artist, author,
    and historian.
Payne, Wanda Hood (July 1934–   ).   Wife of a local rancher in the San Antonio
    River Road area.
Penn, Myrtle Rodgers (19??–19??).   Daughter of Tom "Ball" Rodgers.
Perkins, Jeanette Johnstone (July 1910–   ).   Resident of the community of
    Sarco, Goliad County.
Pettus, June (April 1929–   ).   Member of the Pettus family, one of the earliest
    Anglo families to settle in the area.
Peyton, Jerri Hall (March 1943–   ). A teacher whose Irish ancestors were pioneer
    Victoria settlers and Coleto Creek ranchers.
Phillips, E. "Spec," D.V.M. (August 1921–   ).   Local veterinarian who grew up
    on the Welder Vidauri Ranch, where his father was employed.
Rice, Leo (August 1930–   ).   Member of an African-American farming family
    along the San Antonio River.
Richardson, Gussie Marshall (April 1918–   ).   Wife of Seward Richardson.
Richardson, Seward (June 1915–   ).   Local chauffeur and author of *"Frisco":
    Eighty-One Years in Small-Town Refugio, Texas.* Born and reared in Refugio.
Rigby, Paul "Beans" (January 1904–   ).   Barber. Goliad and Sarco resident.
Robinson, Allie Fay Moore (December 1924–   ).   Retired nurse's aide and Goliad
    resident. Wife of Johnny Robinson.
Robinson, Johnny (March 1919–   ).   Cowboy. Born and reared in Goliad.
Robinson, Troy (April 1917–   ).   Cowboy on the O'Connor Duke Ranch. Grew
    up in the San Antonio River area.
Rodgers, Ida Jenell Blackburn (May 1915–   ).   Daughter of a rancher, she now
    runs the family ranch.
Rodgers, Tom (19??–   ).   Nephew of Tom "Ball" Rodgers.
Rodríguez, Julia O'Riley (March 1913–   ).   Resident of Victoria County and
    member of the pioneering O'Riley family.
Rodríguez, Víctor (February 1915–   ).   *Curandero.* Born on the O'Connor
    River Ranch.
Roell, Constance Kohl (September 1910–   ).   Lifelong resident of Raisin.
Roell, Joseph (May 1917–   ).   Resident of Raisin and husband of Constance
    Kohl Roell.
Rubio, Abel (August 1930–   ).   Author of *Stolen Heritage.* Member of the
    pioneering Carlos De La Garza family.
Rubio, Margaret Pérez-Salazar (October 1929–   ).   Expert on Mexican culture.
    Member of the Pérez family, local musicians. What a beautiful voice!
Rydolph, Simmie (December 1908–   ). Member of prominent African-
    American family of the area; grandson of Anderson Tillman. Grew up in the

Lewis's Bend area. Worked in the dry cleaning business in California. Expert on World War II and the California shipyards.

Schultz, Reatha Morley (August 1916–).   Native of Lavaca County and Tivoli resident since 1937. Wife of Ernest Schultz.

Serrata, José Ángel (1895–1975).   Employee of the O'Connor Melon Creek Ranch.

Shaw, Katharine Kinsler (October 1907–).   Daughter of John Kinsler, an early settler of Tivoli.

Shaw, Monroe "Bailey" (May 5, 1903–September 14, 1996).   Itinerant cowhand and well digger.

Shelton, Vernell Gray (July 1925–).   Former teacher and clerk of the Goliad Manahuilla Missionary Church.

Sievers, Henry Jr., (August 1910–).   DeWitt County native who was reared in Goliad. Member of a family of German ancestry.

Snider, Lucile "Hallie" Fagan (April 1917–).   Author and historian. Born on the Fagan ranch, Refugio County.

Stofer, James N. (September 1937–).   Grandson of Preston Rose Austin, founder of Austwell and Tivoli and partner of Jesse McDowell.

Stubblefield, P. K. (August 1914–).   Retired president of the Victoria Bank and Trust Company. Member of a pioneering merchant family in the San Antonio River and Bloomington areas.

Tatton, Virginia Hallinan (July 23, 1901–April 11, 1993).   Great-granddaughter of Thomas O'Connor I and daughter of Mary O'Connor Hallinan.

Terrell, Josephine Holliman (1910–August 19, 1997).   Granddaughter of Steve Holliman.

Terrell, L. V. (November 26, 1917–July 5, 1989).   Tophand on the O'Connor ranches.

Terrell, Thurman (April 7, 1916–February 11, 1994).   Born on the Terrell ranch; worked for the O'Connors, Welders, Terrells, and Joe Shay. Great-grandson of Martha Perryman.

Terrell, Willie "Luck" (February 1, 1907–May 14, 1981).   Tophand on the Murphy and Fagan ranches of the San Antonio River Road.

Thomas, Milton (1924–).   Grandson of Tom "Ball" Rodgers.

Thompson, Milam (March 17, 1907–January 10, 1991).   Camp cook, philosopher, and preacher.

Tibiletti, Leroy Taylor (1936–1992).   Rancher and descendant of an Italian family that came over during the Italian migration of 1880–1920.

Tijerina, Julián (February 1937–).   Tophand on the O'Connor Brothers Ranches. Descendant of a pioneering Texas ranching family in the San Antonio River area.

Tijerina, Teresa Escalona (October 1939–).   Born and reared on the Braman Spring Creek Ranch, Victoria County. Wife of Julián Tijerina.

Tillman, Eugene (1902–April 9, 1994).   Preacher and farmer. Son of Anderson Tillman of Lewis's Bend.

Tillman, Sarah Sample (19??–19??).   Daughter of Will Sample and sister of Simmie Rydolph.

Tisdom, James "Smokestack" (March 17, 1912–November 5, 1995).   Local cowhand from the Goliad area who sang ballads and told folktales. Also known as "Mr. Jinx."

Traylor, Thomas Pascal (August 11, 1871–May 13, 1952).   Rancher, owner of the Traylor ranches in southeastern Victoria County.

Wade, Reverend Albert (May 1908–).   Preacher who sings the Old One Hundreds.

Warburton, Volney (June 17, 1909–May 15, 1991).   Rancher and farmer who grew up around Kuy Creek. Member of the Stoner family on his mother's side.

Ward, Earl (1918–1986). Itinerant cowhand and foreman for the O'Connor ranches.

Weathers, Will (January 5, 1905–December 2, 1987). Cowboy and preacher.

Wesley, Zearlee Robinson (February 1909–   ). Brought up on the Power ranch, Vidauri. A tomboy in her youth. Loves outside work.

Wieser, Jean Amery (April 1928–   ). Member of the Amery family, which settled Anaqua.

Willemin, Rosie Hornstein (February 23, 1908–December 27, 1993). Grew up on Fleming Prairie.

Williams, Alice Mae Barefield (19??–   ). Grew up in the Tivoli/Austwell area. Wife of Reverend Mack Williams.

Williams, Lela Edwards (September 1909–   ). Born and reared on the O'Connor Brothers River Ranch. Daughter of Alonso "Lonze" Edwards.

Williams, Reverend Mack (November 16, 1914–April 9, 1998). Tophand, O'Connor Peach Mott Ranch. Respected preacher and civic leader. Known as "El Coyote Prieto" and sometimes "Mank" (a nickname for Manchen, his true given name).

Williams, Penceola Terrell (October 1924–   ). Born on the Terrell ranch. Great-granddaughter of Martha Perryman, "Grandma Marthy."

Williams, Royal McKinley (September 11, 1919–March 25, 1994). Tophand on the O'Connor ranches. Son of camp cook Charlie Williams.

Winsor, Joyce Anderson (19??–   ). Irish descendant and Refugio resident. Secretary to regional historian Hobart Huson for many years.

Ybarbo, Jesús (July 2, 1907–November 20, 1990). Itinerant tophand, caretaker of O'Connor cemetery. Member of an old pioneer family in the San Antonio River bottom.

Young, Lee Anna Terrell (April 9, 1911–August 11, 1986). Member of the Terrell family of Lewis's Bend.

Youngblood, Dan (September 9, 1918–May 9, 1987). Tophand, farmer, Welder Vidauri Ranch. Known as "Tea Cakes" and "Wood."

Youngblood, Evelyn Elliot (May 1924–   ). Refugio native, wife of Nathaniel Youngblood.

Youngblood, Nathaniel (May 18, 1922–September 10, 1996). Tophand on the Welder Vidauri Ranch. Known as "Little Baby" and many other names.

Note: For living contributors, birthdates have been omitted for privacy reasons.

Notes

1. The San Antonio River

1. Sister Margaret Rose Warburton, C.D.P., "A History of the Thomas O'Connor Ranch" (master's thesis, Catholic University of America, San Antonio, 1939), 95.

2. Bella French Swisher, "The San Antonio River," in S. H. Dixon, *The Poets and Poetry of Texas* (Austin: Sam H. Dixon & Co., 1885), 308.

3. Kathryn Stoner O'Connor, *Presidio La Bahía del Espritu [Espíritu] Santo de Zúñiga, 1721 to 1846* (Austin: Von Boeckmann-Jones, 1966), 1. Restoring the presidio became one of my grandmother's consuming passions for several years, even though she was already into her eighties.

4. José De Solís, "The Solís Diary of 1767," in *Preparing the Way: Preliminary Studies of the Texas Catholic Historical Society,* Texas Catholic Historical Society Studies in Southwestern Catholic History, no. 1, ed. Jesús F. de la Teja (Austin: Texas Catholic Historical Society, 1997), 109; originally published in 1931 by the Texas Knights of Columbus Historical Commission. My grandmother's notes describe a *mojarra* as a small round fish about six inches long (Kathryn Stoner O'Connor, research notes, O'Connor Family Papers, 1824–1981, Center for American History, University of Texas at Austin; hereafter cited as O'Connor Papers, CAH). Tejanos in the Coastal Bend today say this is the word for "minnow."

5. See Patsy Light and Anne Bode, "San Antonio River Valley (West of Goliad) Rural Historic District," National Register of Historic Places Nomination, 1995, Texas Historical Commission Library, Austin.

6. Hobart Huson, *Refugio: A Comprehensive History of Refugio County from Aboriginal Times to 1953* (Woodsboro, Tex.: Rooke Foundation, 1953), 1:5.

2. They Met Us at the Boat

1. Some historians say the journey lasted six years, others seven. Similarly, the route has long been disputed. For a good summary of the controversy, see Nancy Parrott Hickerson, "The Travels of Cabeza de Vaca," *The Jumanos: Hunters and Traders of the South Plains* (Austin: University of Texas Press, 1994), chap. 1.

2. Howard Roberts Lamar, *Texas Crossings: The Lone Star State and the American Far West, 1836–1986,* George W. Littlefield Lectures in American History (Austin: University of Texas Press, 1991); William H. Goetzmann, "A Long, Long Trail A' Winding," introduction to *No Traveller Remains Untouched: Journeys and Transformations in the American Southwest,* Southwest Writers Collection (San Marcos: Southwest Texas State University, 1995). After his eventual return to Spain, Cabeza de Vaca advocated the benevolent treatment of conquered peoples, a surprisingly advanced view for his time. His efforts are credited with influencing the Spanish government's ultimate decision to end the slave trade in that country.

3. Carol A. Lipscomb, "Karankawa Indians," in *New Handbook of Texas* (Austin: Texas State Historical Association, 1996), 3:1031; Mary Jourdan Atkinson, *The Texas Indians* (San Antonio: Naylor Company, 1935), 194. Later the Tonkawa were reported here, and the Lipan Apache, a Plains tribe, raided the area between 1770 and 1850.

4. Atkinson, *Texas Indians,* 198; W. W. Newcomb Jr., *The Indians of Texas: From Prehistoric to Modern Times* (Austin: University of Texas Press, 1961), 61.

5. John J. Linn, *Reminiscences of Fifty Years in Texas* (New York: D. & J. Sadlier & Co., 1883); Noah Smithwick, *The Evolution of a State or Recollections of Old Texas Days* (Austin: Gammel Book Co., c. 1900; facsimile, Austin: Steck Company, 1935), 13.

6. Kathryn S. O'Connor, research notes, O'Connor Papers, CAH.

7. Jack Jackson, *Los Mesteños: Spanish Ranching in Texas, 1721–1821* (College Station: Texas A&M University Press, 1986), 13.

8. O'Connor, *Presidio La Bahía,* 74–75.

9. Catherine Allan, "Reminiscences of Mrs. Annie Fagan Teal," *By the Way* 1, no. 1 (April 1897), 4, as cited in Kathryn S. O'Connor, research notes, O'Connor Papers, CAH.

10. Kay Blackburn Billingsley, ed., *Blessed Joseph* (Beeville, Tex.: Beeville Publishing Co., 1979), 325.

3. River Bottom Communities: Centers of the World

1. Huson, *Refugio,* 1:7, 2:242.

2. Kathryn Stoner O'Connor, "Anaqua," in *New Handbook of Texas* (Austin: Texas State Historical Association, 1996), 1:161.

3. J. D. B. Stillwell, *Wanderings in the Southwest in 1855,* ed. Ron Tyler, Western Frontiersmen Series, no. 23 (Spokane, Wash.: Arthur H. Clark, 1990), 35–36. Originally published in *The Crayon,* July 11, 1855.

4. Huson, *Refugio,* 1:7, 1:268; O'Connor, "Anaqua."

5. O'Connor, *Presidio La Bahía,* 264.

6. Fredrick Douglas Young, *From These Roots: Cologne—One Hundred Years, 1870–1970* (Houston: Texas Southern University, 1973).

7. Huson, *Refugio,* 2:316.

8. Ibid., 1:579.

9. Lucile Fagan Snider, "Austwell," typescript, n.d., pp. 1–5, O'Connor Papers, CAH, box 2R888, folder 5.

4. Lewis's Bend: The Old Landmark

1. According to 1857 records for Refugio County, county commissioners planned "to lay off the public road from the S. Lewis ferry on the San Antonio River to the Town of Refugio." See Huson, *Refugio,* 1:579. Thomas O'Connor was among the county commissioners who were responsible for determining the route of this public road.

2. *Victoria Advocate,* n.d., O'Connor Papers, CAH. The dates mentioned in the article are uncertain, however. My grandmother told a nephew that Mary Virginia Drake "married Dennis M. O'Connor in Victoria, Texas in 1869 when she was 19 years old. The O'Connor children were Martin, who married Maude Lowe; Thos. who married Kathryn Stoner; Mary who married Jack Hallinan." Kemper Williams to Mrs. C. A. Dickey, July 26, 1968, O'Connor Papers, CAH.

3. Kathryn Stoner O'Connor, research notes, O'Connor Papers, CAH. As a child, I often wondered why Granny, who had the means to buy all the paper she needed, would record valuable history on the back of used envelopes, matchbooks, and other scraps of paper. In a conversation one day with a cousin of mine, Margaret Stoner McLean, I came to understand that in my grandmother's day, paper was much more scarce than it is today. Many people of my grandmother's generation never outgrew the habit of saving every scrap of this precious commodity.

4. Victoria County Probate Records.

5. My research has revealed only one ballplayer of this era who was known by the name "Cool Papa": James Thomas Bell of Mississippi. According to one source, Willie Bell won the sixth game of the first Negro World Series. During his twenty-five-year career (1923–1948), Bell played with not only the Kansas City Monarchs but also five other teams, possibly including a team with the semi-pro Negro Texas League. See Robert Peterson, *Only the Ball Was White* (Englewood Cliffs, N.J.: Prentice-Hall, 1970), 260.

5. Kith and Kin

1. There are numerous accounts of this event, but the exact date is difficult to determine for the one Martha Perryman would have seen. According to *The Encyclopaedia Britannica,* 11th ed. (Cambridge, 1911), 18:261, there were dramatic meteor showers in November of both 1832 and 1833, but records from the Deep South suggest a spring or summer event, possibly in an earlier year. Describing the phenomenon as "the day the stars fell" seems to have had biblical overtones, as the following contemporary record by an African-American indicates: "I left Baltimore, for St. Michael's in the month of March, 1833. I know the year, because it was the one . . . of that strange phenomenon, when the heavens seemed about to part with its starry train. I witnessed this gorgeous spectacle, and was awe-struck. The air seemed filled with bright, descending messengers from the sky. It was about daybreak when I saw this sublime scene. I was not without the suggestion, at the moment, that it might be the harbinger of the coming of the Son of Man . . . . I had read, that the 'stars shall fall from heaven'; and they were now falling." Frederick Douglass, *My Bondage and My Freedom* (New York: Miller, Orton & Co., 1857), 186.

6. Livin' Off the Fat of the Land

1. Stillwell, *Wanderings in the Southwest,* 36, 47–48.

2. Agnes Lutenbacher related this story, which is included in John W. Clark Jr., *Historical and Archaeological Resources of Riverdale, a Company Town in Goliad County, Texas,* ed. Jerry Henderson, Publications in Archaeology, no. 29 (Austin: Texas State Department of Highways and Public Transportation, Highway Design Division, November 1985), Appendix I, 34.

3. Warburton reports that the 1938 pecan crop on the Duke Ranch was 33,000 pounds, which sold for more than $2,400. See "History of the O'Connor Ranch," 47.

4. Mrs. T. C. Allan, comp. "Reminiscences of Mrs. Annie Fagan Teal," *Southwestern Historical Quarterly* 34, no. 4 (April 1931): 324; originally appeared in *By the Way,* a Victoria magazine that was published in 1897. According to my grandmother's notes, the magazine was forced to suspend publication after only five issues because the entire staff went off to fight in the Spanish-American War.

8. Time Has Made a Change

1. Quoted in Mary Ann Noonan Guerra, *The San Antonio River,* 1st rev. ed. (San Antonio: Alamo Press, c. 1987), 43.

Selected Bibliography

Allan, Mrs. T. C., comp. "Reminiscences of Mrs. Annie Fagan Teal." *Southwestern Historical Quarterly* 34, no. 4 (April 1931): 317–328.

Atkinson, Mary Jourdan. *The Texas Indians.* San Antonio: Naylor Company, 1935.

Bannon, John Francis. *Bolton and the Spanish Borderlands.* Norman: University of Oklahoma Press, 1964.

Billingsley, Kay Blackburn, ed. *Blessed Joseph.* Beeville, Tex.: Beeville Publishing Co., 1979.

Billington, Ray Allen. *Westward Expansion: A History of the American Frontier.* New York: Macmillan, 1949.

Bolton, Herbert E. "Defensive Spanish Expansion and the Significance of the Borderlands." In *Bolton and the Spanish Borderlands,* ed. John Francis Bannon. Norman: University of Oklahoma Press, 1964. Originally published in *The Trans-Mississippi West,* ed. James F. Willard and Colin B. Goodykoontz. Boulder: University of Colorado, 1930. Reprinted in *Wider Horizons of American History,* by Herbert E. Bolton. New York: D. Appleton-Century, 1939.

Bolton, Herbert Eugene, ed. *Spanish Exploration in the Southwest, 1542–1706.* New York: Barnes & Noble, 1928.

Bolton, Herbert Eugene, trans. and ed. *Athanase de Mézières and the Louisiana-Texas Frontier, 1768–1780.* Cleveland: Arthur H. Clark, 1914.

Braman, D. E. E. *Braman's Information about Texas.* Philadelphia: J. B. Lippincott & Co., 1857.

Burke, J., Jr., comp. *Texas Rural Almanac and Immigrant's Handbook for 1876.* Houston: Burke and Vasmer, 1876.

By the Way (Victoria), vol. 1, nos. 4 and 5 (1897).

Castañeda, Carlos Eduardo. *Our Catholic Heritage in Texas, 1519–1936.* 7 vols. Austin: Von Boeckmann-Jones, 1936–58.

Castillo-Crimm, Ana Carolina. "Finding Their Way." In *Tejano Journey, 1770–1850,* ed. Gerald E. Poyo. Austin: University of Texas Press, 1996.

Chapman, Charles Edward. *Colonial Hispanic America: A History. New York:* Macmillan, 1933.

Clark, John W., Jr. *Historical and Archaeological Resources of Riverdale, a Company Town in Goliad County, Texas,* ed. Jerry Henderson. Publications in Archaeology, no. 29. Austin: Texas State Department of Highways and Public Transportation, Highway Design Division, November 1985.

De Solís, José. "The Solís Diary of 1767." In *Preparing the Way: Preliminary Studies of the Texas Catholic Historical Society.* Texas Catholic Historical Society Studies in Southwestern Catholic History, no. 1. Ed. Jesús F. de la Teja. Austin: Texas Catholic Historical Society, 1997. Originally published in 1931 by the Texas Knights of Columbus Historical Commission.

Douglass, Frederick. *My Bondage and My Freedom.* New York: Miller, Orton & Co., 1857.

Garrison, George P. Texas: *A Contest of Civilizations.* Boston and Cambridge: Houghton Mifflin/Riverside Press, 1903.

Gatschet, Albert S. *The Karankawa Indians: The Coast People of Texas.* Boston: Peabody Museum, Harvard University, 1891.

Goetzmann, William H. "A Long, Long Trail A' Winding." Introduction to *No Traveller Remains Untouched: Journeys and Transformations in the American Southwest.* Southwest Writers Collection. San Marcos: Southwest Texas State University, 1995.

Guerra, Mary Ann Noonan. *The San Antonio River.* 1st rev. ed. San Antonio: Alamo Press, c. 1987.

Haring, C. H. *The Spanish Empire in America.* New York: Oxford University Press, 1947.

Hickerson, Nancy Parrott. "The Travels of Cabeza de Vaca." In *The Jumanos: Hunters and Traders of the South Plains.* Austin: University of Texas Press, 1994.

Huson, Hobart. *Refugio: A Comprehensive History of Refugio County from Aboriginal Times to 1953.* 2 vols. Woodsboro, Tex.: Rooke Foundation, Inc., 1953.

Jackson, Jack. *Los Mesteños: Spanish Ranching in Texas, 1721–1821.* College Station: Texas A&M University Press, 1986.

Lamar, Howard Roberts. *Texas Crossings: The Lone Star State and the American Far West, 1836–1986.* Austin: University of Texas Press, 1991.

Light, Patsy, and Anne Bode. "San Antonio River Valley (West of Goliad) Rural Historic District." National Register of Historic Places Nomination, 1995, Texas Historical Commission Library, Austin.

Linn, John J. *Reminiscences of Fifty Years in Texas.* New York: D. & J. Sadlier & Co., 1883.

Lipscomb, Carol A. "Karankawa Indians." In *New Handbook of Texas,* vol. 3. Austin: Texas State Historical Association, 1996.

McLean, Malcolm D. "Our Spanish Heritage in Texas." *Humanitas* (Monterrey, Mex.), no. 17 (1976): 569–616.

Myres, Sandra L. *The Ranch in Spanish Texas, 1691–1800.* El Paso: Texas Western Press/University of Texas at El Paso, 1969.

Newcomb, W. W., Jr. *The Indians of Texas: From Prehistoric to Modern Times.* Austin: University of Texas Press, 1961.

O'Connor, Kathryn Stoner. "Anaqua." In *New Handbook of Texas,* vol. 1. Austin: Texas State Historical Association, 1996.

———. *Presidio La Bahía del Espritu [Espíritu] Santo de Zúñiga, 1721 to 1846.* Austin: Von Boeckmann-Jones, 1966.

O'Connor, Louise S. *Cryin' for Daylight: A Ranching Culture in the Texas Coastal Bend.* Austin: Wexford Publishing, 1989.

O'Connor Family Papers, 1824–1981. Center for American History, University of Texas at Austin.

Peterson, Robert. *Only the Ball Was White.* Englewood Cliffs, N.J.: Prentice-Hall, 1970.

Ricklis, Robert A. *The Karankawa Indians of Texas:* An Ecological Study of Cultural Tradition and Change. Austin: University of Texas Press, 1996.

Rubio, Abel G. *Stolen Heritage: A Mexican-American's Rediscovery of His Family's Lost Land Grant.* Austin: Eakin Press, 1986.

Smithwick, Noah. *The Evolution of a State or Recollections of Old Texas Days.* Austin: Gammel Book Co., c. 1900; facsimile, Austin: Steck Co., 1935.

Snider, Lucile Fagan. "Austwell." Typescript, n.d. O'Connor Family Papers, 1824–1981, Center for American History, University of Texas at Austin.

Stillman, J. D. B. *Wanderings in the Southwest in 1855,* ed. Ron Tyler. Western Frontiersmen Series, no. 23. Spokane, Wash.: Arthur H. Clark, 1990. Originally published in *The Crayon,* July 11, 1855.

Swisher, Bella French. "The San Antonio River." In S. H. Dixon, *The Poets and Poetry of Texas.* Austin: Sam H. Dixon & Co., 1885.

Thonhoff, Robert H. *El Fuerte del Cíbolo: Sentinel of the Béxar–La Bahía Ranches.* Austin: Eakin Press, 1992.

Warburton, Sister Margaret Rose, C.D.P. "A History of the Thomas O'Connor Ranch." Master's thesis, Catholic University of America, San Antonio, 1939.

Wright, Robert E. "Spanish Missions." In *New Handbook of Texas,* vol. 6. Austin: Texas State Historical Association, 1996.

Young, Fredrick Douglas. *From These Roots: Cologne—One Hundred Years, 1870–1970.* Houston: Texas Southern University, 1973.

Index